THE WORK OF THE HOLY SPIRIT

AN EXPERIMENTAL AND PRACTICAL VIEW

OF THE

WORK OF THE HOLY SPIRIT

BY

OCTAVIUS WINSLOW

" They that are after the Spirit do mind the things of the Spirit."—
Rom. 8. 5.

THE BANNER OF TRUTH TRUST

1961

First Edition, 1843

First paper-back reprint, March 1961

This book is set in 10-point Pilgrim and
printed and bound in Great Britain by
Billing and Sons Limited, Guildford and
London

J502

PREFACE

TO the subject discussed in the following pages, the Author earnestly bespeaks the prayerful consideration of the Christian reader. It cannot occupy a position too prominent in our Christianity, nor can it be a theme presented too frequently for our contemplation. All that we spiritually know of ourselves, all that we know of God, and of Jesus, and His Word, we owe to the teaching of the Holy Spirit; and all the real light, sanctification, strength and comfort we are made to possess on our way to glory, we must ascribe to Him. To be richly anointed with the Spirit is to be led into all truth; and to be filled with the Spirit is to be filled with love to God and man. The *gift* of the Spirit he has not felt it his duty to plead for in these pages. *It is already given.* God *has* given the Spirit to the church, dwelling in, and for ever abiding with her. "I will pray the Father," says Christ to His disciples, "and he shall give you another Comforter, that he may *abide with you for ever;* even the Spirit of truth; whom the world cannot receive, because it seeth him not, neither knoweth him: but ye know him; for he *dwelleth* with you, and shall be *in* you." John 14. 16-17. God has never revoked this gift. He has never removed His Spirit from the church—He is still her divine, personal and abiding Resident. And to plead for the bestowment of that which God has *already* so fully and graciously given, seems to mark an unbelief in, and an overlooking of the mercy, as ungrateful to the Giver as it is dishonouring to the Gift.

But *for a larger degree of His reviving, anointing and sanctifying influences*, we do most earnestly plead. The Spirit, though the ever-blessed and abiding Occupant of the church of Christ, and of the individual believer, may not always be *manifestly* present. The prayerless, unholy and trifling walk of a believer will cause Him to withdraw His sensible presence. The coldness, formality, worldliness and divisions of a church will compel Him to withhold the plentiful rain or the gentle dew of His precious influence. He may be so disowned, dishonoured, wounded and grieved as to retire within the curtains of His secret glory, leaving for a while the scene of worldliness and strife to the curse and the reproach of barrenness. To impress the mind more deeply with the glory of His person and with the necessity and value of His work, and to awaken a more ardent desire and more earnest and constant prayer for a greater manifestation of His influence, and a more undoubted evidence of His glory and power in the church and in the believer, are the object of the writer in the following treatise. All we want, brethren beloved in the Lord, is a richer and more enlarged degree of the reviving, sealing and witnessing influence of the Holy Ghost. This will sanctify and bless the learning, the wealth and the influence, now so rich an endowment of Christ's redeemed church, and without which that learning, wealth and influence will but weaken her true power, impede her onward progress, and beget in her a spirit of human trust and vain-glory. This, too, will consume in its holy fire the unhallowed spirit of jealousy and party strife now the canker-worm of the *one body*; and, without asking for the compromise of truth, will yet, in the love it shall enkindle, so cement the hearts of the brotherhood, and so throw around them the girdle of a heaven-born and uniting charity, as will establish an evidence of the truth of Christianity—the last that Christ will give—which all its enemies shall not be able to gainsay or resist. Descend, holy and blessed Spirit, upon all Thy churches, Thy ministers, and Thy people! Descend Thou upon Jew and Gentile; everywhere, and among all people, manifest Thy glory, until the church scattered up and down the earth shall acknowledge, receive and welcome Thee, her ever-blessed and ever-abiding Indweller, Sanctifier and Comforter.

It is with much reluctance that the Author, in consequence of the unexpected size to which this treatise has grown under his hand, has been compelled to omit some important aspects of the Spirit's work; two subjects especially—the one on " Grieving the Spirit "; the other on the " Outpouring of the Spirit." It is his intention, however, to introduce them in a work now in preparation, to be entitled, " Personal Declension and Revival, a Plea for the Outpouring of the Spirit," to appear in a short period, if the Lord permit.[1]

Leamington, May, 1840.

This book, under a slightly different title—*Personal Declension and Revival of Religion in the Soul*—was published in 1891 and reprinted by the present publishers in 1960. It contains a chapter on *Grieving the Spirit,* but the subject of the *Outpouring of the Spirit* is not dealt with. Probably Winslow devoted a separate book to the latter subject. Can any reader confirm this? We should also be grateful to borrow a copy of Winslow's work, *Eminent Holiness Essential to an Efficient Ministry.*—The Publishers.

CONTENTS

CONTENTS

CHAPTER I

The Godhead and Personality of the Holy Spirit

THE NATURE AND NECESSITY OF EXPERIMENTAL RELIGION

" *Go, teach all nations, baptizing them in the name of the Father, and of the Son, and of the Holy Ghost.*"—Matt. 28. 19.

IT is essential to a proper and just exhibition of the work of the Holy Spirit that, at the outset of the discussion, the basis of that work be deeply and broadly laid. He is not " a wise master builder," who, in rearing the great structure of Divine truth, does not commence with a clear and scriptural exposition of the foundation. While every portion of God's Word, whether it be a doctrine, a precept or a promise, must be regarded as bearing upon the salvation, sanctification and consolation of the believer, there yet are doctrines which have ever been held and maintained as forming the *ground-work*, essential to the very existence, security and harmony of the entire system of revealed truth. For example, the self-existent being of GOD forms the foundation doctrine of revelation, the basis of all revealed truth. If this were to be renounced, not a step could be advanced in demonstrating to an unbeliever the attributes of God, His moral government, and the holiness and equity of His claims to the supreme obedience of the creature. If there be no true God, there can be no true religion. The same observation will apply with equal propriety and force to the mediatorial work of the Lord Jesus. The basis of Christ's work is His proper and essential deity. If he be not JEHOVAH in the highest sense, we lose all confidence in

the vicarious character of His death, and are compelled to resign our long and fondly cherished hope of salvation through
His cross—the perfection of His atoning work falling with the
dignity of His person.

Yet another confirmation of the truth of this thought will
be found in a consideration of the work of the Holy Spirit.
The basis of that work is His DIVINE PERSONALITY.   All the
dignity, efficacy and glory of His office, work and various
operations spring from this truth.   We must relinquish all dependence upon His influences, if we cannot scripturally maintain the doctrines of his Deity and Personality.   And here let
it be remarked, that a believer's views of the necessity and
the nature of the gracious operations of the Spirit will be
materially affected by the strength of his faith in the doctrine
of the personal glory of the Spirit.   Low views of the dignity
of His person will engender low views of the necessity and
nature of His work.   The one must be essentially modified by
the other. The Lord, in His wisdom, has so ordered it. " Them
that honour me I will honour, and they that despise me shall
be lightly esteemed."   Let this gracious promise and solemn
threatening be applied to our conduct in relation to the Holy
Spirit, and how true will they appear!   Where He is honoured, and adoring thoughts of His person, and tender, loving
views of His work are cherished, *then* are experienced, in an
enlarged degree, His quickening, enlightening, sanctifying and
comforting influences.   On the contrary, where He is robbed
of His glory, dishonoured and denied, all is darkness and desolation—presenting the dreariness and barrenness of winter,
the very coldness and torpor of death!   Come, eternal and
blessed Spirit! impart to our minds life, light, and unction,
while investigating Thy all-important and glorious work. Give
to him that writes, and to those who read the words of this
book the " anointing that teacheth all things "—the blessing
shall be ours; Thine the honour and the praise!

In considering this, it will materially aid the reader in his
clear perception of the truth, if a simple order of arrangement
be observed. In the present chapter, therefore, the distinct
personality of the Holy Spirit will be first proved—this will

necessarily lead to a vindication of His *deity*; a brief glance at the relation which these two doctrines bear to the entire revelation of God, and the reality and growth of the believer's experience of Divine truth, will close the chapter.

We commence with the distinct PERSONALITY of the Holy Spirit. In adducing scriptural testimony to the truth of this doctrine, we need scarcely pause upon the threshold of our subject to state at length opposite and antagonistic views of the Spirit. And yet, for the information, possibly, of a few into whose hands this treatise may fall, and for the more full and irresistible conviction on the minds of all, of the bearing and force of the numerous passages we shall adduce in proof, it may be proper briefly to state what those views of the Holy Spirit are, the fallacy and the fatal tendency of which it is our humble desire to refute and expose.

It is asserted by those who impugn the doctrine in question, that the Holy Spirit is but another name for the Father—that all the operations and influences which we ascribe to His personal and Divine agency are but so many emanations of Deity, or the exercise of one or more of the Divine attributes—either the wisdom, power or mercy of God. And to evade the force of the many passages in the Scriptures of truth which substantiate the doctrine of His distinct personal existence, it is argued that every passage thus adduced is to be interpreted, not in a literal, but in a *figurative* sense. And thus, the Holy Spirit, the third person in the glorious Trinity, the Author of Divine life, and the great Testifier of Jesus, is reduced to a mere figure of speech, an oriental metaphor! And what stamps the hypothesis with such glaring absurdity is that an attribute, a principle, an emanation, is allowed to possess the organs and faculties, both physical and mental, of a distinct person and a sentient being! An error more fatal to an experimental and practical reception of Divine truth, we cannot imagine to exist. O that the Holy Spirit may now enable us to vindicate His glory, and from His own word and work prove Him to be, what He truly is—*a distinct Person in the Godhead*.

If it be inquired what we mean by the term *person* as applied to the Spirit, we briefly reply—such a distinction in the Trinity as demonstrates a separate mode of existence, to which belong *personal attributes*; and yet this distinct intelligent Agent, coalescing in, and constituting in union with the Father and the Son, the one God.   Because of His union with the Godhead, we ascribe to Him *divinity*; and because of His personal properties and acts, we ascribe to Him *personality*. We now proceed to the proof.

In opposition to the idea that the Holy Spirit is a mere *quality* or *influence*, let us adduce two or three passages in which the Spirit is spoken of as a *person*, and *distinguished* from an *attribute*. Acts 10. 38: "God anointed Jesus of Nazareth with the Holy Ghost and with power." Rom. 15. 13: "Now the God of hope fill you with all joy and peace in believing, that ye may abound in hope, through the power of the Holy Ghost." 1 Cor. 2. 4: "And my speech and my preaching was not with enticing words of man's wisdom, but in demonstration of the Spirit and of power." We now ask, is it not plain and intelligible to the most common understanding that the Spirit is a distinct and intelligent Agent, and is never to be confounded with the Divine attributes? In these passages, the distinction is clearly drawn between the Spirit and the Divine attribute of power. To interpret both as meaning one and the same thing would be to throw contempt upon the Word of God.

The personality of the Spirit rejected, in what light shall we interpret the sin of BLASPHEMY AGAINST THE HOLY GHOST? Matt. 12. 31, 32: "Wherefore I say unto you, All manner of sin and blasphemy shall be forgiven unto men : but the *blasphemy against the Holy Ghost* shall not be forgiven unto men. And whosoever speaketh a word against the Son of man, it shall be forgiven him : but whosoever *speaketh against the Holy Ghost*, it shall not be forgiven him, neither in this world, neither in the world to come." Reserving our views of the precise *nature* of the sin here spoken of, we at present confine our remarks to the evidence the passages afford to the doctrine of the *personality* of the Spirit.   Here is an action spoken of as against, and terminating in, a *person*.   It certainly cannot be interpreted, with any correct knowledge of the Word of God, as a sin against a distinct attribute, for the reason assigned, that " all manner of sin and blasphemy against God shall be forgiven unto men, but the blasphemy against the Holy Ghost shall not be forgiven unto men." The inference, plain and logical, is that the Holy Ghost is not an attribute, or an emanation, but a distinct *person*. " It is therefore incredible, and certainly inexplicable," are the words of a distinguished writer, " that *all manner of blasphemy* against the whole character of God, particularly against his moral character, *should be forgiven*; and yet that blasphemy against a single natural attribute should never be forgiven." And what shall be thought of a doctrine that teaches that blasphemy committed against the Divine *attribute* of *power*, is more heinous and *unpardonable* than blasphemy committed against *God Himself?* And yet, to this awful conclusion does the denial of the personality of the Holy Spirit lead us.

The Spirit is spoken of as a SERVANT. John 15. 26, 27: " But when the Comforter is come, whom I will send unto you from the Father, even the Spirit of truth, which proceedeth from the Father, He shall testify of me." John 16. 7: " Nevertheless, I tell you the truth; it is expedient for you that I go away: for if I go not away, the Comforter will not come unto you; but if I depart, I will send Him unto you." What language can more clearly and forcibly convey to the mind the idea of *personality* than this? Surely Christ did not speak allegorically here. His language cannot on any just principles be figuratively interpreted. If He spake figuratively when alluding to the Holy Spirit, we are compelled for the same reasons, and in the same way, to interpret His words when referring to Himself. But who will believe that when speaking of Himself He spake of a *figurative being?* No one, surely. But He spake of the Comforter as a person; " when He "—let the reader note the frequent and peculiar use of the masculine personal pronoun—" when *He*, the Spirit of truth, is come," " The Comforter, the Holy Ghost, which the Father will send in my name, *He* shall teach you all things," " *He* shall testify of me." Who does not see, unless he willingly closes his mind to the truth, that, to suppose the Lord Jesus speaking thus gravely of a mere figurative personage, is awful trifling with the Word of God? If a distinct personage is not spoken of in these passages, language has lost its power to describe what a person really is, or to convey to us an intelligent idea of his existence. But our Lord was speaking of an exchange of persons. It was a Divine and intelligent *person* that was to depart, and it was a Divine and intelligent *person* that was to supersede Him in the church, abiding with it for ever.

And what shall be said of *the ordinance of baptism* being administered into His name, in union with the Father and the Son? Matt. 28. 19: " Go, teach all nations, baptizing them in the name of the Father, and of the Son, and of the Holy Ghost." Is an *attribute* or a distinct intelligent *person* spoken of here, as associated in this Divine ordinance with the Father and the Son? Note the emphatic expression—" In the name of the Holy Ghost." In the name of an *attribute*? of a *principle*? of a *quality*? What vain tautology then would this be—the first example of unmeaning and unnecessary repetition found in the Word of God. We have already shown, that when God the Father is spoken of, all the Divine attributes are included—for what are the attributes of God, but God Himself? To baptise then, first in the name of the Father, and then in the name of one of His attributes, is an interpretation which the weakest judgment must reject.

For a further illustration of our argument, let us refer to the description given of Satan in contradistinction to the Holy Spirit, by our Lord. Matt. 12. 26-28: " And if Satan cast out Satan, he is divided against himself; how shall then his kingdom stand? And if I by Beelzebub cast out devils, by whom do your childre cast them out? Therefore they shall be your judges. But if I cast out devils by the Spirit of God, then the kingdom of God is come unto you." Satan is here spoken of as a *person*, by whose influence, they blasphemously affirmed, Christ performed His miracles. In contradistinction to this, the Holy Spirit is spoken of as a *person*, by whose power Christ actually did cast out devils. We have no authority to interpret His meaning, when speaking of Satan, as *literal*, and when speaking of the Spirit, as *figurative*. We think it as clear as it is possible for language to make it, that the *personality* of the *Spirit* is affirmed equally with the *personality* of *Satan*.

We pass now to a consideration of a few of the *attributes*, *personal acts* and *properties* ascribed to the Holy Spirit.

Is *speaking* a personal action? Then it is ascribed to the Holy Spirit. Mark 13. 11: "Whatsoever shall be given you in that hour, that speak ye; for it is not ye that speak, but the *Holy Ghost*." Again, Acts 13. 2: "As they ministered to the Lord, and fasted, *the Holy Ghost said*, Separate me Barnabas and Paul for the work whereunto I have called them." Acts 21. 11: "And when he was come unto us, he took Paul's girdle, and bound his own hands and feet, and said, *Thus saith the Holy Ghost*, So shall the Jews at Jerusalem bind the man that owneth this girdle, and shall deliver him into the hands of the Gentiles." 1 Tim. 4. 1: "Now *the Spirit speaketh* expressly, that in the latter times some shall depart from the faith." Rev. 2. 7: "He that hath an ear, let him hear what *the Spirit saith* unto the churches." We will not multiply proofs. Had we quoted but one from among the several thus adduced, it had been sufficient to explode the hypothesis that an attribute, an energy or an influence could assume to itself and exercise the faculty of speech, one of the personal properties and acts of a distinct, intelligent agent. We will content ourselves with presenting a summary view of the kindred personal properties and actions which are ascribed to the Holy Spirit.

The power of REVEALING is ascribed to him. Luke 2. 26: "And it was *revealed unto him by the Holy Ghost*, that he should not see death, before he had seen the Lord's Christ." Now the Apostle speaks of our blessed Lord as a *revealer*. In this passage, the same faculty is ascribed to the Holy Spirit; what is the inference? That, if it were a personal act in the one, it must also be so in the other. Interpreting this passage upon the anti-trinitarian hypothesis, how unintelligible would it read: " And it was revealed unto him by a revelation, that he should not see death," &c. God may reveal an attribute, but an attribute cannot reveal itself.

The Holy Spirit is spoken of as a WITNESS. Acts 5. 32: " We are his witnesses of these things: and *so is also the Holy Ghost.*" Are we to understand that the witness which the apostles bore to the Messiahship and the miracles of Christ was but figurative? Surely not. And yet the same personal action accorded to them is also ascribed to the Holy Spirit. If the witness of the apostles was literal and not figurative, so was also the witness which the Holy Ghost bore to the same facts a literal and not a figurative one. Again, Rom. 8. 16: " *The Spirit itself beareth witness* with our spirit, that we are the children of God." Who is it that testifies to the believer's calling, pardon, adoption and acceptance? Who applies the atoning, peace-speaking blood to the conscience? An attribute, an energy, an emanation? Ask the child of God if *this* were sufficient to remove his guilt, calm his fears, and assure him of his acceptance in Christ. O no! None but the Spirit of God Himself can accomplish this. "The Spirit itself"— not an attribute, nor an influence, but "the Spirit itself[1] beareth witness with our spirit, that we are the children of God." Let no professor of the Gospel rest short of this evidence. Without it, all other is false. Holy and blessed is he that has it!

KNOWLEDGE is ascribed to the Holy Spirit. 1 Cor. 2. 10, 11: " The Spirit searcheth all things, yea, the deep things of God. For what man knoweth the things of a man, save the spirit of man which is in him? Even so the things of God knoweth no man, but *the Spirit of God.*" We ask, in the words of another, " whether any man can conceive, that *knowledge*, one essential attribute of God, can, with any meaning, be said to be an attribute of *power*, which is another? Or whether power can, in any words that have meaning, be said to know anything?"

The Spirit was the *immediate Agent* of all the MIRACLES

---

[1] The meaning of this phrase is brought out more fully in the R.V. which translates this as " the Spirit himself."

performed by the apostles. Rom. 15. 19: "Through mighty signs and wonders, *by the power of the Spirit of God*."

SPIRITUAL LIFE is ascribed to Him. John 6. 63: "It is the Spirit that quickeneth." 1 Pet. 3. 18: "Put to death in the flesh, but quickened by the Spirit." Are these the evidences of an attribute, or are they the actions of a person? Can a mere influence work miracles? Can a mere emanation impart life?

The Holy Spirit is represented as SENDING FORTH. Acts 13. 4: The apostles "being *sent forth by the Holy Ghost*, departed unto Seleucia."

AS DESIGNATING TO AN OFFICE. Acts 20. 28: "Take heed therefore unto yourselves, and to all the flock over which *the Holy Ghost hath made you overseers*."

AS EXERCISING HIS OWN PLEASURE. Acts 15. 28: "*It seemed good to the Holy Ghost* and to us." 1 Cor. 12. 11: "But all these worketh that one and the selfsame Spirit, dividing to every man severally *as he will*."

AS BEING VEXED. Isa. 63. 10: "They rebelled, and *vexed his Holy Spirit*."

AS BEING GRIEVED. Eph. 4. 30: "And *grieve not the Holy Spirit*."

AS BEING RESISTED. Acts 7. 51: "Ye stiff-necked and uncircumcised in heart and ears, ye do always *resist the Holy Ghost*: as your fathers did, so do ye."

Here we rest the evidence in favour of the *distinct personality* of the Spirit. Sufficient has been advanced, we believe, with His blessing, to allay every suspicion, to remove every doubt and to confirm and settle the mind in the full belief of this important truth. And yet, aside from his own Divine illumination, what avails the multiplicity of scriptural proof to the truth of His character, or the reality of His work? The Spirit is the great illuminator of the soul. We may spread the most momentous and spiritual truths before the mind, the evidence that confirms them may be collected from every source, and poured, as with focussed power, upon the intellect; yet until the Spirit of life and light moves upon the moral chaos, all is darkness, disorder and confusion.

We pass now to a consideration of the DIVINITY of the Holy Spirit.

Not less full and satisfactory is the evidence afforded by the Scriptures of truth to the absolute and essential DEITY OF THE SPIRIT. It will not be expected that the argument sustaining this doctrine be a laboured and a lengthened one; seeing that, if we have shown the fallacy of a mere attribute having grafted upon it all the other Divine attributes, or a mere influence or quality clothed with the properties and exercising the actions of a person—if, in a word, we have been enabled to establish upon a scriptural, and therefore a satisfactory and an immovable basis, the doctrine of the distinct *personality* of the Spirit—the GODHEAD of the Spirit may be legitimately and logically inferred. The very actions that prove Him a *person* demonstrate that person *Divine*. We now proceed to the proof.

And in the first place let us inquire, is it no evidence of the supreme deity of the Spirit that the very NAMES of Deity are given to Him? For so we read, 2 Cor. 3. 17: "Now the Lord (Jehovah) is that Spirit." 2 Cor. 3. 18: "But we all with open face beholding as in a glass the glory of the Lord, are changed into the same image from glory to glory, even as by the Spirit of the Lord."

He is also called GOD, in that remarkable passage recorded in Acts 5. 3, 4: "But Peter said, Ananias, why hath Satan filled thine heart to lie to the Holy Ghost, and to keep back part of the price of the land? Why hast thou conceived this thing in thine heart? Thou hast not lied unto men, but unto God." So self-evident is the conclusiveness of the argument drawn from this passage, that comment is deemed needless. "Thou hast not lied unto *men*"—the Holy Spirit, though a person, not a creature—"but unto the Holy Ghost—unto God." To the experienced believer, how delightful is this evidence of the divinity of Him whom he loves, honours and adores as the Author of his renewed nature!

There are *parallel passages* in which the name of God is ascribed to the Spirit. Thus, 1 Cor. 3. 17: "The temple of God is holy, which temple ye are." Compare 1 Cor. 6. 19:

"Know ye not that your body is the temple of the Holy Ghost?" What is the true inference but that the Holy Ghost is GOD—God dwelling in the renewed, recovered soul?

1 Cor. 2. 11: "The things of God knoweth no man." Compare 1 Cor. 2. 14: "But the natural man receiveth not the things of the Spirit of God." The only distinction here made between God and the Spirit of God, is one that establishes the *personality*, while it affirms the *divinity* of the Spirit.

Luke 11. 20: "If I with the finger of God cast out devils." Compare Matt. 12. 28: "If I with the Spirit of God cast out devils." The "finger of God" is metaphorical of the immediate agency of God. When, therefore, it is said that devils were cast out by the "finger of God," the obvious sense of the expression is that they were cast out by God Himself. But from the text of the evangelist Matthew, this special and supernatural act was ascribed to the *Spirit*; the inference is in favour of the deity of the Holy Ghost.

Not only the names, but the ATTRIBUTES and WORKS of God are ascribed to the Spirit.

ETERNITY. Heb. 9. 14: "How much more shall the blood of Christ, who through the ETERNAL SPIRIT offered himself without spot to God," &c.

OMNISCIENCE. 1 Cor. 2. 10: "The Spirit searcheth all things, yea, the deep things of God." Of whom speaks the apostle this language, but of a distinct, intelligent, and Divine person? Both the personality and the divinity of the Spirit are clearly and conjointly stated. The properties of His *person* are His understanding and knowledge united with His power of communicating that knowledge to others. The argument for His *divinity* is His faculty of foretelling things to come, by an intuitive power and underived knowledge, which faculty can belong to Deity alone. Let the spiritual reader pause and reflect for a moment upon this Divine attribute of the eternal Spirit. He is here represented as *searching*. Searching what? Searching where a finite mind, though it were an angel's, would be lost in maze and doubt. What else is the meaning of the verse immediately preceding?—"But as it is written, Eye hath not seen, nor ear heard, neither have entered into the heart of man, the things which God hath prepared for them that love him." And then it is added, " But God hath revealed them unto us by his Spirit: for the Spirit searcheth all things, yea, the deep things of God." But what things are those which a finite mind, whether human or angelic, cannot penetrate or reveal? The eternal love of God towards His covenant people—what finite intellect can fully comprehend or adequately reveal this?—that ocean whence flows " the river that makes glad the city of God "—that Divine source of all blessedness to the believer; in which originated the wondrous plan of his salvation. O, what but a *Divine* mind could fathom this sea of love, and lead down its sweet streams into a believer's soul? " The deep things of God "—His nature, perfections, government, the eternal covenant of grace, the incarnation of Jesus, the nature and operations of Divine grace upon the soul of man, the mysteries of providence, the glories of the world to come—who can understand, and who can search these " deep things of God," but God Himself? " Who hath known the mind of God, or who hath been his counsellor?" who, save the eternal and blessed Spirit, the third person in the adorable Trinity? "The Spirit searcheth all things, yea, the deep things of God."

OMNIPRESENCE. Psalm 139. 7: " Whither shall I go from Thy Spirit? or whither shall I flee from Thy presence?"

OMNIPOTENCE. Rom. 15. 18, 19: " For I will not dare to speak of any of those things which Christ hath not wrought by me, to make the Gentiles obedient by word and deed, through mighty signs and wonders, by the power of the Spirit of God." And so also in Zech. 4. 6: " Not by might, nor by power, but by my Spirit, saith the Lord of hosts."

SOVEREIGNTY. 1 Cor. 12. 11: " But all these worketh that one and the self-same Spirit, dividing to every man severally as he will." To whom can this properly apply, but to God? No creature has a right to do as he wills. This right belongs to God alone. It is a Divine prerogative, incommunicable to a creature. The highest happiness of angels, and of the " spirits of just men made perfect " in glory, is to do the will of God. Even our dear Lord, when speaking of Himself in His mediatorial character, in which alone He was subordinate to the Father, says, "I came not to do mine own will, but the will of Him that sent me." When, therefore, it is declared of the Spirit that He worketh "as He will," we have the strongest positive evidence of His absolute divinity. Of none could this be predicated, but God Himself.

We have by no means exhausted the Scripture testimony to the doctrine of the DIVINE PERSONALITY of the Holy Spirit, although it is necessary, having other topics to discuss in connection with this truth, that the evidence should close here. As we advance more fully into the consideration of His work, collateral evidences in favour of His personal dignity will press themselves upon the mind of the reflective reader, which perhaps may afford him confirmation of the truth of the doctrine as strong and satisfactory as a direct and positive argument. With earnest prayer for that "anointing which teacheth of all things," his mind shall be led into the blessed truth, and the happy result will be—a crowning of the Spirit equally with the Father and the Son.

We proceed now, in accordance with our design, to point out the essential relation which the doctrine of the Divine personality of the Holy Spirit holds to the entire revelation of God, and the reality and growth of Christian experience. We argue that a denial of the personal dignity of the Spirit renders the Word of God incomplete. For instance:—

Without a full an unequivocal recognition of the doctrine in question, there is a want of harmony and coherence in those numberless passages which teach the doctrine of the Trinity in the Godhead. Take Isa. 48. 16: "And now the Lord God, and his Spirit, hath sent me." Who is the speaker here? The Lord Jesus, who, in verse 12, says, "Hearken unto me, O Jacob and Israel, my called; I am he; I am the first, I also am the last." Eph. 2. 18: "For through him (Christ) we both (Jews and Gentiles) have access by one Spirit unto the Father." Yet further; Matt. 3. 16, 17: "And Jesus, when he was baptized, went up straightway out of the water: and lo, the heavens were opened unto him, and he saw the Spirit of God descending like a dove, and lighting upon him; and lo, a voice from heaven, saying, This is my beloved Son, in whom I am well pleased." Matt. 28. 19: "Go ye therefore, and teach all nations, baptizing them in the name of the Father, and of the Son, and of the Holy Ghost." Now can the doctrine of three distinct persons in the Godhead be more clearly and unequivocally taught than it is in these passages? And yet if the DIVINE PERSONALITY of the Spirit be denied, these, and kindred texts, must be rendered totally obscure and nugatory. The Christian reader will require no extended argumentation to convince his understanding, that a regard to the perfection and analogy of truth demands a full belief in the doctrine which in this chapter we have sought to establish. We must either deny the doctrine of the Trinity to be a part of Divine revelation, and consequently, render perfectly unintelligible the numerous passages which declare and confirm it, or we must admit the Holy Spirit to be a distinct person in the Godhead, to whom belongs equal honour and dignity with the Father and the Son.

Again, *viewed as a Spirit of revelation*, His claims to Divine dignity must be conceded; for if His deity be denied, the entire revelation of God falls to the ground. For we read that "prophecy came not in old time by the will of man, but holy men of God spake as they were moved by the Holy Ghost." We must then either deny the Divine inspiration of the Word of God, or admit that the Holy Spirit is God. All that we know of God, truly and perfectly, we know by the revelation of the Holy Spirit. He is the great Revealer of the glory, perfections, love and grace of Jehovah; and until the mind of man has been brought under His gracious influence, it is ignorant of God and of itself. All is dark, yes, darkness itself, until the Divine light of the Spirit breaks through the gloom, and chases that darkness away.

In venturing upon this remark, let it not be supposed that we undervalue the contributions brought to the confirmation of the truth of revealed religion by what is termed natural theology. We are never reluctant to acknowledge our indebtedness to this source of evidence. We cannot forget that the God of revelation is the God of nature, that in exploring this vast territory we trespass upon the domain of no foreign potentate, we invade no hostile kingdom, we tread no forbidden ground. The spiritual mind, fond of soaring through nature in quest of new proofs of God's existence, and fresh emblems of His wisdom, power and goodness, exults in the thought that it is his *Father's* domain he treads. He *feels* that God, *his* God, is there. And the sweet consciousness of His all-pervading presence, and the impress of His great perfections which everywhere meets his eye, overwhelm his renewed soul with wonder, love, and praise. O the delight of looking abroad upon nature, under a sense of pardoning, filial love in the soul when enabled to exclaim, " this God is *my God!*" Let it not therefore be supposed that nature and revelation are at war with each other. A spiritual mind may discover a close and beautiful relation and harmony between the two. The study of God in His external operations, is by no means discouraged in His word. " The heavens declare the glory of God, and the firmament sheweth his handywork. Day unto day uttereth speech, and night unto night sheweth knowledge." Referring to the rejection of this source of evidence by the heathen, the apostle argues, " The invisible things of Him from the creation of the world are clearly seen, being understood by the things that are made, even his eternal power and Godhead; so that they are without excuse."

But if natural theology has its advantages, it also has its *limitations*. It must never be regarded as taking the place of God's Word. It may just impart light enough to the mind to leave its *atheism* " without excuse," but it cannot impart light enough to convince the soul of its sinfulness—its guilt—its exposure to the wrath of a holy God, and its need of such a Saviour as Jesus is. All this is the work of the eternal and blessed Spirit; and if my reader is resting his hope of heaven upon what he has learned of God and of himself in the light of nature only, and is a stranger to the teaching and operations of the Holy Ghost upon his mind, he is awfully deceiving himself. Natural religion can never renew, sanctify and save the soul. A man may be deeply schooled in it as a science; he may investigate it thoroughly, defend it ably and successfully, and even from the feeble light it emits grope his dark way to the great edifice of revelation—but beyond this it cannot conduct him; it cannot open the door and admit him to *the fulness of the gospel* therein contained. It may go far to convince him that the Word of God is true, but it cannot " open the book and loose the seals thereof " and disclose to the mind its rich and exhaustless treasures. O no! Another and a diviner light must shine upon his soul; another and a more powerful hand must break the seals. That light, that hand, is God the Holy Ghost. He only can make the soul acquainted with this solemn truth—" The heart is deceitful above all things, and desperately wicked." He only can explore this dark chamber of imagery, and bring to light the hidden evil that is there. He only can lay the soul low in the dust before God at the discovery, and draw out the heart in the humiliating confession—" Behold, I am vile! " He only can take of the precious blood of a precious Saviour, and the glorious righteousness of the God-Man Mediator, and, working faith to receive it, through this infinitely glorious medium seal pardon, acceptance and peace upon the conscience. O thou blessed and loving Spirit! this is Thy work, and Thine alone. Thine to empty, Thine to fill. Thine to lay low, Thine to exalt. Thine to wound, Thine to heal. Thine to convince of sin, and Thine to lead the soul, all sinful, guilty and wretched as it is, to the precious blood of Jesus—" the fountain opened for sin and uncleanness." Thou shalt have the praise and wear the crown!

It remains for us to glance at *the relation of the personal character of the Spirit to the existence, reality and advance of the believer's experience.*

A believer's experience of the truth of God is no mere fancy. However severely experimental godliness may have been stigmatised by an unrenewed world as the offspring of a morbid imagination and the product of a fanatical mind, " he that believes in the Son of God hath the witness in himself " that he has yielded the consent of his judgment and his affections to no " cunningly devised fable." A sense of sin, brokenness and contrition before God, faith in the atoning blood of Christ, a sweet consciousness of pardon, acceptance, adoption and joy in the Holy Ghost, are no mere hallucinations of a disordered mind. To read one's pardon fully, fairly written out —to look up to God as one accepted, adopted—to feel the spirit going out to Him in filial love and confidence, breathing its tender and endearing epithet, "Abba, Father"—to refer every trial, cross, and dispensation of His providence to His tender and unchangeable love—to have one's will, naturally so rebellious and perverse, completely absorbed in His—to be as a weaned child, simply and unreservedly yielded up to His disposal, and to live in the patient waiting for the glory that is to be revealed—oh, *this is reality*, sweet, blessed, solemn reality! Holy and happy is that man, whose heart is not a stranger to these truths. But rob the Spirit of His personal glory, divest Him of his great offices in the covenant of grace, reduce Him to a mere influence, attribute, or principle, and the believer's experience of the truth dwindles down to an airy nothing. All *is* fancy, fanaticism and delusion, if the Holy Spirit be not a *distinct person in the Godhead*. But so long as this doctrine is brought home with convincing power to the soul that the Holy Spirit is a distinct person *from*, yet co-essential, co-equal and co-eternal *with* the Father and the Son, then we have the comforting assurance that the experience of the truth in the heart, of which He is the Author and we the subjects, is a supernatural work—the work of God the Holy Ghost. And this assurance gives stability to the soul.

The doctrine of the Spirit's personal dignity also affords a pledge that the work thus commenced shall be carried forward to a final and glorious completion. Because He is God, He will finish what He has begun. And let it not be forgotten that the *growth* of the believer in the experience of the truth is as much the work of the eternal Spirit as was the first production of Divine life in the soul. The dependence of the believer on the Spirit by no means ceases in conversion. There are after stages along which it is His office to conduct the believing soul. Deeper views of sin's exceeding sinfulness, a more thorough knowledge of self, more enlarged discoveries of Christ, a more simple and habitual resting upon His finished work, increasing conformity to the Divine image, the daily victory over indwelling sin, and a constant preparation for the inheritance of the saints in light—all these are the work of the one and the self-same Spirit who first breathed into his soul the breath of spiritual life. Not a step can the believer advance without the Spirit. Not a victory can he achieve without the Spirit. Not a moment can he exist without the Spirit. As he needed Him at the first, so he needs Him all his journey through. And so he will have Him, until the soul passes over Jordan. To the last ebbing of life, the blessed Spirit will be his Teacher, his Comforter and his Guide. To the last, He will testify of Jesus. To the last, He will apply the atoning blood. And to the very entrance of the happy saint into glory, the eternal Spirit of God—faithful, loving to the last—will be present, to whisper words of pardon, assurance and peace. Holy Spirit! build us up in the infinite dignity of Thy person, and in the surpassing greatness and glory of Thy work!

I cannot allow myself to close this chapter, without addressing a few solemn and earnest considerations to the *denier* of the personal dignity of the Spirit. You and I will soon stand at the bar of God. In view of that day, how solemn, how awful is your present position! If you have read the preceding pages with any degree of thought and candour, you must have closed the argument with the conviction that truly the Spirit is a distinct person in the Godhead—so full, so clear and so conclusive is the testimony of the Divine Scriptures to the truth of this doctrine. In rejecting the doctrine and in resisting the conviction of evidence, you assume responsibilities and incur guilt of a fearful kind. In denying the Spirit's personal dignity, you deny God Himself; in refusing the evidence, you turn your back upon His *revelation*. Can imagination conceive of a position more truly solemn? You may think lightly of *experimental* truth; you may deride the religion of a man who hopes that he is "born of the Spirit" and has found pardon and acceptance through Christ, as the very wildness of enthusiasm; you may press to your heart more closely and fondly than ever your religion of nature, your form of godliness, your cold, lifeless, soulless creed; but, O remember, you have to do with a God who searches the heart and tries the reins of men—a God of spotless holiness and inflexible justice—with whom the *form*, without the *power* of godliness, is a mockery—and to whom prayer, without the Spirit, is a sin! Do not be deceived in a matter so momentous, and involving interests so precious and eternal. Do not think to offer to God an acceptable oblation, while you refuse Divine honour, homage and love to the third person in the glorious Trinity. Do not wonder that the details of Christian experience of a child of God, are all a mystery, an enigma to you; that when he speaks of a broken heart, of a contrite spirit, of a mourning over sin, of regeneration, of pardon, of acceptance, of the joys of God's salvation, of the comfort of the Holy Ghost, and of a good hope through grace of eternal glory, that he speaks to you of a kingdom whose splendours you have never seen, of a territory whose wealth you have never ransacked, of a world whose glories have never beamed upon you, whose odours have never been wafted to you, whose breezes have never fanned you, whose music has never fallen on your ears, and whose Spirit has never breathed into your heart. *You deny the Holy Ghost*; this is your sin, and your sin is your punishment. You deny the Author of Divine life, light and revelation; do not marvel that all which appertains to experimental godliness is to you death, darkness and mystery. Without this blessed Spirit, you can never know yourself, nor Christ, nor God, nor heaven. Trifle no longer with this subject, refuse Him no longer Divine honour, lay aside the prejudices of education and of creeds, and fall down and plead for the teaching of this Spirit, whose personal dignity you have so long denied, whose word you have so long rejected, whose voice you have so long disregarded, and all whose influences you would, were it possible, this moment quench. Yet He is faithful, kind and forgiving. You have denied Him, but "He cannot deny himself"; though you believe not, yet "He abideth faithful." He can dissolve your heart, give you true contrition, and lead you to the atoning blood of Jesus for the pardon of your sin.   But if resolved to adhere to your present views, remember the awfully solemn words of our Lord—may they sink down into your ears— " Whosoever speaketh a word against the Son of man, it shall be forgiven him : but whosoever speaketh against the Holy Ghost, it shall not be forgiven him, neither in this world, neither in the world to come."

CHAPTER II

The Spirit a Quickener

THE SOUL BEFORE CONVERSION

" *It is the Spirit that quickeneth.*"—John 6. 63.

HAVING laid the basis of the Holy Spirit's work in His PERSONAL DIGNITY, it will now be an easy and a more delightful (because less controversial) task to raise the super-structure.

Commencing from such a foundation—the GODHEAD of the Spirit—what dignity and glory attach to His various offices and operations, as contained in the covenant of redemption, and as unfolded in the work of grace upon the heart! How important that we should enter upon its discussion deeply im-pressed with the spirituality of our theme, with its essential relation to the eternal happiness of the soul, and with fervent prayer for His own Divine illumination!

It will be perceived that, in unfolding His work, we com-mence with the Spirit's first gracious and Divine act—*the breathing of spiritual life in the soul.* This must be regarded as an operation preceding all others. The Spirit's work as a *Quickener* must ever precede His work as a Sanctifier and a Comforter. If we look for Him in any of His offices before we have received Him as the Author of Divine life in the soul, we reverse His own order and cover ourselves with disappoint-ment. We enter upon the discussion of this subject the more readily and, we trust, prayerfully, from the conviction that the modern views of the doctrine of regeneration, as held and preached by many, are not only widely different from the old standards of doctrinal truth, but, which is more serious and deeply to be deplored, are such as the Word of God clearly and distinctly disowns, and upon which there rests the dark-

31

ness of its frown. Regeneration, as taught by many in the present day, differs widely from the doctrine as preached in the days of the apostles and reformers. In their writings and discourses the basis was deeply and broadly laid in the original and total depravity of man; this doctrine is now by many greatly modified, if not absolutely denied. In the days of primitive Christianity, the utter helplessness of the creature, and the absolute and indispensable necessity of the Holy Spirit's influences in the regeneration of the soul, were distinctly and rigidly enforced; sentiments the reverse of these, subversive of the Scripture doctrine of regeneration, and destructive of the best interests of the soul, are now zealously and widely promulgated. Surely this is a cause of deep humiliation before God; may He restore to His ministers and people a pure language, and graciously revive the precious, soul-humbling, Christ-honouring truths, once the safeguard and the glory of our land. We propose in this and the following chapter to present a simple and scriptural delineation of the doctrine of regeneration, the office of the Holy Spirit in its production, and some of the holy effects as traced in the life of a believer. May there descend on the reader the anointing of the Holy One, and may the truth empty, sanctify and comfort the heart.

Regeneration is a work standing alone and distinct from all the other operations of the Divine Spirit. It is to be carefully distinguished from conversion, adoption, justification and sanctification, and yet must be regarded as forming the basis and the spring-head of them all. For instance, there can be no conversion without a principle of *life* in the soul, for conversion is the exercise of a spiritual power implanted in man. There can be no sense of adoption apart from a renewed nature, for adoption confers the privilege only, not the nature, of sons. There can be no comforting sense of acceptance in the Beloved until the mind has passed from death unto life, nor can there be the smallest advance in a conformity of the will and of the affections to the image of God while there is wanting in the soul the very root of holiness. Faith is a purifying grace, but faith is only found in the heart " created anew in Christ Jesus." There must necessarily be the spiritual renewal of the whole man, before the soul can pass into an adopted, justified and sanctified state. Reader, ponder seriously this solemn truth. It will probably aid us in arriving at a clearer and more accurate knowledge of the true nature of regeneration, or the new birth, if we briefly look at the subject first from a *negative* point of view.

Notice first of all that *regeneration is not an act of grace conferred upon an individual in the external rite or ordinance of baptism.* An error so untenable on scriptural grounds and so fatal to the spiritual interests of the soul, we could scarcely believe would find an advocate professing to be taught of the Spirit, in this gospel-illumined age. And yet from the pulpit and from the press, both professing to be the guardians of evangelical truth, this doctrine is zealously propagated; thousands receive it as a Divinely revealed truth, and live and die in the fatal delusion. Oh, did every professed minister of Christ but study the third chapter of John's Gospel, with earnest prayer for the teaching of the Spirit, before he attempted to expound to others the way of salvation, how soon would the heresy of baptismal regeneration be expelled from our pulpits, and banished from the land! Let us endeavour to pour the light of Divine truth upon this dark and fatal error.

We observe that the application of water in any mode, as a sacramental rite, is utterly impotent in the production of this mighty change in man. It cannot impart spiritual life to a soul " dead in trespasses and sins." The following are some of the strong and emphatic expressions which the Word of God employs in describing the new birth : " Born again "— " born of the Spirit "—" quickened by the Spirit "—" created anew in Christ Jesus "—" made alive "—" new creature." Claims that the external application of water, even as a sacred rite, could effect the great change implied in these phrases, are utterly incredible to a spiritual and reflecting mind.

To regard the ordinance of baptism as a vehicle by which the Spirit of God operates on the heart is equally unscriptural and dangerous. As a means of grace, it cannot be relied upon.

B

If regeneration has not transpired in the soul *before* the act of baptism, we are nowhere in the Scriptures of truth authorised to believe that mere submission to the external ceremony confers spiritual life upon the subject. The ordinances both of baptism and the Lord's supper are to be considered, as far as they relate to the receiver, merely as sources of spiritual nourishment and comfort to the grace *already* implanted in the soul, through the omnipotent and effectual operation of the Spirit of God. The one may more properly be regarded as a *witness* to the grace that is there; the other, as a Divinely instituted source of *nourishment* to that grace. If it is not so; if this setting aside the two ordinances of Christ's church as causes of spiritual life is not scriptural and proper, then it must follow that all who have submitted to these external institutions are actually regenerated; and so, in reference to the departure into eternity of the avowed unbeliever, on the ground that baptismal regeneration be true, death is to him the birth-day of a glorious immortality! If this be not a most awful inference, properly and legitimately drawn from the error we have stated, we know not what is. The advocate of baptismal regeneration cannot evade it. It is a fair, legitimate and logical conclusion deduced from his own premises. If all those who have ever been baptised were, in the act, made the subjects of renewing grace, then thousands are now shut up in the regions of hopeless despair who ought not to be there. They were baptised and yet they lived in open rebellion against God and died, as the record of many testifies, with the "terrors of the Lord" already in their consciences. And, if baptism is a rite *essential* to salvation, it must follow that vast numbers are now in glory, who, never having submitted to that institution, are admitted there on *other* grounds than the mere observance of an external ceremony. We cite from among many, the case of the thief upon the cross, as illustrating our idea. There is no record of his having received Christian baptism, either in the early part of his life, for he was a pagan, or at the period of his death. And yet, here is presented to us the amazing spectacle of a *heathen malefactor*, passing from spiritual death unto spiritual life at the very extremity of his ignominious existence; and, without having washed in the laver of baptism, going from the cross to receive a kingdom and a crown. If water baptism be *essential* to salvation, let the advocate of the doctrine explain to us the nature and the cause of this remarkable conversion and this triumphant death.

Reader, your baptism, whether received in infancy or in riper years, will avail you nothing if you are not a new creature. You may be baptised, and yet be lost; you may not be baptised, and yet be saved. " In Christ Jesus, neither circumcision availeth any thing, nor uncircumcision " (and the same is true of *baptism*), " but a new creature." Gal. 6. 15. Your baptism infused into you no principle of life; it conferred upon you no saving grace. You must be born again of the Spirit, be washed in the blood of Christ and be clothed in His righteousness before you can enter the kingdom of grace on earth, or be admitted within the kingdom of glory in heaven.

Again, *an outward reformation of habit does not constitute the spiritual change under investigation.* The influence of education, early moral instruction, attendance upon an evangelical ministry, combined with the moral restraints of society, will go far in effecting an outward reformation of human character. There may be much unfolding itself which bears strong resemblance to the sweet flower of Divine grace —gentleness—kindness—amiability; there may be the heart that pours forth its deep sympathies over the picture of human suffering—the tear that falls upon the pallid cheek of sickness—the arm that is nerved to shield the oppressed—the hand that is extended to relieve the widow and the fatherless; and yet " repentance toward God, and faith toward our Lord Jesus Christ " (the spring of all true holiness and goodness)— may be strangers to that bosom. In others, there may be the excision of outward sins, the giving up of sinful habits long indulged in, even a love of virtue, an approval of things that are excellent, and a diligent observance of the means of grace, marking the character and deportment; and all the while, the heart—self-deceived—may know nothing of the renewing, transforming, humbling power of God the Holy Ghost. Regeneration is a mighty and a deep work. It does not rest upon the surface. It has to do with the deep, hidden principle of evil in the heart of man. It allows nothing for the tender and kindly instincts of our fallen nature. It does not destroy or weaken them in the wonderful process through which the mind passes at the period of its renewal, but rather invests them with a new character and directs them into another and a holier channel; yet in the effecting of this mighty moral revolution they take no part, and can lay claim to none of the glory.

This chapter may possibly arrest the attention of the rigid moralist, who, up to the present, has been enveloping himself in the thick and silken foldings of a self-complacent and self-righteous spirit, not for a moment suspecting the existence of a deep taint of ungodliness within, which, in the eye of a holy and a heart-searching God, mars all his moral virtues, and renders of none effect all his moral duties. Reader, may the Lord the Spirit in His infinite mercy bring you out of this awful state of self-deception; and, as one step towards it, He warns you in His word to trust to no view of yourself presented by the false mirror of your own heart. That "heart is deceitful above all things, and desperately wicked." Do not trust in it, it is treacherous; expect nothing truly good from it, it is a depth of undiscovered depravity. Is this harsh language? Are these sentiments revolting to you? *I speak but the truth of God* when I say that your heart, in its present unrenewed state, is your worst enemy. Does it speak soothingly? It speaks but to flatter. Does the surface look fair and pleasant to the eye? Beneath is every thing that defiles, and that works abomination. O the awful picture your renewed heart would present to your view were the Holy Spirit *now* to put in the plough of conviction, break up the hard and fallow ground, and bring to the surface the hidden evil that is there. How would you shudder at the discovery, and shrink away from the sight!

Again, shall we add, after the exceptions we have made, *that an outward profession of the Gospel may exist, and yet the heart be a stranger to this spiritual process?* And yet the age we live in demands a distinct avowal of this. If in the days of our Lord and of His faithful and vigilant apostles—the days when a public profession of attachment to Christ was to mark a man for the cross and the stake—if in their days and under these circumstances there were found those who could take refuge in a mere outward profession, is it astonishing that *now*, when it costs a man nothing to profess Christ, but rather adds to his worldly influence and emolument, thousands should run upon this quicksand and make shipwreck of their souls? Oh, it is no marvel. Our blessed Lord foresaw and forewarned men of this evil. Let His words—searching and solemn as though now uttered from the judgment-seat—sink down into our ears: "Not every one that saith unto me, Lord, Lord, shall enter into the kingdom of heaven; but he that doeth the will of my Father which is in heaven. Many will say to me in that day, Lord, Lord, have we not prophesied in thy name? and in thy name have cast out devils? and in thy name have done many wonderful works? And then will I profess unto them, I never knew you: depart from me, ye that work iniquity." Matt. 7. 21-23.

Yet we would go farther than this. In reviewing the negative evidences of regeneration, it is of the utmost importance that we do not overlook *that close approximation to this work, which in numberless cases may take place, but which when brought to the test of God's Word proves but an awful deception.* Few, save those who have been taught of the Spirit and who have accustomed themselves to analyse closely the evidences of true conversion, are aware how far an individual may go, not merely in an outward reformation of character and in an external union to Christ, but in a strong resemblance to the positive and manifest evidences of the new birth, without the actual possession of a single one. If there is one aspect in which our subject may be viewed as more solemn than another, it is this. May the eternal Spirit lead us into deep self-examination and prayer, while examining these false evidences of regeneration.

We have observed that there may be in an individual's

frame of mind and outward conduct, much that bears a strong
affinity and resemblance to many of the positive evidences of
the new birth, without a single step towards that state having
been taken. There may be, as regards the state of mind, a deep
and clear knowledge of Divine truth, a strongly enlightened
judgment, and a sound and scriptural creed. There may be a
strong attachment to, and a zealous maintenance of, some of
the distinguishing doctrines of grace—even a desire to hear
of Christ, and an ability to judge between sound and unsound
preaching—and all the while the *heart* may be encased in the
hardness of impenitence and unbelief, a stranger to the regenerating influence of the Spirit of God. Do not misinterpret
our meaning. We are not saying anything against a true
spiritual and experimental acquaintance with Divine truth.
We do not forget that there can be no faith in Christ without
some knowledge of Christ. The very existence of faith in the
heart implies the existence of, and an acquaintance with, the
object of faith—the Lord Jesus. We are not against an enlarged possession of Divine knowledge. It would be well for
the Church of Christ, and would greatly promote her stability
and real spirituality, were the standard of Divine knowledge
more elevated in her midst. It would screen her from much
of the unsound theology and false philosophy, which, at this
moment, threaten her purity and her peace. It cannot with
perfect truth be said, as far as an elevated and spiritual taste
and thirst for experimental truth are concerned, that
"wisdom and knowledge are the stability of our times."
Much of the prevalent religion is characterised by "itching
ears," 2 Tim. 4. 3; habit of "change," Prov. 24. 21; "unstable-
ness," 2 Pet. 3. 16; affected by "every wind of doctrine," Eph.
4. 14; and which, in its influence, is "barren and unfruitful,"
2 Pet. 1. 8. Were there a more diligent and prayerful study
of God's word, a more regular and constant attendance upon
a stated ministry (if that ministry be found productive of
spiritual benefit), connected with frequent seasons of retirement consecrated to meditation, self-examination and secret
prayer, there would be less of that superficial Christianity
which marks the many in this day of high and universal

profession. We want more depth of knowledge, more spirituality, more experience, more of the life and power of true godliness; in a word, more of the anointing and sanctifying influences of the Holy Ghost in the church.

But in the exception that we make, we refer to a knowledge of the truth that is not saving in its effects, is not influential in its character, and which has its place in the *judgment* only. Here the truth may be assented to, approved of, and even ably and successfully vindicated, while the *soul*, the seat of life—the *will*, the instrument of holiness—and the *heart*, the home of love, are all unrenewed by the Holy Spirit. You cannot be too distinctly nor too earnestly informed that there is a great difference in Divine knowledge. There is a knowledge of the truth, in the attainment of which a man may labour diligently, and in the possession of which he may look like a believer, but which may not come under that denomination of a knowledge of Christ, in allusion to which our dear Lord in His memorable prayer uses these words, "This is life eternal, that they might know thee the only true God, and Jesus Christ, whom thou hast sent." John 17. 3. The fatal error to which you are exposed is—O that you may have escaped it!—the substitution of knowledge of Divine truth in the judgment for the quickening grace of God in the heart. It is surprising how far an outwardly moral individual may go in Divine attainments—spiritual knowledge—eminent gifts—and even great usefulness, and yet retain the carnal mind, the rebellious will, the unhumbled and unbroken heart. If the volume of Divine truth had not informed us of this, and supplied us with some striking and solemn cases in proof, we should be perpetually beguiled into the belief that a head filled with rational, speculative, theoretical truth must necessarily be connected with some degree of Divine grace in the affections. But not so. Balaam's knowledge of Divine things was deep; he could ask counsel of God and prophesy of Christ, but where is the undoubted evidence that he "knew the grace of God in truth"? Saul prophesied, had "another spirit" given him, and asked counsel of God; but Saul's heart was unchanged by the Holy Spirit. Herod sent

for John, and "heard him gladly, and did many things," and
yet his heart and his life were strangers to holiness. Addressing the Pharisees, the apostle employs this striking language,
"Behold, thou are called a Jew, and restest in the law, and
makest thy boast of God, and knowest his will, and approvest
the things that are more excellent, being instructed out of the
law" : and yet deep hypocrisy was their crying sin. O let no
man be so deceived as to substitute *knowledge* for *grace*.
Better that his knowledge of the truth should be limited to its
mere elements, its first principles, and yet with it be enabled
to say, " ' Behold, I am vile,' but ' He hath loved me and given
himself for me,' " than to possess " all knowledge," and live
and die destitute of the renewing grace of God upon the
heart.

Still farther may an individual go in an approximation to
the evidences of true godliness, and yet remain unregenerate.
He may possess *eminent spiritual gifts*—fluency of expression
in prayer—great exhortatory powers—eloquence in preaching—clear discrimination in spiritual subjects—the discerning
of spirits—the gift of speaking and of interpreting of tongues;
yet continue a graceless soul, retaining the "carnal mind"
and the "heart of stone." What, we ask, is the most instruc-
tive and solemn page in the history of the Corinthian church?
—that which teaches us that *great gifts may exist in union
with great impiety*; in other words, that gifts are not graces,
that an individual, or a community of individuals, may
possess the gifts that edify, and at the same time be destitute
of the grace that humbles and sanctifies. On the other hand,
how frequently is the union found to exist of feeble natural
and acquired gifts with great grace, deep spirituality, and
even extensive usefulness! The tongue has stammered in
prayer; thought, deep welled in the mind, has found no
adequate utterance; feelings, burning in the heart, no outlet;
a glowing and spiritually-chastened imagination, no conduc-
tor; and yet in the man's secret life, there has been the holy
and close walk of a patriarch, and in his public one, the self-
consuming zeal of an apostle. God has revealed to him the
secret of His love; Christ has opened to him the treasures of

His grace; and the Holy Spirit has sealed him to the day of redemption. Well might an eminent prelate exclaim, as he surveyed a spectacle like this—" The poor illiterate world attain to heaven, while we, with all our learning, fall into hell."

One step farther would we go. There may be strong light and conviction of sin in the conscience (Heb. 6. 4)—deep distress of soul in the near prospect of death and eternity (Acts 24. 25)—this succeeded by solemn vows, purposes and resolutions (Exod. 9. 27, 28)—and this by a species of joy (Matt. 13. 20)—connected with an external mortification of sin (Acts 8. 12, 13)—and yet the mighty and spiritual process of regeneration may not even have commenced in the soul. Far be it from us to say that the Spirit of God may not employ these as means of conversion—He may, He often does; yet they may exist alone and apart from any connection with a work of grace. We are aware that, in showing what regeneration is *not*, we have assumed high and solemn ground, and have advanced statements which, if supported by the Scriptures of truth (and we have endeavoured to fortify every position by the Word of God), will break up the lying refuges, undermine the spurious hopes, explode the false evidences, and rip apart the specious covering of many now dwelling in the outer courts of Christianity and making a "fair show" of religion "in the flesh." Gal. 6. 12. But the vast importance of the subject and its vital relation to the eternal happiness of the soul demanded from us a close investigation of the false evidences of this great work. We now proceed to view *positively* the nature of regeneration.

Need we enlarge upon the moral state of the soul which is the reverse of true regeneration? It may be helpful to glance briefly at it. It is described in God's Word in dark colours, and by gloomy images. The *heart* is spoken of as depraved—the *understanding* as darkened—the *will* as perverted—the *affections* as estranged. Look at the description of the *heart* in its natural state. Jer. 17. 9: "The *heart* is deceitful above all things, and desperately wicked." Matt. 15. 19: "For out of the *heart* proceed evil thoughts, murders,

adulteries, fornications, thefts, false witness, blasphemies."
Awful picture of the natural heart!—the picture of *all* yet in
an unrenewed state. There may not be the overt act of sin,
the actual commission, the outbreaking of the evil—but *the
evil is there*, deeply imbedded and hidden there, and only
restrained by the power of God. Read again, Eccles. 8. 11:
"Because sentence against an evil work is not executed
speedily, therefore the *heart* of the sons of men is fully set in
them to do evil." Eccles. 9. 3: "The *heart* of the sons of
men is full of evil, and madness is in their *heart* while they
live." Can language present the natural state of the heart in
more affecting and awful terms? Here it is represented as
"fully set to do evil"—"full of evil and madness"—"deceitful"—"desperately wicked." The surface may be fair
to the eye—there may be kindness, affection, benevolence
dwelling there; but beneath that surface is deep, deep ungodliness. No love to God there—no affection for Jesus there—
no thirst for holiness there—no crucifixion of sin and self
there; and until the Holy Spirit enters and creates all things
new, all things will remain as they were, under the unbroken dominion and tyranny of sin.

The *understanding* is dark. Eph. 4. 18: "Having the
understanding darkened." Hence there can be no true knowledge of God and of Christ; no proper acquaintance with His
word, His law, His commands; no just realisation of eternity,
no proper estimate of time. All is spiritual darkness in the soul.

The *will* is perverted. It is in opposition to God and
holiness. It has no bias towards spiritual and heavenly things.
Its natural bent and disposition is to evil; evil only, and evil
continually.

But there is more. There is *positive enmity* in the natural
man to God. Rom. 8. 7: "The carnal mind is enmity against
God: for it is not subject to the law of God, neither indeed
can be." This is a strong expression; the apostle states that
the carnal mind is not only alienated from God, averse to
Him, but is actual enmity. Had he represented the carnal
mind as an *enemy* to God, that would have sounded startling;
but when he describes it as "*enmity*" itself, we have the

most vivid and awful idea of man's state by nature. An *enemy* may be reconciled, but *enmity* cannot. The ground of this enmity the apostle states to be "the law of God": "It is not subject to the law of God." The enmity of the carnal heart is against God as the *moral Governor* of the universe. Let not the reader, especially if there be the honest conviction in his conscience of the existence of the carnal mind, overlook this important fact. There is danger of turning aside from the true cause of man's enmity to God. We repeat then, all are enemies to God who do not submit to His kingly authority. Men may imagine they admire and love God under other characters, but hate Him as a Lawgiver. But this cannot be. If God be not loved, adored and obeyed as a Lawgiver, He cannot, without denying Himself and throwing contempt upon His own law, recognise the supposed love and adoration of any of His creatures. Supreme dominion is essential to His character, and to be properly and truly loved He must be loved as a *King*. Among men, the person and the office may be separable. A man may be the personal friend of the king, and yet an enemy to his government. As a *man*, he may be loved; as a *magistrate*, he may be hated. We can imagine that many who lived in the days of the Commonwealth were sincerely attached to the *person* of Oliver Cromwell, but disapproved of his *government*, and condemned as unjustifiable his usurpation of authority and power. But not so in reference to God, the moral Governor of the world. His nature and His office, His attributes and His government are inseparable: and no one can possibly be a friend to God who hates His government and refuses obedience to His law.

Now "the carnal mind is enmity against God" because of His moral government. The question is, "who shall reign, God or the sinner?" This is the only ground of controversy. Decide this question in *favour* of the sinner, and so far as it relates to him, the controversy ceases. Only let God drop the reins of His government—let Him descend from His throne, lay aside His sceptre, give up His law—and the enmity of the carnal mind ceases. Man would revel in His goodness admire His wisdom, and adore His power. But God can as soon cease to be, as give up His right to dominion. He must assert His claim to the throne. He is bound to maintain the dignity, shield the purity and support the honour of His law; and sooner can heaven and earth pass away than one jot or one tittle of that law fail. This the carnal mind cannot bear, "for it is not subject to the law of God, neither indeed can be."

Enmity against God, O awful thought! Enmity to the best of beings, the dearest of friends! Enmity to Him whose nature and whose name is love!—who is holy, yes, *holiness* itself—good, yes, *goodness* itself—true, yes, *truth* itself! Enmity to Him, out of whom nothing is good, nothing holy, nothing true; who is the Fountain from whence all the streams flow, the Sun from which all the rays emanate. Enmity to Him, who gave His Son to die for *sinners*! "For God so loved the world, that he gave His only begotten Son, that whosoever believeth in Him should not perish, but have everlasting life." "God commendeth His love toward us, in that, while we were yet *sinners*, Christ died for us." Yes, to die for His *enemies*. "When we were *enemies*, we were reconciled to God by the death of His Son." Romans 5. 10. Enmity to *Jesus* who thus died; who flew on wings of love to the rescue and the redemption of fallen man; who took the place, bore the sins, endured the curse, all this for rebel man; who gave His life, His obedience, all He could give—*Himself*; all this for the poor, the vile, the worthless; who suffered, bled and died —was not *this* enough? Could He have done more? The law said, "it is enough"; Justice said, "I am satisfied"; all this—and who can estimate it? all this for *sinners*, for *rebels*, for *enemies*! Son of God, is it for *this* they hate Thee, despise Thee, reject Thee? Oh, the enmity of the carnal mind!

If possible, the Word of God gives a yet more awful description of the unrenewed state of man. It is represented under the image of *death*. The natural condition of the soul is moral death. Thus is it described. Eph. 2. 1: "*Dead* in trespasses and sins"; and verse 5: "When we were *dead* in

sins." Col. 2. 13 : "You being *dead* in your sins." Rom.
5. 15 : "Through the offence of one, many are *dead*." This is
his awful state—spiritually, legally and (if the quickening
power of the eternal Spirit of God does not interpose) judicially
dead. Insensibility to all spiritual things marks the unrenewed mind. To things that are *carnal*, it is all feeling, all
sensitiveness, all life. *Here* all its natural faculties are in full
vigour and play. The *understanding*, the *will*, the *affections*
find ample range for their carnal propensities, powerful incen-
tives to their indulgence, and revel and exult and expatiate
amid the world of sensual delight—limited it is confessed—
that opens to their view. O yes, all is life *here*. The *mind*
can think, reason, compare and arrange; the *will* can select,
and the *affections* pour forth their tender yearnings—and still
the pall of spiritual death covers the soul!

What are the symptoms? Is *insensibility* a mark of death?
Then it is here. No spiritual sensation—no feeling—no emotion; all is stagnant, quiet and motionless as the river of death.
True, the *natural conscience* may for a moment be aroused,
and the agitated and alarmed soul may exhibit some signs of
feeling—and so will a *corpse* under the influence of galvanic
power—the eye may roll, and the lip may move, and every
feature in the countenance assume the expression of life, *but
it is a corpse still.* We speak to the soul dead in trespasses
and sins; we employ the language of *terror*; we preach the
law; we unfold its authority, its purity, its demands; we announce its curse, its threatening, its fearful doom. We speak
of a holy God, a sin-seeing, sin-hating, sin-avenging God; we
uncover *hell* and reveal its darkness, its quenchless flame, its
undying worm, the smoke of its eternal torments; we look—
but not a bosom heaves, not an eye weeps, not a lip quivers,
not a feature wears the aspect of terror—all, all is still, cold
and motionless; *death* is there!

We change our theme. We speak in the language of *persuasive tenderness*. We preach the *Gospel*. We proclaim its
divinity, its design, its fulness, its freeness, the mercy it
promises, the blessings it breathes, the glory it unfolds. We
lift up *Jesus*, as loving sinners, dying for sinners, receiving

sinners, saving sinners. We unveil *heaven*, and bring to view
its light, its holiness, its cloudless day, its eternal sunshine, its
deep songs of joy, its never-dying, ever-growing bliss; we look
—but not a heart throbs, not an eye glistens, not a lip praises,
not a countenance beams with delight—all, all is quiet, cold,
and silent—for *death* is there! Awful picture of the unrenewed man!

Does the absence of *breath*—the vital principle of life—
denote a state of death? *Then it is here*. *Prayer* is the vital
energy of a quickened soul, the spiritual breath of one "born
from above." It is the first symptom of sensibility—the first
and strongest evidence that "the Spirit that quickens" has
entered the soul, breathing over the whole man the "breath
of life." The pulse may at first beat but faintly, even as the
first gentle heaving of an infant's bosom; still it is not less the
product of the Spirit, the breath of God. "Behold he
prayeth" is the announcement that sends gladness through
the church of Christ on earth, and kindles joy among the
angels of God in heaven. God the Father hastens to welcome
the returning and resuscitated soul, and exclaims, "This my
son was *dead*, and is *alive* again. Luke 15. 24. It will follow
then that the *absence of prayer* marks the soul yet "dead in
sins." What evidence can be more convincing? It is a symptom that cannot mislead. The *praying* soul is a *quickened*
soul. The *prayerless* soul is a *lifeless* soul. The individual
that has never truly prayed has never known what one throb
of spiritual life is. He may content himself with the external
form—he may kneel in the outer court of the tabernacle, and,
as the holy Leighton[1] expresses it, "breathe his tune and air
of words," and yet continue an utter stranger to true prayer.
Are *you* such a one? Let the voice of tender affection now
lead you to a serious consideration of your real state. Do not
mistake the outward form for the inward spirit of prayer.
The soul may be dead, with all the appearance of life. But
where there is *true prayer*, there is *real life*; for prayer is the
ascending of the Divine life to God from whom it came. It

---

[1] Robert Leighton (1611-1684), author of a once famous commentary
on the *First Epistle of Peter*.

came from God, and returns to Him again. As the river flows towards the ocean, or as the infant turns to its mother, the author of its existence and the source of its nourishment, as the "well of water" in a renewed soul "springing up" rises heavenwards—so a soul born of God turns to God, its Author, its Sustainer, its Keeper.

But it is proper that we detain the reader no longer from a consideration of the real nature of the spiritual change. It is the reverse of what we have, with some minuteness and at some length, been describing. The Word of God shall be the speaker here.

It is a passing from death unto life. John 5. 24: "Verily, verily, he that heareth my word, and believeth on him that sent me, hath everlasting life, and shall not come into con- demnation; *but is passed from death unto life.*" Col. 2. 13: "And you, being *dead* in your sins, and the uncircumcision of your flesh, hath he *quickened.*" 1 John 3. 14: "We know that we have passed from death unto life."

It is a new creature. 2 Cor. 5. 17: "Therefore if any man be in Christ, he is a *new creature*: old things are passed away; behold, all things are become new." Gal. 6. 15: "For in Christ Jesus neither circumcision availeth anything, nor uncircum- cision, but a *new creature.*"

It is a Divine nature. 2 Pet. 1. 4: "Partakers of the Divine *nature.*" Heb. 12. 10: "Partakers of *his holiness.*"

A new birth. John 3. 3: "Except a man be *born again* (marg. *from above*) he cannot see the kingdom of God." John 1. 13: "Which were born, not of blood, nor of the will of the flesh, nor of the will of man, but of God." 1 Pet. 1. 23: "Being *born again*, not of corruptible seed, but of incor- ruptible, by the Word of God, which liveth and abideth for ever."

A turning from darkness to light. 1 Pet. 2. 9: "But ye are a chosen generation, a royal priesthood, an holy nation, a peculiar people; that ye should shew forth the praises of him who hath *called you out of darkness into his marvellous light.*"

A change from enmity to love. Col. 1. 21: "And you, that

were sometime *alienated*, and *enemies* in your mind by wicked works, yet now hath he *reconciled*." 1 John 4. 19 : "We love him." Rom. 5. 5 : "The love of God is shed abroad in our hearts."

A restoration of the Divine image. Col. 3. 10 : "And have put on the new man, which is renewed in knowledge *after the image of him* that created him." Rom. 8. 29 : "For whom he did foreknow, he also did predestinate *to be conformed to the image of his Son.*" 1 John 2. 29 : "If ye know that he is righteous, ye know that *every one that doeth righteousness is born of him.*"

Thus clearly and emphatically does the Word of God speak when unfolding the nature of true regeneration. Reserving for the next chapter the consideration of the Author and the evidences of this work, we close the present one by holding up more distinctly and prominently to view a few of the broad lineaments of the new creature.

The Holy Ghost testifies that "if any man be in Christ, he is a *new creature.*" This testimony is true. For first, *he loves and worships a new God.* The natural man is a god to himself, and he has many other gods as well. Whether it be self-righteousness, self-gratification, the world, wealth, family, in whatever form it appears, "other lords have dominion over him," to the exclusion of the one true and living God. The nature of the human mind is such that it must love and worship some object supremely. In his state of innocence, Jehovah was the one and supreme object of the creature's love and adoration. Seduced from that state of simple and supreme affection by the tempter's promise that, if they ate of the fruit of the tree forbidden of God, "they should be as gods," in one moment they threw off their allegiance to Jehovah, renounced him as the object of their supreme love, the centre of their holiest affections, *and became gods to themselves.* The temple was ruined, the altar was thrown down, the pure flame was extinguished, God departed and "other lords" entered and took possession of the soul. But what a change does grace produce! It repairs the temple, rebuilds the altar, rekindles the flame and brings God back to man! God in

Christ is *now* the supreme object of his love, his adoration and his worship. The idol *self* has been cast down, self-righteousness renounced, self-exaltation crucified. The " strong man armed " has entered, cast out the usurper, and, " creating all things new," has resumed his rightful supremacy. The affections, released from their false deity and renewed by the Spirit, now turn to and take up their rest in God. God in Christ! how glorious does He now appear! Truly it is a *new God* the soul is brought to know and love. Never did it see in Him such beauty, such excellence, such blessedness as it *now* sees. All other glory fades and dies before the surpassing glory of His character, His attributes, His government, and His law. God in Christ is viewed as *reconciled* now; enmity ceases; hatred has passed away; opposition grounds its weapons; hard thoughts of His law, and rebellious thoughts of His government, subside; love kindles in the soul and, in one precious Christ the one Mediator, God and the sinner meet, embrace and blend. Truly they become one. God says, "Thou are mine." The soul responds, "Thou art my God— other lords have had dominion over me, but henceforth, Thee only will I serve, Thee only will I love. 'My soul followeth hard after thee; thy right hand upholdeth me.' 'One thing have I desired of the Lord, that will I seek after, that I may dwell in the house of the Lord all the days of my life, to behold the beauty of the Lord, and to inquire in his temple.' "

God in Christ is his *Father* now. " I will arise, and go unto my *Father*," is the first motion of a renewed soul. " Father, I have sinned against Thee," is the first confession rising from the broken heart. The Father hastens to meet and embrace His child, and clasping him to His bosom exclaims, " This My son was *dead*, and is *alive* again." Reconciled, he now looks up to Him truly as his *Father*. " And because ye are sons, God hath sent forth the Spirit of his Son into your hearts, crying, Abba, Father." "Thou shalt call me, My Father; and shalt not turn away from me." Jer. 3. 19. Does God speak? it is the voice of a *Father* he hears. Does God chasten and rebuke? it is from his *Father*, he feels. Are his hopes disappointed, his plans crossed, his cisterns broken, his gourds withered? "My *Father* has done it all," he exclaims. Blessed Spirit of adoption! sweet pledge and evidence art Thou of the new creature.

God in Christ is now the object of *confidence* and *trust*. Trust in a reconciled God and Father was no mark and portion of his unrenewed state. It was *then* trust in self, in its imagined wisdom, strength and goodness. It was *then* trust in the arm of flesh, in second causes. *Now* the soul trusts in God, trusts Him at all times and under all circumstances, trusts Him in the darkest hour, under the gloomiest dispensation, trusts Him when his providences look dark and lowering, and God seems to hide Himself; it even trusts Him "though He slay." *Now* "though the fig tree should not blossom, and there be no fruit in the vines; the labour of the olive fail, and the fields yield no meat; though the flocks be cut off from the fold, and there be no herd in the stall, he will rejoice in the Lord, and joy in the God of his salvation." Oh, how *safe* he feels in God's hands and under His government now! His soul, his body, his family, his business and his cares are completely surrendered, and God is all in all. Reader, *this* is to be born again.

Second, the regenerate soul possesses and acknowledges *a new Saviour*. How glorious, suitable and precious is Jesus to him now! Not so formerly. *Then* he had his saviours, his "refuges of lies," his many fatal confidences. Jesus was to him as "a root out of a dry ground, having no form nor comeliness." It may be that he denied His deity, rejected His atonement, scorned His grace and slighted His pardon and His love. Christ is all to him *now*. He adores Him as the "mighty God, the everlasting Father, the Prince of peace"; as "over all, God blessed for ever"; as "God manifest in the flesh"; as stooping to the nature of *man*, becoming bone of our bone and flesh of our flesh; as offering Himself up as the "propitiation for our sins"; as dying, "the Just for the unjust." His *righteousness* is glorious as "justifying from all things"; His *blood* is precious as "cleansing from all sin"; His *fulness of grace* is valued as "supplying all need." Oh, how surpassingly glorious, inimitably lovely and unutterably precious is Jesus to a renewed soul!

Truly a *new Saviour*! "Other lords" he has renounced; "refuges of lies" he has turned his back upon; "false Christs" he no longer follows. He has found another and a better Saviour—Jesus, the mighty God, the Redeemer of sinners; the "end of the law for righteousness to every one that believeth." All is new to his recovered sight; a new world of glory has floated before his mind. Jesus the Lamb is the light and glory thereof. Never did he suppose there was such beauty in His person, such love in His heart, such perfection in His work, such power and such willingness to save. That blood which was trampled under foot is now precious. That righteousness which was scorned is now glorious. That name which was reviled is now as music to the soul, even "a name that is above every name."

Jesus is his *only* Saviour. Not an allowed confidence has he out of Christ. The covenant of "dead works" he has renounced. The Spirit, having brought him out of and away from it, has led him into the covenant of grace, the substance and stability and glory of which is Jesus. On the broad basis of Immanuel's finished, atoning work he rests his whole soul; and the more he presses the foundation, the more he leans upon the "corner-stone," the stronger and the more able to sustain him does he find it. True, he feels a self-righteous principle closely adhering to him all his journey through the wilderness. When he prays, it is there; when he speaks, it is there; when he labours, it is there; when he reflects, it is there: he detects it when suspicion of its existence would be most at rest. But in the sober moments of his judgment, when prostrate beneath the cross and looking up to God through Jesus, this principle is searched out, abhorred, confessed and mourned over; and with the eye of faith upon a suffering Saviour the language of his expanding heart is,

> "*Other* refuge have I none,
> Hangs my helpless soul on *Thee*."

Third, *new and enlarged views of the Holy Spirit mark a*

regenerate mind. Having received the Holy Ghost as a Quickener, he feels the need of Him now as a Teacher, a Sanctifier, a Comforter and a Sealer. As a *Teacher*, discovering to him more of the hidden evil of the heart, more knowledge of God, of His word and of His Son. As a *Sanctifier*, carrying forward the work of grace in the soul, impressing more deeply on the heart the Divine image, and bringing every thought and feeling and word into sweet, holy and filial obedience to the law of Jesus. As a *Comforter*, leading him in the hour of his deep trial to Christ; comforting, by unfolding the sympathy and tenderness of Jesus, and the exceeding preciousness and peculiar fitness of the many *promises* with which the word of truth abounds for the consolation of the Lord's afflicted. As a *Sealer*, impressing upon his heart the sense of pardon, acceptance, and adoption; and Himself entering, as the "earnest of the inheritance, until the redemption of the purchased possession." Oh, what exalted views does he *now* have of the blessed and eternal Spirit—of His personal glory, His work, His offices, His influences, His love, tenderness, and faithfulness! The ear is open to the softest whisper of His voice; the heart expands to the gentlest impression of His sealing, sanctifying influence. Remembering that he is "a temple of the Holy Ghost," he desires *so* to walk —humbly, softly, watchfully and prayerfully. Avoiding every thing that would grieve "the Spirit," resigning every known sin that would dishonour and cause Him to withdraw; the one single aim of his life is to walk so as to please God, that "God in all things may be glorified."

Fourth, *a new spring of action* is a distinguished feature of the renewed man which must not be overlooked. Every unconverted man has his rule of action; or, in other words, some great governing principle, which is his rule and standard in all that he does. The controlling principle of an unrenewed mind is *self.* His rule is to adopt such a course, and to do such things, as either gratify or elevate himself. Beyond this narrow circle he never moves. Other and more spiritual motives he is a stranger to. But quickened by the Spirit, "born of God," "created anew in Christ Jesus," *the will of God* is now his rule of action, *the glory of God* his aim, and *the love of Christ* his constraining motive. " The expulsive power of a new affection " has found a home and a dwelling-place in his heart; and when his own will comes into competition with God's will, under the holy sway of this " new affection "—the love of Christ—self is renounced, yea swallowed up in God, and God in Christ is all in all.

Fifth, it would be an imperfect enumeration of some of the strong features of the new creature did we omit to notice *the growing nature and tendency of the vital principle of grace thus implanted in the heart of the regenerate.* Nothing more strikingly and truly proves the reality, we would say the divinity, of the work within, than the growing energy and holy tendency that ever accompany it. It is the property of that which has life in itself, to increase—to multiply itself. The seed cast into the earth will germinate. Presently will appear the tender sprout; this will advance to the young sapling, and this in time to the gigantic tree with its overshadowing branches and richly laden with fruit. Obeying the law of its nature, it aspires to that perfection which belongs to it. It *must* grow. Nothing can prevent it but such a wound as will injure the vital principle, or the cutting of it down entirely. *The life of God in the soul of man* contains the principle of *growth.* He that is not *advancing*—adding grace to grace, strength to strength; fruitful in every good word and work; increasing in the knowledge of God, of his own heart, of the preciousness, fulness and all-sufficiency of Jesus; and in Divine conformity " growing up into Christ in all things "—has great reason to suspect the absence of the Divine life in his soul. There may be much that suggests a *resemblance* to the new birth; there may be the portrait finely executed, the marble statue exquisitely chiselled, but there is not the *living* man, " the new creature." We can expect no increase of perfection in a finished picture or in a piece of statuary; that which has not *life* in it cannot grow. This is self-evident.

An individual may look *like* a believer, and even *die*, with a false peace, like the righteous, and all the while retain his dwelling among the tombs. But the spirit we are now considering is that of a man truly "born again." Phil. 3. 12-14: "*Not as though I had already attained*, either were already perfect: but I follow after, if that I may apprehend that for which also I am apprehended of Christ Jesus. Brethren, I count not myself to have apprehended: but this one thing I do, forgetting those things which are behind, and reaching forth unto those things which are before, *I press toward the mark*," &c. O holy resolve of a regenerate man! Here is the springing up of the well of *living* water in the heart. Here is the turning of the soul to God. See how the fountain rises! See how the flame ascends! It is the mighty energy of God the Holy Ghost drawing the soul upward, heavenward, Godward.

Let not the Christian reader close this chapter with a burdened heart. Let no dear child of God "write hard and bitter things against himself" as he reads this last sentence. Let him not come to any hasty, unbelieving, doubting and God-dishonouring conclusions. What are you to *yourself*—worthless—vile—empty? What is Jesus to you—precious—lovely—all your salvation and all your desire? What is *sin* to you—the most hateful thing in the world? And what is *holiness*—the most lovely, the most longed for? What is the throne of grace to you—the most attractive spot? And the cross—the sweetest resting-place in the universe? What is God to you—*your* God and Father—the spring of all your joys—the fountain-head of all your bliss—the centre where your affections meet? Is it so? *Then* you are born again—*then* you are a child of God—*then* you shall never die eternally. Cheer up, precious soul! the day of your redemption draws near. Those low views of yourself—that brokenness, that inward mourning, that secret confession, that longing for more spirituality, more grace, more devotedness and more love does but prove the existence, reality and growth of God's work within you. God the Holy Spirit is there, and these are but the fruits and evidences of His indwelling. Look up, then, reader, and let the thought cheer you—*that soul never perished that felt itself to be vile, and Jesus to be precious.*

Thus have we endeavoured to unfold some of the prominent and essential attributes of the great work of regeneration. The next chapter will exhibit the Author of the work, and a more experimental and practical view of its nature and tendency. And may the anointing of the Holy Ghost rest upon the reader while perusing it.

CHAPTER III

The Spirit a Quickener

THE SOUL AFTER CONVERSION

" *That which is born of the Spirit is spirit.*"—John 3. 6.

NO truth shines with clearer lustre in the Divine word than that salvation, from first to last, is of God. It is convincingly and beautifully shown to be the work of the glorious Trinity in unity : each person of the Godhead occupying a distinct and peculiar office, and yet all engaged upon, and, as it were coalescing in this mighty undertaking. The *Father* is represented as giving His elect in covenant engagement to His Son, John 17. 2. The *Son* is represented as assuming in eternity the office of Surety, and in the "fulness of time" appearing in human form, and suffering for their sins upon the cross, Rom. 8. 3. The *Holy Ghost* is represented as convincing of sin, working faith in the heart, and leading to the atoning blood, John 16. 8. Thus is salvation shown to be the entire work of the Triune God, distinct in office, yet one in purpose. We have now more immediately to do with that department in the stupendous plan which is ascribed especially and peculiarly to God the eternal Spirit.

We have already viewed the sinner in the various phases of his unconverted state. How awful did that state appear! The understanding, the will, the affections were all dark, perverted and alienated from God, with *enmity* and *death* marking every unconverted man. We have seen this state *reversed*; the temple restored, and God dwelling again with men; the heart brought back to its lawful Sovereign, and clinging to Him with all the grasp of its renewed affections; darkness succeeded by light, enmity by love, ingratitude by praise—and the whole soul turning with the rapidity and certainty of the magnetic needle to God, the centre of its high and holy attraction. To whose power are we to attribute this marvellous change? To the sinner himself? That cannot be; for the very principle that led to the first step in departure from God, and which still urges him on in every successive one, supplies him with no adequate power or motive to return. To the mere exercise of some other human agency? That is equally impossible; for in the whole empire of created intelligence God has nowhere delegated such power and authority to a single individual. We must look for the secret of this spiritual change out of the creature, away from men and angels, and seek it in God the eternal Spirit. God looks *within Himself* for the power, and He finds it there, even in His own omnipotent Spirit. This is the great and spiritual truth we are now to consider: *regeneration, the sole and special work of the Holy Spirit.*

The doctrine that assigns to *human power* an efficient part in the new birth is based upon the supposition that there is in man an inherent principle, the natural bias of which is to holiness; and that, because God has created him a rational being, endowed with a will, understanding, conscience, affections and other intellectual and moral properties, therefore the simple, unaided, voluntary exercise of these powers—a simple choosing of that which the conscience and the understanding point out to be good in view of certain motives presented to the mind—is all that is required to bring the soul into the possession of the Divine nature. With all meekness and affection, yet uncompromising regard for the glory of God, would we expose, on scriptural grounds alone, the *fallacy* and the *dangerous tendency* of this hypothesis.

Begging the reader to bear in mind that which in the previous chapter has been advanced touching the actual state of the natural man, we would earnestly call his attention to the following passages. John 3. 6: " That which is born of the flesh is flesh." It is, morally, nothing but flesh. It is carnal, corrupt, depraved, sinful and has no discernment or perception whatever of spiritual things. This is the sense in which the term *flesh*, as opposed to *spirit*, is to be interpreted in

God's Word. It signifies the corruption of nature. Gal. 5. 17 : " For the flesh lusteth against the Spirit, and the Spirit against the flesh : and these are contrary the one to the other." Again, Rom. 8. 5-8 : " For they that are after the flesh do mind the things of the flesh; but they that are after the Spirit the things of the Spirit. For to be carnally minded is death; but to be spiritually minded is life and peace. Because the carnal mind is enmity against God; for it is not subject to the law of God, neither indeed can be. *So then they that are in the flesh cannot please God.*" What further proof do we need of the natural sinfulness and impotence of man? And yet the powerful testimony borne to this by God's Word is by no means exhausted.

Do we speak of his *mind*? Eph. 4. 18 : " Having the understanding darkened." Of his *knowledge*? 1 Cor. 2. 14 : " The natural man receiveth not the things of the Spirit of God; for they are foolishness unto him : neither can he know them, because they are spiritually discerned." Of his *heart*? Eccles. 9. 3 : " The heart of the sons of men is full of evil." Of his *love to God*? Rom. 8. 7 : " Enmity." Of his *ability to believe*? John 12. 39 : " They could not believe." Of his *power to acknowledge Christ*? 1 Cor. 12. 3 : " No man can say that Jesus is the Lord, but by the Holy Ghost." Thus minute, clear and solemn is the testimony of the Holy Ghost Himself, touching the real amount of *human power* brought to bear upon the production of spiritual life in the soul of man.

So far from co-operating with the Spirit in the new creation, the natural man presents every *resistance* and *opposition* to it. There is not only a passive *aversion* but an active *resistance* to the work. The stream of man's natural inclinations, as we have fully proved from the Scriptures of truth, runs counter to all holiness. A strong and steady current has set in against God, and all that God loves. The pride of reason, the perverseness of the will, the enmity of the mind, the heart's love of sin, all are up in arms against the entrance of the Holy Spirit. Satan, the great enemy of God and man, has been too long in quiet and undisturbed possession of the soul to resign his dominion without a strong and a fearful struggle to maintain it. When the Spirit of God knocks at the door of the heart, every ally is summoned by the "strong man armed" to "resist" the Spirit, and bar and bolt each avenue to His entrance. All is alarm, agitation and commotion within. There is a danger of being dispossessed, and every argument and persuasion and contrivance must be resorted to, in order to retain the long undisputed throne. The *world* is summoned to throw out its most enticing bait—ambition, wealth, literary and political distinction, pleasure in her thousand forms of fascination and power—all are made to pass, as in review, before the mind. The *flesh* exerts its power—the love of sin is appealed to, affection for some long-cherished lust, some long-indulged habit, some "fond amusement," some darling taste—these, inspired with new vigour, are summoned to the rescue. Thus Satan, the world, and the flesh, are opposed to the Father, the Son, and the Spirit, in the great work of spiritual regeneration. Oh let no individual be so deceived as to believe that when God the eternal Spirit enters the soul, He finds the temple swept and garnished, and prepared for His reception—that, without the exercise of His own omnipotent and irresistible power, the *heart* bounds to welcome Him, and *reason* bows submissively to His government, and the *will* yields an instant and humble compliance. O no! If He that is in the regenerate were not greater and more powerful than he that is in the world, such is the enmity of the heart to God, such the strong power and love of sin, such the supreme control which Satan exerts over the whole empire of man, God would be for ever shut out, and the soul for ever lost. But see how clearly regeneration is proved to be *the work of the Spirit*. A few quotations from His own Word will set the question at rest.

Examine the following. "Except a man be born of water and of the Spirit, he cannot enter into the kingdom of God." "It is the Spirit that quickeneth, the flesh profiteth nothing." "That which is born of the flesh is flesh; and that which is born of the Spirit is spirit." "Not by works of righteousness which we have done, but according to his mercy he saved us, by the washing of regeneration, and renewing of the Holy Ghost." Other passages show the *power* exerted in regeneration to be *infinite*. God says, " A new heart also will I give you, and a new spirit will I put within you: and I will take away the stony heart out of your flesh, and I will give you an heart of flesh." The same power that called the material creation from nothing into existence, effects the new and spiritual creation. " God, who commanded the light to shine out of darkness, hath shined in our hearts, to give the light of the knowledge of the glory of God in the face of Jesus Christ." The same power that raised up Jesus from the dead—" And what is the exceeding greatness of his power to us-ward who believe, according to the working of his mighty power, which he wrought in Christ, when he raised him from the dead." We need not multiply proof. God has written it as with a sunbeam, that "we are His workmanship," and that the eternal Spirit is the mighty Agent.

We now proceed to show in *what manner* the blessed Spirit commences, carries forward and sustains this great work in the soul.

First, the commencement of spiritual life is *sudden*. We are far from confining the Spirit to a certain prescribed order in this or any other part of His work. He is a *Sovereign*, as we shall presently show, and therefore works according to His own will. But there are some methods He more frequently adopts than others. We would not say that all *conversion* is a sudden work. There is a knowledge of sin, conviction of its guilt, repentance before God on account of it; these are frequently slow and gradual in their advance. But the first communication of Divine *light* and *life* to the soul is always *sudden*—sudden and instantaneous as was the creation of *natural light*. " God said, Let there be light, and there was light." It was but a word, and in an instant chaos rolled away, and every object and scene in nature was bathed in light and glory. Sudden as was the communication of life to Lazarus—" Jesus cried with a loud voice, Lazarus, come forth!" It was but a word, and in an instant " he that was dead came forth, bound hand and foot with grave-clothes." So is it in the first communication of Divine light and life to the soul. The eternal Spirit says, " Let there be light," and in a moment there is light. He speaks again, " Come forth," and " in a moment, in the twinkling of an eye, the *dead* are raised incorruptible, and are changed."

Striking illustrations of the suddenness of the Spirit's operation are afforded in the cases of Saul of Tarsus, and of the thief upon the cross. How sudden was the communication of light and life to their souls! It was no long and previous process of spiritual illumination—it was the result of no lengthened chain of reasoning—no laboured argumentation. In a moment, and under circumstances most unfavourable to the change—as *we* should think—certainly at a period when the rebellion of the heart rose the most fiercely against God, " a light from heaven, above the brightness of the sun," poured its transforming radiance into the mind of the enraged persecutor; and a voice conveying life into the soul reached the conscience of the dying thief. Both were translated from darkness into light, " in a moment, in the twinkling of an eye."

How many who read this page may say, " Thus was it with me! God the eternal Spirit arrested me when my heart's deep rebellion was most up in arms against Him. It was a sudden and a short work, but it was mighty and effectual. It was unexpected and rapid, but deep and thorough. In a moment the hidden evil was brought to view—the deep and dark fountain broken up—all my iniquities passed before me, and all my ' secret sins seemed placed in the light of God's countenance.' My soul sank down in deep mire—yea, hell opened its mouth to receive me."

Do not overlook this wise and gracious method of the blessed Spirit's operation in regeneration. It is instantaneous. The *means* may have been simple—perhaps it was the loss of a friend—an alarming illness—a word of reproof or admonition dropped from a parent or a companion—the singing of a hymn—the hearing of a sermon—or some text of Scripture winged with His power to the conscience; in the twinkling of an eye, the soul " dead in trespasses and sins " was

" quickened," and translated into " newness of life." O blessed work of the blessed and eternal Spirit! O mighty operation! O inscrutable wisdom! What a change has now passed over the whole man! Overshadowed by the Holy Ghost, that which is begotten in the soul is the *Divine life*, a holy, influential, never-dying principle. Truly he is a new creature, " old things passing away, and all things becoming new."

For this change let it not be supposed that there is, in the subject, any previous *preparation*.[1] There can be no preparation for light or life. What preparation was there in chaos? What preparation was there in the cold clay limbs of Lazarus? What in Paul? What in the dying thief? The work of regeneration is supremely the work of the Spirit. The *means* may be employed, and *are* to be employed, in accordance with the Divine purpose, yet are they not to be *deified*. They are *but* means, " profiting nothing " without the power of God the Holy Spirit. Regeneration is His work, and not man's.

We have remarked that the first implantation of the Divine life in the soul is sudden. We would however observe that the *advance* of that work is in most cases *gradual*. Let this be an encouragement to any who are writing hard and bitter things against themselves in consequence of their *little* progress. The growth of Divine knowledge in the soul is often slow—the work of much time and of protracted discipline. Look at the eleven disciples—what slow, tardy scholars were they, even though taught immediately from the lips of Jesus; and " who teacheth like him?" They drank their knowledge from the very Fountain. They received their light directly from the Sun itself. And yet, with all these superior advantages—the personal ministry, instructions, miracles, and example of our dear Lord, how slow of understanding were they to comprehend, and how " slow of heart to believe," all that He so laboriously, clearly, and patiently taught them!

[1] The author is not affirming that the Holy Spirit has no dealings with a sinner prior to regeneration but that the sinner does nothing to prepare himself for this saving act of God.

Yes, the advance of the soul in the Divine life—its knowledge of sin, of the hidden evil, the heart's deep treachery, intricate windings, Satan's subtlety, the glory of the Gospel, the preciousness of Christ, and its own interest in the great salvation—is not the work of a day, nor of a year, but of many days, perhaps many years of deep ploughing, long and often painful discipline, of "windy storm and tempest."

But this life in the soul is not less *real*, nor less Divine, because its growth is slow and gradual; it may be small and feeble in its *degree*, yet in its *nature* it is the life that *never dies*. The figures and illustrations employed by the Holy Ghost to set forth the character and advance of His own work in the soul, are frequently such as convey the idea of feebleness. Thus, Isa. 40. 11 : " He shall feed his flock like a shepherd : he shall gather the lambs with his arm, and carry them in his bosom, and shall gently lead those that are with young." Can language more strikingly and more touchingly unfold the *feebleness* and often *burdened state* of God's dear saints? Again, ch. 42. 3 : " A bruised reed shall he not break, and the smoking flax shall he not quench." Had it been described as a " reed " only, *that* had been deeply expressive of its weakness; but a " *bruised* reed," seems to unfold the very lowest degree of feebleness. Had this gracious work been compared to " flax " merely, we should have thought it small indeed; but " smoking flax " seems to represent it as "ready to die." And still both are the product of the eternal Spirit; never shall the " bruised reed " be quite broken, nor the " smoking flax " be quite extinguished; the Lord will tenderly bind up and strengthen the one, and will carefully watch over and nourish the other. How many of the Lord's beloved ones, the children of godly parents brought up in the ways of God, are at a loss in reviewing the map of their pilgrimage, to remember the starting point of their spiritual life! They well know that they left the city of destruction, that by a strong and a mighty arm they were brought out of Egypt; but so gently, so imperceptibly, so softly and so gradually were they led—"first a thought, then a desire, then a prayer"—that they could no more discover when the first dawning of Divine life took place in their soul than they could tell the instant when natural light first broke upon chaos. *Still it is real.* It is no *fancy* that he has inherited an evil principle in the heart; it is no fancy that that principle has been subdued by grace. It is no fancy that he was once a child of darkness; it is no fancy that he is now a child of light. He may mourn in secret over his little advance, his tardy progress, his weak faith, his small grace, his strong corruption, his many infirmities, his startings aside like "a deceitful bow," yet he can say, "though I am the ' chief of sinners,' and the ' least of all saints'; though I see *within* so much to abase me, and *without*, so much to mourn over, yet this ' one thing I know, that, whereas I was blind, now I see.' I see that which I never saw before—a hatefulness in sin and a beauty in holiness; I see a vileness and emptiness in myself, and a preciousness and fulness in Jesus." Do not forget then, reader, that *feeble* grace is yet *real* grace. If the soul but "hungers and thirsts," if it "touches but the hem," it shall be saved.

We must also point out the *sovereignty* of the Spirit's operations in the production of this work. There is a sovereignty in all the works and dealings of God. If it be asked what God's own definition of His sovereignty is, we refer the inquirer to His words. "I will have mercy upon whom I will have mercy." Here is the Sovereign! How like Himself he speaks! He carries forward His gracious purposes of infinite wisdom and love—chooses or rejects—reveals or withholds, "working all things after the counsel of his own will," "giving no account," either to angels or to men, "of any of his matters." Now, notice the unfolding of *sovereignty* in the operations of the blessed Spirit. Thus did Christ declare it. John 3. 8: "The wind bloweth where it listeth, and thou hearest the sound thereof, but canst not tell whence it cometh, and whither it goeth: *so is every one that is born of the Spirit.*" Here is His sovereignty. Mark how striking is the figure. The wind bids defiance to man's governing power. It is as irresistible in its influence as it is mighty in its strength. We cannot command it nor can we control it. It is alike out of our power to summon as it is to soothe it. It comes, we know not whence; it goes, we know not whither. " *So is every one that is born of the Spirit.*" We do not say that the Spirit is *not resisted*—He *is resisted*, strongly and persever-ingly. But He is not *overpowered*. All the enmity and car-nality of the heart rises in direct opposition to Him; but when bent upon a mission of love, when in accordance with the eternal purpose He comes to save, not all the powers on earth or in hell can effectually resist Him. Like the mighty element, He bears down all opposition, sweeps away every barrier, overcomes every difficulty, and the sinner, " made willing in the day of His power," is brought to the feet of Jesus, there meekly and gratefully to sit, " clothed and in his right mind." His power, who can withstand? Whether He speaks in the " still small voice " of tender, persuasive love, or whether He comes in the " mighty rushing wind " of deep and overwhelming conviction, His influence is unquenchable, His power is irresistible. He " *effectually* worketh " in them that believe.

But His operation is as *sovereign* as it is mighty. He comes to *whom* He will; He comes *when* He will; He comes in the *mode* He will. We cannot bring Him by an effort of our own will, nor can we by an effort of our will compel Him to de-part. He bloweth where He listeth; we hear the sound, we see the effects; but *how* He works, *why* He works, and why in a *particular way* He works, He does not reveal to mortals. Even so, O thou blessed and eternal Spirit, for so it seemeth good in Thy sight.

We will not expand this part of the subject by citing the numerous *examples* of this truth which abound in the Scrip-tures of truth. The reader may refer to them at his leisure, if they do not spontaneously recur to his recollection at this moment. We would merely now urge him to examine the cases of Jacob and Esau—the publican and Pharisee—Saul of Tarsus, and the men who journeyed with him—the two thieves upon the cross, and see if the *sovereignty* of the Divine choice and the operation of the eternal Spirit are not written out in their histories as with a sunbeam.

Is the reader a child of God? Then we will not confine him

C

to the word of Divine truth. We summon *him* as a witness
to the sovereignty of the blessed Spirit's operation. "Ye are
my witnesses," saith God. *Who* and *what* made you to
differ? You have been taken out of your family, your kindred, your friends, your companions. From this circle it may
be that *you alone* have been selected, called, and made a child
of grace, an heir of glory. The others, *where are they?* Still
dead in trespasses and sins. *Where are they?* Living *in* the
world and *to* the world, lovers of pleasure, lovers of self,
lovers of sin, hating God, rejecting Christ, and warring against
the Spirit speaking to them in the Word, through providences,
and by the conscience. *Where are they?* Bursting through
every restraint, and bending their footsteps down to the doom
of the lost. *Where are they?* Gone, many of them, into
eternity—past the confines of mercy, "in hell lifting up their
eyes, being in torments." *And what are you?* A sinner saved
by grace, a sinner chosen and called, pardoned and justified,
washed and clothed, adopted and sanctified, brought to the
foot of the cross, constrained to welcome Jesus, to take up the
cross and to follow Him. O the electing love of God! O the
distinguishing grace of Jesus! O the sovereign operation of
the eternal Spirit! "Who art *thou*, O man, that repliest
against God?" Bow down to the sovereignty of His will;
silently wonder and adore Him who says, "Be still, and know
that I am God."

Has my reader hitherto found this doctrine a "hard saying"? Has he been prone to object to it and pass it by? I
would, with all meekness and affection, urge him seriously,
candidly and prayerfully to examine it by the light of the
Divine Word. Let him not object to it, lest he be found to
"fight against God"; let him not pass it by, lest he "grieve
the Spirit," and rob his own soul of an inestimable blessing.
O precious truth! It stains the pride of human merit—it lays
the axe at the root of self—it humbles and abases—it empties
and lays "low in a low place," and ascribes all the praise,
honour and glory, might, majesty and dominion of the *new
creation* in the soul, to the Triune God.

Intimately connected with the sovereignty, is *the free grace* of the Spirit's operation. No worthiness of the creature allures Him to the sinner's breast. What *worthiness* can be supposed to exist; what *merit* can there be in an adjudged criminal, an outlawed rebel, a poor insolvent, one whose mind is enmity, whose heart is swelling with treason against God, His government, and His Son, one who owes ten thousand talents, and has "nothing to pay"? None whatever. And that the eternal Spirit should enter the heart of such a one—convincing of sin—subduing the hatred—breaking down the rebellion—leading to Jesus, and sealing pardon and peace upon the conscience—oh! what but free grace—unmerited mercy—sovereign love, could thus have constrained Him? And as He exercises His sovereignty in conversion, let none suppose that that which decides Him in the selection of His subject is anything more worthy, or more lowly, which He may discover in one more than in another. O no! He often selects the poorest, the vilest, the most depraved and fallen, as if utterly to explode all idea of human merit, and to reflect in its richest lustre the free grace of His heart. Behold then, the grace of the blessed Spirit's operation; He comes, He knocks, He unbars, He enters, and creates all things new, irrespective of any merit of the creature, if merit that may be called which is so wretched and poor that language fails adequately to describe it. O the riches of His grace! How it is magnified—how it is illustrated—how it shines in the calling of a poor sinner! "Lord, what didst Thou see in me," exclaims the convinced soul, "that moved Thee with compassion, that drew Thee to my breast, and that constrained Thee to make me Thy temple? Nothing on my part, but poverty, wretchedness, and misery—on Thy part, nothing but love, sovereignty, and unmerited favour." Reader, do not turn from this glorious feature of the blessed Spirit's operation—it glorifies God, while it humbles man—it exalts Jesus on the ruins of the creature. Poor in spirit! blessed are you! You are rich in your poverty—you are exalted in your lowliness. All the love that is in God—all the grace that is in Jesus—and all the tenderness that is in the Spirit, all, all is for you. Lift up your head then, and let your heart sing for gladness.

Though poor, though nothing, though despised, though worthless in your own eyes—ah! and worthless in the eyes of the
vaunting Pharisee—yet, for *you*, Jehovah pours out all the
treasures of His grace—gives His well-beloved Son, and sends
His blessed Spirit. " All things are yours," you poor in spirit,
you broken in heart—" all things are yours "—how vast the
compass of your blessings! " All things are yours, for ye
are Christ's, and Christ is God's." Oh, could you know how
dear you are to the heart of God—could you know with what
tenderness Jesus yearns over you—how the blessed Spirit
delights to make you His dwelling-place, you would rejoice in
that you are made low. "For thus saith the high and lofty
One that inhabiteth eternity, whose name is Holy; I dwell in
the high and holy place, with him also that is of a contrite
and humble spirit, to revive the spirit of the humble, and to
revive the heart of the contrite ones." (Isa. 57. 15.)

The operation of the Spirit is *effectual*. As we have necessarily touched upon this feature in former parts of the chapter,
especially in the preceding sentences, it seems to demand a
less extended unfolding here. Still, it presents an important and
glorious aspect of the Spirit's work, upon which we cannot
reflect without clearer, more elevated and sanctifying views
of His operations in the work of regeneration. The reader
will not need to be reminded that the great change which
takes place in the soul at regeneration is frequently termed by
the Holy Ghost, in various parts of His Word, a *calling*. A
reference to a few passages will prove it. Gal. 1. 15: Paul
speaks of his being " *called* by grace." Rom. 8. 28: The
saints of God are spoken of as the " *called* according to his
purpose." 1 Pet. 2. 9: " *Called* out of darkness." Rom.
8. 30: "Whom he did predestinate, them he also *called*."
Jude 1: "Preserved in Jesus Christ, and *called*." 2 Tim. 1. 9:
" Who hath *called* us with an holy calling." Heb. 3. 1: " Partakers of the heavenly *calling*." 2 Pet. 2. 10: "Make your
calling and election sure." Thus is it clear that he who is
raised from the dead, brought out of darkness, and born
again is *called*. The blessed Agent by whom he is called is the
eternal Spirit. " It is the Spirit that quickeneth," and *calleth*.

The point with which we have now especially to deal is the *effectual nature of His calling.*

There is an *external* and also an *internal* call of the Spirit. The *external* call is thus alluded to. Prov. 1. 24: "I have *called*, and ye refused." Matt. 22. 14: "Many are *called*, but few are chosen." This outward call of the Spirit is made in various ways: in the Word, in the glorious proclamation of the gospel, through the providences of God—those of mercy and those of judgment—the warnings of ministers, the ad-monitions of friends, and, not less powerful, the awakening of the natural conscience. By these means does the Holy Spirit "call sinners to repentance." In this sense, every man who hears the gospel, who is encircled with the means of grace, and who bears about with him a secret but ever-faithful monitor, is called by the Spirit. The *existence* of this call places the sinner in an attitude of fearful responsibility; and the *rejection* of this call exposes him to a still more fearful doom. God has never poured out His wrath upon man with-out first extending the olive-branch of peace. Mercy has invariably preceded judgment. "I have called, and ye have refused." "All day long I have stretched forth my hands." "Behold, I stand at the door, and knock." He reasons, He argues, He expostulates with the sinner. "Come, let us reason together," is His invitation. "Bring your strong argu-ments." He instructs, warns and invites; He places before the mind the most solemn considerations, urged by duty and interest; He presses His own claims and appeals to the indi-vidual interests of the soul, but all seems ineffectual. Oh, what a view does this give us of the long-suffering patience of God towards the rebellious! That He should stretch out His hand to a sinner—that, instead of *wrath*, there should be *mercy*—instead of *cursing*, there should be *blessing*—that, instead of *instant punishment*, there should be the *patience* and *forbearance* that *invites*, *allures* and "*reasons*"—Oh, who is a God like unto our God? "I have called, and ye refused; I have stretched out my hand, and no man regarded."

But, there is the *special*, *direct* and *effectual* call of the Spirit, in the elect of God, without which all other calling is

in vain. God says, "I will put my Spirit within them."
Christ says, "The hour is coming, and now is, when the dead
shall hear the voice of the Son of God; and they that hear *shall
live*." And in the following passages reference is made to the
effectual operation of God the Spirit. Eph. 3. 7. "Whereof I
was made a minister, according to the gift of the grace of God
given unto me by the *effectual* working of his power."
1 Thess. 2. 13: "The word of God which *effectually* worketh
in you that believe." Thus, through the instrumentality of
the *truth*, the Spirit is represented as effectually working in
the soul. When He called *before*, there was no inward, supernatural, secret power accompanying the call to the conscience.
Now there is an energy put forth with the call which
awakens the conscience, breaks the heart, convinces the judgment, opens the eye of the soul and pours a new and an
alarming sound upon the hitherto deaf ear. Notice the
blessed effects. The scales fall from the eyes, the veil is torn
from the mind, the deep fountains of evil in the heart are
broken up, the sinner sees himself lost and undone—without
pardon, without a righteousness, without acceptance, without a God, without a Saviour, without a hope! Awful condition! "What shall I do to be saved?" is his cry: "I am
a wretch undone! I look within me, all is dark and vile; I
look around me, everything seems but the image of my woe;
I look above me, I see only an angry God: whichever way I
look, there is hell!—and were He now to send me there, *just*
and *right* would He be." But blessed be God, no poor soul
that ever uttered such language, prompted by such feelings, ever died in despair. That faithful Spirit who begins
the good work, effectually carries it on and completes it.
Presently, He leads him to the *cross of Jesus*—unveils to his
eye of glimmering faith, a suffering, wounded, bleeding, dying
Saviour—and yet a Saviour with stretched-out arms! That
Saviour speaks—oh, did ever music sound so melodious?—
"All this I do for *you*—this cross for *you*—these sufferings
for *you*—this blood for *you*—these stretched-out arms for
you. Come unto Me, all ye that labour and are heavy laden,
and I will give you rest—him that cometh to Me, I will in

no wise cast out—look unto Me, and be ye saved—only believe. Are you lost? I can save you. Are you guilty? I can
cleanse you. Are you poor? I can enrich you. Have you
sunk to the depths? I can raise you. Are you naked? I can
clothe you. Have you *nothing* to bring with you—no price,
no money, no goodness, no merit? I can and will take you
to Myself, just as you are; poor, naked, penniless, worthless;
for such I came to seek, such I came to call, for such I came
to die." "Lord, I believe," exclaims the poor, convinced soul,
"help thou mine unbelief. Thou art just the Saviour that I
want. I wanted one that could and would save me with all
my vileness, with all my rags, with all my poverty—I wanted
one that would save me fully, save me freely, save me as
an act of mere unmerited, undeserved grace—I have found
Him whom my soul loveth—and will be His through time
and His through eternity." Thus *effectually* does the blessed
Spirit call a sinner, by His *special*, *direct* and *supernatural*
power, out of darkness into marvellous light. "I will
work," says God, "and who shall let it?" (marg. *turn it
back*).

This great work the Holy Spirit *sustains* in the soul. As he
is the Author, so he is the Supporter. He breathed the spiritual life, and He keeps, and nourishes, and watches over it.
Let it not be supposed that there is anything in this life that
could keep itself. There is no principle in Divine grace that
can keep this life from decline and decay. If it be not watched
over, nourished, sustained, and revived perpetually by the
same omnipotent power that implanted it there, it is liable
to constant decline. What experienced child of God has not
felt this? Where is the believer who has not been made,
solemnly and painfully, to learn it? That there is not a grace
of the Spirit in him, but that grace needs, at times, greatly
invigorating; not a particle of faith, but it needs strengthening; not a lesson, but he needs to re-learn; not a precept, but
requires to be re-written upon his heart. Now this is the
work of our ever-watchful, ever-loving, ever-faithful Spirit.
He watches over, with a sleepless, loving eye, the work He
has wrought in the soul. Not a moment but He has His eye

upon it. By night and by day, in summer and in winter, when it decays and when it revives, He is there, its Guardian and its Protector, its Author and its Finisher.

And how does He nourish it? *Spiritually*. As the *life* is *spiritual*, so the *support* is *spiritual*. 1 Pet. 2. 2: " As new-born babes, desire the sincere milk of the word, that ye may grow thereby." 1 Tim. 4. 6: " Nourished up in the words of faith and of good doctrine." How does He nourish it? By leading the soul to *Jesus*, the substance of all spiritual truth. By unfolding His *fulness* of all grace, strength and sanctification. By leading constantly to His blood and righteousness. By teaching the believer the sweet lesson of living out of himself, his convictions, his enjoyments, his fruitfulness, upon Christ, and Christ alone. What is there in a child of God, in his best estate, that can supply adequate nourishment and support for this principle of Divine life? He has no resources within himself. He cannot live upon *evidences*; how soon they are clouded! He cannot grow upon *enjoyment*; how soon it is gone! He cannot find nourishment in any part of the work of the Spirit within him, precious and glorious as that work is. *Christ* is the " true bread " that sustains the life of God in the soul of man. Jesus said, " I am the living bread which came down from heaven: if any man eat of this bread, he shall live for ever." Again, " As the living Father hath sent me, and I live by the Father: so he that eateth me, even he shall *live by me*." The renewed soul only lives, as it lives on Jesus; it only advances, grows, and " brings forth much fruit," as it draws its vigour, its nourishment, its support and fruitfulness simply and entirely from Christ. These again are His words, " Abide in me, and I in you. As the branch cannot bear fruit of itself, except it abide in the vine; no more can ye, except ye abide in me." Reader, it may be that for a long time you have been looking to yourself for nourishment, for strength, for comfort and for fruitfulness. And the more you have looked within yourself, the more emptiness, poverty and barrenness you have discovered. And now the blessed Spirit, the nourisher as He is the author of the life within you, may give you such a new and enlarged view of Jesus as you have never had before. It may be that He will unfold to your soul such a fulness in Him—strength for your weakness, wisdom for your folly, grace for every corruption, tenderness and sympathy for every trial—as will bring you out of your bondage, introduce you into a "large room," and cause you to exclaim, "Thanks be unto God for his unspeakable gift!" Thus does the Spirit nourish and sustain the work He has wrought in the soul. He leads to Jesus.

I must not omit to notice the use of *sanctified trial* as one means frequently made, by the Spirit, subservient to this great end. In order to stir up His own grace within us, the Lord often places us under some heavy affliction. Did He not thus deal with his servant Job, and with a host more of the Old Testament saints? Messenger upon messenger arrives, and billow upon billow rolls, but bearing the precious tidings—though they may speak roughly, as Joseph did to his brethren —of God's love to our souls, that our Brother lives, that Joseph is alive and loves us still, that there is plenty of corn in Egypt, and that all we need do is simply to come and partake of it. What new life the news infuses into us! What new energy! What an impulse, what a new spring to hope, faith, joy and wondering gratitude! Blessed result when our afflictions are thus sanctified, when they arouse our souls, when they impart new energy to prayer, new vigour to faith, a new spring to hope, a new thirst for holiness, and a new motive and encouragement to trust in God. We can then truly say, "It has been *good* for me that I have been afflicted." Do not despise then, tried and afflicted soul, the chastenings of the Lord. He may now be about to communicate some of the most costly blessings of your life. Who can tell what mercies now await you, what covenant favours are in reserve, what new views of truth, what enlarged views of Christ, what an abiding sense of His love, what advances in holiness your covenant God and Father may, through this painful yet needed discipline, be on the eve of making you the happy partaker of? Then look up and say, "I will trust him, and not be afraid. Though he slay me, yet will I trust in him." In this way does the Spirit often stir up, strengthen and invigorate the Divine life in the soul by sanctifying the discipline of the covenant.

Although the limits assigned to this chapter have already been exceeded, we cannot properly close it without a brief exposition of some of the *effects* or *fruits* of regeneration as manifest in the spirit and life of a believer. We have incidentally touched upon some of them as we have passed along, yet there remains a few essential and prominent marks to be considered.

The first evidence we would mention is *holiness*. This appears to be the order of the Holy Ghost. 1 John 3. 9: "Whosoever is born of God doth not commit sin; for his seed remaineth in him: and he cannot sin, because he is born of God." This is a solemn and important point. None more so. When we think how Satan can counterfeit God's work; when we remember how much false, spurious Christianity there is in the world, yes, even in the professing world, we cannot but feel peculiar solemnity here. But God has stamped His own work with His own seal, and a mind taught of the Spirit cannot fail to recognise it.

Let us repeat the passage: "Whosoever is born of God doth not commit sin; for his seed remaineth in him: and he cannot sin, because he is born of God." These words have received two interpretations, which we believe are equally true. The more general one is that he who is born of God does not *willingly* sin. Having "put on the new man, which after God is created in righteousness and true holiness," he cannot sin with the full consent and concurrence of the will. He hates it, he fights against it, he resists it. But, it may be inquired, is not all sin an act of the will? We reply, not the *renewed* will. The apostle speaks of two wills in a believer, or rather, the same will under two opposite influences. Thus Rom. 7. 15: "That which I do, I allow not: for what I would, that do I not; but what I hate, that do I." Ver. 19: "For the good that I would, I do not: but the evil which I would not, that I do." Few will question that Paul here speaks of himself as a regenerate man. And yet he refers to two antagonistic principles dwelling in him; one is on the side of *holiness*, the other on the side of *sin*. What I *hate*, that I *do*." No man can possibly *hate* sin, unless he is "born of the Spirit." "The fear of the Lord is to *hate* evil." And still he says, "what I hate"—the sin that is so abhorrent to me, "that I do." Is there *volition* in the act? True philosophy demands that we reply, "Yes." Every sin must be voluntary; if not so, it cannot be sin. Is there the *concurrence* and *consent* of the *renewed* will in the act? True grace demands that we reply, "No." "For what I *hate*"—*there* is the mark of the regenerate man, "*that do I*"—*there* is the act of the will under the influence of indwelling sin.

But, there is another and a stronger interpretation of which the passage is susceptible. It is this. He that is born of God, *as such* does not sin at all; there is in him a regenerate soul, an indwelling, living principle of grace and holiness, whose natural and constant bias is to *holiness*. "He (the new man) *cannot* sin, because he is born of God." "He *cannot* sin." Why? "Because his seed remaineth in him." And what is that seed? 1 Peter 1. 23, "incorruptible"; being born again, "not of corruptible seed, but of *incorruptible*." In accordance with Christ's own words, "That which is born of the flesh is flesh; and that which is born of the Spirit is spirit." It is *spiritual*, *holy*, "from above," "the Divine nature"; it "CANNOT sin, because it is born of God."

Here then is the great evidence of regeneration. Let not the reader mistake it. Aware how tender the conscience of a dear child of God often is—how acutely alive to every view of truth that appears condemnatory, how prone to self-accusation, thinking hard and bitter things, calling that nature which is grace, extracting sometimes from the very consolations of God's word material for self-condemnation—We would here tenderly caution the Christian reader against a misinterpretation of what we have advanced in the preceding sections. We are far from asserting that sin does not still exist in the regenerate. Paul himself speaks in Rom. 7. 20 of the "sin that dwelleth in me." The entire testimony of God's Word and the histories of all the saints recorded in its pages go to confirm the doctrine that indwelling sin remains in a believer.

The Lord has wisely, we must acknowledge, so ordained it that sin should yet remain in His people to the very last step of their journey. And for this he has graciously provided His word as a storehouse of promises, consolations, cautions, rebukes, admonitions, all referring to the indwelling sin of a believer. The covenant of grace—all its sanctifying, strengthening, invigorating and animating provision—all was designed for this very state. The gift of Jesus—all His fulness of grace, wisdom, strength, and sympathy, His death, resurrection, ascension and advocacy—all this was given with a special view to the pardon and subjection of sin in a child of God. *Perfect holiness, entire sinlessness*, is a state not attainable in this life. He who has settled down with the conviction that he has arrived at *such* a stage, has great reason to suspect the soundness, or at least the depth of his real knowledge of himself. He, indeed, must be but imperfectly acquainted with his own heart who dreams of *perfect sanctification* on this side of glory. With all meekness and tenderness, we would earnestly exhort such an individual to review his position well, to bring his heart to the touchstone of God's Word, to pray over the seventh chapter of the epistle to the Romans, and to ascertain if there are not periods when the experience of an inspired apostle, once " caught up to the third heaven," will not apply to him—" I am carnal, sold under sin "—the " sin that dwelleth in me." The writings and the preaching of men, mistaken views of truth—yes, I would add, even what was once a sincere and ardent desire for sanctification—any one of these, or all combined, may have led to the adoption of such a notion as sinless perfection, the nature and tendency of which is to engender a spirit of human pride, self-trust and self-complacency; to throw the mind off its guard, and the heart off its prayerful vigilance, and thus render the man an easy prey to that subtle and ever-prowling enemy, of whose " devices " (and this is not the least one) no believer should be " ignorant."

O yes, sin, often deep and powerful, dwells in a child of God. It is the source of his greatest grief, the cause of his acutest sorrow. Remove this, and sorrow in the main would be a stranger to his breast. Go and ask that weary, dejected, weeping believer the cause of his broken spirit, his sad countenance, his tears. "Is it," you inquire, "that you are poor in this world?" "No." "Is it that you are friendless?" "No." "Is it that worldly prosperity does not shine upon you—your plans are blasted—your circumstances are trying —your prospects are dark?" "No." "What is it then that grieves your spirit, clouds your countenance, and that causes those clasped hands and uplifted eye?" "It is sin," the soul replies, "that dwells in me; sin is my burden, sin is my sorrow, sin is my grief, sin is my confession, sin is my humiliation before my Father and God; rid me of this, and the outward pressure would scarcely be felt." Truly does the apostle say—and let the declaration never be read apart from its accompanying promise—"If we say that we have no sin, we deceive ourselves, and the truth is not in us. If we confess our sins, he is faithful and just to forgive us our sins, and to cleanse us from all unrighteousness. If we say that we have not sinned, we make him a liar, and his word is not in us. My little children, these things write I unto you, that ye sin not. And if any man sin, we have an Advocate with the Father, Jesus Christ the righteous."

Again, we beg the reader to note this great evidence of regeneration: "Whosoever is born of God doth not commit sin." He doth not commit it with the total, absolute, and complete assent and concurrence of the renewed will. He does not give himself over to sin "with greediness." "He would do good." He hates sin. Grace reigns, not sin. Sin *dwells* in him, but does not *govern*; it has *power*, but does not *rule*; it torments, but does not reign with a continued, unbroken supremacy. His experience accords with the promise, "sin shall not have dominion over you." It may for a moment triumph, as it did in David, in Peter, and in a host of other eminently holy men; yet still the promise is verified—as we see in the restorings of the blessed Spirit in their spirit and conduct, in their humblings and confessions, and holy and upright walk with God in after years—"sin shall not have *dominion* over you." Reader, have you ever been made aware of the plague of sin within you? What do you know of warfare in the soul, of "the flesh lusting against the Spirit, and the Spirit against the flesh"? Your honest reply will decide the great question whether or not you are born of God.

Secondly, there is a *positive* mark of regeneration. 1 John 2. 29: "Every one that doeth righteousness is born of him." Negative holiness, the abstaining from outward sins, does not always describe a regenerate soul. Associated with this there must be *positive evidence*. "Every one that *doeth righteousness* is born of him." Where there is *life*, there is *action*, *motion* and *energy*. The life of a regenerate man is a life of the highest activity. The principles that influence him are Divine and heavenly; their tendency is to *holy action*. The more we resemble Christ "in righteousness and true holiness," the stronger the evidence to ourselves and to others that we are born again. We possess professedly and, if not self-deceived, actually the life of Christ. That life is holy in its *tendency* and vigorous in its *acting*. The renewed soul longs for holiness. He pants for Divine conformity. He does not rest in the mere longing; he arises and *labours* for the blessing; he " *works out* his salvation with fear and trembling." He prayerfully and diligently uses the *means* the Lord of sanctification has given him for the attainment of holiness; he is active in his pursuit of the blessing. He does not resemble the sluggard, who rests in mere desire. "The soul of the sluggard desireth, and hath nothing." But he resembles the "diligent soul," of whom it is said, "Blessed is the man that heareth me, watching daily at my gates, waiting at the posts of my doors." He *seeks* the blessing. He seeks it *diligently*, *perseveringly*. He "watcheth daily at the gates," he "waits at the posts of the doors." If he does not find it in one way, he seeks it in another. Should one door of grace be closed, he turns to another—for grace has many doors of blessing. If the *ministry* conveys no nourishment, he seeks it in a more retired walk. Perhaps he turns to the *communion of saints*, but he may find no refreshing here—for God sometimes makes his people a "dry tree." Disappointed in this channel, he turns to the *revealed Word*. This he finds a sealed book; no promise meets his case, no consolation speaks from its sacred page. Driven from this " door," he flies to the *throne of grace*. (Precious pavilion! ever verdant spot of a tempest-tossed, wearied spirit!) But alas! a cloud overshadows the mercy-seat, this last sanctuary of his soul; not the cloud of the Shekinah—the visible glory of the Lord—but the dark cloud of guilt and unbelief.

> " *Just ready all hope to resign*,"

he goes out into the "highways and hedges" of sin and wretchedness. He enters a hovel, goes down into the cellar, or climbs up to the garret, the gloomy abode of some child of sickness, sorrow and want. He inquires for the Sabbath school child, or delivers a tract, or drops a word of reproof, rebuke, exhortation, comfort, or prayer; and while like his Divine Master he is *going about* DOING GOOD, the Lord the Spirit meets him with a blessing, the Sun of righteousness breaks in upon his soul, every cloud is gone, and he looks up to God's serene countenance and calls Him " Abba, Father!" Thus is he made to experience the blessedness of "the man that heareth [God], watching daily at [his] gates."

Thirdly, *victory over the world* may be specified as another and a strongly marked feature of a regenerate man. 1 John 5. 4: "Whatsoever is born of God overcometh the world." How does victory over the world mark one born of God? It proves it in this way. That which overcomes the world must be superhuman, of almighty power. It cannot be anything of the world, nor can it be of the flesh; for the flesh has no power over the flesh, and the world will never oppose itself. The flesh loves itself, and the world is too fond of power, quietly and unresistingly to yield its dominion. What then is that which overcomes the world? John goes on to reply, " And this is the victory that overcometh the world, even our *faith*." *Faith* then is the conquering grace; this it is that gives the victory; this it is that crushes this tremendous foe. And what is faith but the " gift of God," and the work of the eternal Spirit in the soul? So that he who possesses that faith which is of the operation of the Spirit is " born of God "; and " whatsoever is born of God overcometh the world," and the instrument by which he overcomes the world is faith. "Who is he that overcometh the world, but he that *believeth* that Jesus is the Son of God?"

And *how* does faith overcome the world? By leading the believer to the cross of Jesus. True faith deals with its great object, Jesus. It goes to Him in the conflict, it goes to Him when hard pressed, it goes to Him in its weakness, it goes to Him in deep distress; on Him it leans, and through Him it always obtains the victory. Of the martyrs it is recorded that they "overcame through the blood of the Lamb," and Paul employs similar language in describing his victory: "God forbid that I should glory, save in the cross of our Lord Jesus Christ, by whom the world is crucified unto me, and I unto the world." It is *faith in Christ* that gives us the victory. How could a feeble saint, with no strength or wisdom in himself, overcome so powerful and subtle an enemy as this without supernatural aid? He never could. Look at the world! There are its ten thousand temptations, its temptations of pleasure, its temptations of ambition, its temptations of wealth, its false religion, its temporising policy, its hollow friendship, its empty show, its gay deceptions, its ten thousand arts to ensnare, beguile, allure and charm. Oh, how could one poor weak believer ever crush this fearful, powerful foe but as he is "strong in the grace that is in Christ Jesus"? The cross of Christ gives him the victory. Christ has already conquered the world, and faith in His blood will enable the feeblest soul to exclaim, while the enemy lies subdued at his feet, "Thanks be unto God, which always causeth me to triumph in Christ."

Reader, have you obtained the victory over the world, or has the world obtained the victory over you? One of the two is certain; either you are warring against it, or you are its passive and resistless victim; either you are "born of God," and "have overcome the world," or you are yet unregenerate, and the world has overcome you. On whose side is the victory? Perhaps you profess faith in the Lord Jesus, yet love the world, and conform to its maxims, its policy, its principles, its fashions, its dress, its amusements, even its very religion—for it has its hollow forms of religion. Is it so? Then

hear what the Word of the Lord says to *you*. 1 John 2. 15:
" Love not the world, neither the things that are in the world.
*If any man love the world, the love of the Father is not in
him.*" A solemn declaration for you, you who profess faith
in Christ, and who are still lovers of the world! You cannot
love God, and love the world at the same time. Do not be
deceived! The outward garb will not save you. The mere
name, the empty lamp—these will avail you nothing when
you come to die. If the world has never been ejected from
your heart, if you have never been crucified to it, then the
love of God is not there; if the love of God is absent, then
you are a stranger to the new birth.

There is another and a peculiar snare of the world to which
the saints of God are exposed; and because many have fallen
into it, and not a few have in consequence greatly embittered
their happiness, retarded their holiness and dishonoured God,
we would briefly, and in this connection, touch upon it with
all tenderness and affection. We allude to *the formation of
matrimonial alliances between the saints of God and the unregenerate world.* The Word of God is *against* a union so unholy and so productive of evil as this. Not a precept author-
ises it, not a precedent encourages it, not a promise sanctions
it, not a blessing hallows it! Indeed, so far is God from
authorising it, that He expressly *forbids* it. Thus, 2 Cor. 6.
14-18: " Be ye not unequally yoked together with unbelievers:
for what fellowship hath righteousness with unrighteousness?
and what communion hath light with darkness? and what
concord hath Christ with Belial? or what part hath he that
believeth with an infidel? And what agreement hath the
temple of God with idols? for ye are the temple of the living God; as God hath said, I will dwell in them, and walk in
them; and I will be their God, and they shall be my people.
Wherefore come out from among them, and be ye separate,
saith the Lord, and touch not the unclean thing; and I will receive you, and will be a Father unto you, and ye shall be my
sons and daughters, saith the Lord Almighty." How strong
the command, how conclusive the argument, and how persuasive and touching the appeal! Could it be more so? The

command is—that a *believer* be not yoked with an *unbeliever*. The *argument* is—he is a temple of God. The *appeal* is—God will be a Father to such, and they shall be His children, who walk obediently to this command. There are many solemn considerations which seem to urge this precept upon the believer. A child of God is not his own. He does not belong to himself. " Ye are not your own." His soul and body are redeemed by the precious blood of Christ, and therefore he is Christ's. He must not, he cannot, dispose of himself. He belongs to the Lord, and has no authority to give away either soul or body. O that this solemn fact could be written upon every believer's heart, " Ye are not your own. Ye are bought with a price, therefore glorify God in *your body, and in your spirit, which are God's.*" May the eternal Spirit *now* engrave it deeply and indelibly there! But more than this, if this were not enough to urge the command upon a believer, *his body is the " temple of the living God "!* How solemn and weighty is *this* consideration! And shall he take " the temple of God," and unite it with one who is a stranger to His grace, to His love, to His Son? with one whose " mind is enmity against God," and whose heart beats not one throb of love to Jesus? God forbid! " Know ye not," says James, " that the *friendship* of the *world* is *enmity* with God?" Then for a believer to form with an unbeliever an alliance so close and so lasting as this, involving interests so important and so precious, is to enter into a league with an *enemy* of God. It is to covenant, and that for life, with a *despiser* of the Lord Jesus!

It is no extenuation of this breach of God's command that the Lord has frequently, in the exercise of His sovereign grace, made the believing party instrumental to the conversion of the unbelieving party. He can, and often does, bring good out of evil, order out of confusion, " making the wrath of man to praise him," and causing events that were designed to thwart His purposes to be the very means of promoting them. But this is no encouragement to sin; and when sin is committed, this is but poor consolation. And to enter into a compact of the nature we are deprecating, with a conscience quieted and soothed with the reflection that "the wife may save the husband, or the husband may save the wife," is presumption of the highest kind, a presumption which God may punish with a disappointment as bitter as it is overwhelming. Let no dear child of God be allured into an alliance so unholy, by a consideration so specious as this. Many have fallen into the snare, and have covered themselves with shame and confusion.

To the believer himself, forming an alliance so contrary to the express injunction of God's Word, the evils arising from it are many and grievous. To say nothing of the want of what must ever be considered essential to the mutual happiness of the union—oneness of mind, harmony of sentiment, congruity of spirit—there are lacking the higher elements of happiness—the mutual faith of each other in Christ, the communion of redeemed spirits, the holy intercourse of renewed minds, the unutterable sweetness of talking of Jesus by the way, and as "heirs together of the grace of life," the joy of looking forward to the re-union of the glorified beyond the grave. It is, from the very nature of things, impossible that these elements of happiness should exist in the relation we are considering. The individuals thus united are inhabitants of different countries; one is an "alien from the commonwealth of Israel, a stranger and a foreigner," the other is a "fellow-citizen with the saints, and of the household of God"; they speak different languages, are travelling opposite roads, and are journeying towards different countries. Surely we may ask what real union and communion can exist here?

But more than this. There are not merely negative but *positive* evils resulting from such a connection. The influences that are perpetually exerting their power are hostile to all growth in grace, to any advance in sanctification and to an upright and holy walk with God. The temptations to inconsistency of Christian conduct are many, perpetual and alarming. The constant influence of worldly conversation, worldly example and worldly pursuits weakens by slow but certain degrees the spiritual life of the soul, impairs the taste for (and lessens the enjoyment in) spiritual duties, unfits the mind for communion with God and opens the door for an almost endless train of departures. We do not claim that *all* these evils are realised; but we do say that the believer who so shapes his course is fearfully exposed to them; and that he has not been, or may not be, overcome of them is of the mere grace of God. The evils themselves are the necessary sequences of his departure from God's Word; and that he is preserved from the direst of them is only of the covenant mercies of that God, who, in the midst of all their temptations, is alone able to keep His people from falling.

A child of God, passing through this vale of tears, requires all the spiritual assistance he can meet with to urge him on his way. All the strength, the comfort, the encouragement, and all the support it is possible for him to obtain from any and every quarter, he needs to call into full exercise, in order to bear up against the many and peculiar difficulties that throng his path, and would keep him from advancing. Infirmities within and impediments without, inward corruptions and outward trials, the strugglings of sin and the assaults of Satan, all conspire to cast him down, and often to extort from him David's exclamation, " My soul cleaveth to the dust." At such a period, how strengthening, how supporting, how encouraging and how animating the communion and soothings of a kindred spirit—a spirit *one* with himself! If it be true—and most true it is—that "as iron sharpeneth iron, so doth the countenance of a man his friend," to a much greater degree, and in a more endearing sense, is this reciprocity experienced in the high and endearing relation we are considering. The godly husband and the godly wife are true helpmeets to each other. They belong to the same family, speak the same sweet language, are travelling the same happy road, and are journeying to the same blissful home. For a child of God, then, to unite himself to one who can be of no assistance to him in his journey, but rather a hindrance—who, when he speaks of conflicts, cannot understand them; of burdens, cannot lighten them; of perplexities, cannot guide them; of trials, cannot share them; of sorrows, cannot soothe them; and of joys and hopes, cannot participate in them—is indeed to mark out for himself a lonely and a desolate path, which may know no termination of its trial until it conducts him to the grave.

To the Christian reader who may already have taken the step, we would say, with much affection, guard vigilantly against its hurtful consequences. Necessary as they are, they may, in a degree, be greatly mitigated. Draw largely from the grace that is in Christ Jesus, treasured up for all the circumstances and the necessities of His people. Be doubly prayerful, watchful, and humble; let your whole deportment be marked by the fear of God, a jealous regard for His honour, and a beautiful harmony with the high " vocation wherewith you are called "—and may God overrule the event to His glory and your real good.

To others we would say, guard against this needless and unscriptural entanglement with the world. Marry " only in the Lord." " In all your ways acknowledge him." Let His Word be your guide, His fear your rule, His glory your aim, and He will direct your paths through life, sustain you in death and conduct you safely to His heavenly kingdom.

As we review the subject of this chapter, many important considerations suggest themselves, which in closing can be allowed but a brief and passing notice. The first is, how high the obligation to live to God! Are we born again? Can we think of the " horrible pit, the miry clay," the " valley of bones," the " rock whence we were hewn," and then remember, that if we are born again, we have in our souls at this moment the buddings of eternal life? Oh, can we think of this, and not desire an unreserved surrender of all we are and all we have to God? Christian! watch over your principles, your daily walk, your intercourse with the world, and see that the evidences of the new birth signalise every action of your life. The world is a close observer. Narrowly and vigilantly are you watched. It weighs your actions, scrutinises your motives, sifts your principles, and ponders all your steps, waiting for your halting. Disappoint it! Live out your religion, carry out your principles; they are designed not merely for the Sabbath, but for the week; not merely to be exhibited in the place and at the hour of prayer, and in social Christian intercourse, but they are to be carried into your haunts of business, into your shop, your counting-house, your study, your profession. You are to exhibit them, not in a spirit of vain-glory, but in "lowliness of mind" in all your intercourse with a world lying in wickedness. To be born again! Oh, it is a mighty work! Let the evidences of its reality in you be such as shall compel the gainsayer to admire the work, though he may hate the change. Oh, be in spirit—in temper—in life —like Jesus.

Have not even you, who may be *tried and afflicted*, much to make you praise God? Born again! How light are your afflictions when compared with this! Take the scales and weigh the two. Place in one your every sorrow. Is it domestic?—place it there. Is it personal—a nervous frame, a feeble constitution, trying circumstances?—place it there. Are friends unfaithful, are saints unkind, does the world frown?—place it all there. Then in the other put your hidden life, your sense of pardon and your hope of heaven; *these* outweigh them all. "For I reckon," says Paul, "that the sufferings of this present time are not worthy to be compared with the glory which shall be revealed in us."

Unconverted reader, what solemn truth does this subject address to you! You must have perceived that the Word of God sets before you a new mould into which you must be cast. It professes to work a great change in you, in the hands of the eternal Spirit, not of opinions only, but of your *nature*, of your *heart*. Is this done? Do not turn away from the question; do not lightly pass it by—your all depends upon the answer to it. Eternity hangs upon the issue. I ask not what you hold, what you know, or what you profess, but— *what you are*. Are you born again? Are you a new creature? Do not say, " peace, peace, when there is no peace." You may persuade yourself, or be persuaded by others, that regeneration is all enthusiasm, a delusion and a lie, and yet,

> " This fearful truth will still remain,
> The sinner must be born again,
>   Or sink to endless woe."

CHAPTER IV

The Indwelling of the Spirit

THE BELIEVER A TEMPLE

" What! know ye not that your body is the temple of the Holy Ghost which is in you?"—1 Cor. 6. 19.

THAT the religion of our adorable Immanuel is a reality— no airy fiction, as is the Mahomedan, and no " cunningly devised fable," as is the Romish—many, conclusive and precious are the evidences. There is however, to the true believer, one evidence which, apart from, and superior to all others, affixes the seal of credibility; this is the conviction of its truth arising from *the indwelling of the Spirit in the heart.* There is in this great truth, something so palpable, so undoubted and so self-evident, that no sophistry of man, no ingenuity of Satan and no knowledge of the deep evil of our fallen nature can weaken or overthrow it. It is God Himself, as it were, taking the witness-stand and, setting aside all other testimony, challenging everything that would reduce His own work to a mere nonentity and exclaiming, " Who is he that condemneth?" Clad in the armour of *this* evidence, the feeblest disciple of Jesus takes higher ground in vindication of the truth of the Gospel than the acutest reasoner who is destitute of the indwelling of the Holy Ghost. It is true that the conviction arising from this source of evidence is the strongest and most convincing to his own mind; yet there is, in the simplicity, the honesty and the boldness with which his belief is declared, that which carries a powerful conviction to the minds of others. He may be challenged by the sceptic, there may be objections which he cannot meet, arguments which he cannot answer, difficulties which he cannot explain and sophisms which he cannot unravel; and yet the " witness within himself" shall throw such vigour into his reasoning and tenderness into his spirit, and shall invest his whole demeanour with an air of sincerity so touching that his accusers shall be compelled to pay him the tribute once awarded to his Lord, " he speaks as one having authority." He believes and has *experienced* what he declares, and thus God has given him a " mouth and wisdom, which all his adversaries shall not be able to gainsay nor resist."

But let it not be supposed that we regard the indwelling of the Spirit in the believer as presenting merely, or even mainly, an evidence in favour of the truth of the Gospel. This undoubtedly demands a distinct and grateful recognition. But we must not rest here. We are to take a more enlarged view of the glory of God, as unfolded in this most holy and blessed doctrine—His glory as secured to Him in the comfort, holiness and filial walk of the believer who is conscious that he is a temple of the Holy Ghost. We feel the subject to be one of great and solemn importance. Its vastness is almost overpowering. The bare thought that the " high and lofty One, inhabiting eternity, whose name is Holy," should dwell with man, yes, *in* him—that He should take out of the fallen race of His creatures a people whose hearts should be so renewed and sanctified as to form a dwelling-place of the Holy Ghost —that this heavenly visitant should take up His abode there in all His regenerating, sanctifying, sealing and comforting influences—the bare thought of this seems almost too illimitable and glorious for a poor finite mind to grasp. And yet, reader, the consolation flowing from this subject is so great, and the motives to holiness drawn from it so persuasive, and God so glorified by it, that we feel constrained to place it in the foreground of this treatise. May He Himself draw near, unfold His own truth to our minds, and sanctify us through its holy influence.

The first thought that presents itself to the mind as we look into this great subject is that suggested by the passage placed at the head of this chapter: " Know ye not that your body is the *temple* of the Holy Ghost which is in you?" The great idea here conveyed is that the believer is a *temple*, the resident of that temple being God the Holy Ghost. With the converted Corinthians, to whom these words were addressed, the figure would be at once striking and significant; the magnificent city in which they dwelt abounded with gorgeous temples erected to the honour of supposed deities, at whose idolatrous and superstitious rites they had frequently attended in the days of their ignorance. Drawing their minds away from the service of idols (while at the same time using the concept of a heathen temple as an illustration of his fine idea) the apostle, by an easy and a beautiful transition of thought, leads them to consider *themselves* as temples in an eminent and holy sense—formed, consecrated and adorned for the indwelling of God the Holy Ghost. There is a depth of important and spiritual truth in this idea which we desire to unfold, as the Divine Teacher shall Himself "anoint us with that anointing which teacheth us of all things."

In contemplating the believer as a temple of the Holy Ghost, it is natural and proper to consider the condition of the soul previous to the entrance of the Spirit of God. Man, in his original constitution, was a glorious temple. Two facts will prove it. First, he was like God in his moral image; and second, God dwelt in him. He was in every respect worthy of such a resident. He was the holy temple of a holy God. Not a flaw was there. The entire man was holy. There was perfect knowledge in the judgment, perfect holiness in the will, and perfect love in the heart. "Holiness to the Lord," was the inscription written on every window and every door, yes, on every part of this temple. A beautiful structure was man in his original state! Well did the mighty Architect, as He gazed upon His work, pronounce it "very good"!

But behold what *sin* has done! Man has lost his original resemblance to God. It is true that he still retains his spiritual, intelligent and immortal nature; these he can never lose. But as for his *moral* likeness to God in knowledge, purity, justice, truth and benignity, these glorious lineaments are blotted from his soul, and darkness, impurity, desolation and death reign there. With the obliteration of moral resemblance, the soul has lost all *love* to God. More than this; there is not only the absence of love but, as we have shown in a former chapter, there is positive *enmity*. "The carnal mind is enmity against God," that enmity showing itself in a thousand ways, principally in its seeking to *dethrone* God. From his affections he *has* dethroned Him. To eject Him from the throne of His moral government in the universe is the great and constant aim of the carnal mind. If this is not so, why this perpetual war against God—against His being, His law, His will, His supreme authority to govern and reign? Why this refusal to acknowledge and obey Him? "Who is the Lord God, that I should obey him?" Oh, there is no mystery in the case! Man has revolted from God and, having thrown off all allegiance to Him as his Sovereign, *he seeks to be a God to himself*. Self is to him what Jehovah once was—the object of supreme delight. Having cast out God, he moves in a circle of which he himself is the centre—all he does is *from* self, and *for* self. From this all the lines diverge, and to this they all again return.

It needs not the argument or the illustration of a moment to show that such being the moral destitution of man, God has ceased to dwell in him. The temple polluted, defaced and destroyed, the Divine Resident has gone, and the heart, once so sweet a home of Deity, is now the dwelling-place of all sin. Another occupant has taken possession of the ruin; and, like ancient Babylon, it has become the den of every ravenous beast, a habitation of dragons and the impure abode of every foul, malignant passion. Reader, it is as impossible that God can make your heart His dwelling-place, while every thought and feeling and passion is up in arms against Him, as it would be for Christ to dwell with Belial, or light to commingle with darkness. You must be renewed in the spirit of your mind. You must be born again.

But it was God's eternal and gracious purpose to restore this temple. Satan had despoiled His work, sin had marred His image; but both usurpers He would eject, and the ruin of both He would repair. Oh, what mercy, infinite, eternal and free, was this that set Him upon a work so glorious! What could have moved Him but His own *love*, what could have contrived the plan but His own *wisdom*, and what could have executed it but His own *power*? In the restoration of this temple, man was no auxiliary. He could be none. His *destruction* was his own, his *recovery* was God's. He ruined himself; that ruin he could not himself repair. The work of *restoration* is a greater achievement of Divine power than was the work of *creation*. To repair the temple when ruined was more glorious than to create it. In one day He made man; He was four thousand years in *redeeming* man. It cost Him nothing to create a soul; it cost Him His dear Son to *save* it. And who can estimate that cost? He met with no opposition in creating man; in *re-creating* him, Satan, the world, even man himself, is against Him.

We have said that it was God's gracious and eternal purpose to restore this ruined temple. The first step which He took in accomplishing this great work was *His assumption of our nature*, as though He Himself would be the model from which the new temples should be formed. This was one of the profoundest acts of God's wisdom, one of the greatest demonstrations of His love. " The Word was made flesh, and dwelt among us " (marg. *tabernacled* among us). His human body, the temple; his Godhead, the indwelling Deity. Was ever a temple so glorious as this? " Immanuel, God with us." " God manifest in the flesh." O awful mystery! what imagination can conceive, what mind can fathom it? We can but stand upon the shore of this vast ocean of wisdom and love, and exclaim, " O the depth!" " Great is the mystery of godliness, God was manifest in the flesh." This was the first step towards His work of replenishing the earth with spiritual temples, to be filled now and eternally with the Divine presence and glory. The entire success and glory of His undertaking rested here. This was the foundation of the structure. He could only obey the law, as He was " made of a woman "; he could only " redeem them that were under the law," as He was God in our nature. The absolute *necessity*, then, of His Godhead will instantly appear. Had the basis of the great work He was about to achieve been laid in any other doctrine, anything inferior, less holy, less dignified; had the foundation been laid in *mere creature* excellence, however exalted that excellence might be, there could have been neither strength, permanency, nor glory in the temple. It would have fallen before the first storm of temptation, and fearful would have been its destruction. God well knew at what cost the work of redemption would be achieved. He knew what His violated law demanded, what His inflexible justice required, and through what costly channel His love must flow; therefore " He laid help upon one that was mighty "—" mighty to save." And what was the secret of His might?—*His absolute deity*. Take a lower view than this, and you reduce the work of Christ to nothing; you tear the soul from the body, pluck the sun from the firmament, wrench the keystone from the arch and the foundation from the building. But look at His work *through His Godhead*, and oh, how vast, how costly, how glorious does it appear; what a basis for a poor sinner to build upon; what a resting-place for the weary soul; what faith, hope, and assurance does it inspire; how perfect the obedience, how infinitely efficacious the blood, and how prevailing the intercession—all derived from the Godhead of Jesus. Glorious temple wast Thou, blessed Son of God!

But this temple was to be destroyed. *Jesus must die!* This was the second step in the accomplishment of the great work. Thus did he announce the fact to the obtuse and incredulous Jews: " Jesus answered and said unto them, Destroy this temple, and in three days I will raise it up." " He spake of the temple of his body." His death was as necessary to the satisfaction of justice, as His life of obedience had been to the fulfilling of the law. As the Substitute of His people, He must yield up His life; as the Surety of the covenant, He must completely surrender Himself into the hands of Divine justice; as the Testator of His own will, there must of necessity be His death, otherwise the testament would have been of no force at all while He lived. There was no possible avenue for His escape, even had He sought it. He or His people must die. He must taste the bitterness of the death that was temporal, or His elect must have tasted of the bitterness of the death that was eternal. O yes, Jesus *wished* to die. Never for one moment did He really shrink from the combat.

He well knew the conditions upon which He had entered into a covenant engagement on behalf of His people. He knew that the price of their pardon was His own blood, that His death was their life, and that His gloomy path through the grave was their bright passage to eternal glory. Knowing all this, and with the awful scene of Calvary full in view—the cross, the sufferings of the body, the deathly sorrow of the soul—He yet panted for the arrival of the moment that was to finish the work His Father had given Him to do. How *ready* was Jesus thus to die? Whence this eagerness? It sprang from His *great love* to sinners. Oh, this was it! We must go down to the secret depth of His love, if we would solve the mystery of His willingness to die. "God commendeth his love toward us, in that, while we were yet sinners, Christ died for us." Thus was the "temple of His body" destroyed, that "through death he might destroy him that had the power of death, that is the devil, and deliver them who through fear of death were all their lifetime subject to bondage." See, reader, the source of your free pardon, the ground of your humble trust, the secret of your "strong consolation." It is all involved in the death of Jesus. You cannot *ask* too much, you cannot *expect* too much, you cannot *repose* too much at the foot of the cross. All is mercy here—all is love —all is peace. Sin cannot condemn, Satan cannot tempt, the world cannot allure, conscience cannot accuse; "there is no condemnation" to a poor soul that shelters itself beneath the cross of Jesus. *Here* every dark cloud withdraws, and all is sunny; *here* every tear is dried, but that of joy; and every voice is hushed, but that of praise.

But a third step in the accomplishment of this stupendous design was the *resurrection of Christ*. This formed an essential and glorious part of His work, in preparing a way for the personal and permanent residence of the Holy Ghost. "Destroy this temple, *and in three days I will raise it up again*." Great stress is laid upon this doctrine in the Word. And the child of God may be but imperfectly aware what an essential pillar it is to his hope, and how sanctifying and comforting the blessings are that spring from a full belief in it. The re-

surrection of Jesus is the great seal to the character and perfection of His work. Indeed, without this Divine attestation
His work would never have effected our salvation. His perfect
keeping of the law and His suffering unto death were but parts
of the vast plan, and, taken separately and distinctly, were
not capable of perfecting the salvation of the church. The
apostle so reasons. 1 Cor. 15. 14-18: "If Christ be not risen,
then is our preaching vain, and your faith is also vain. Yea,
and we are found false witnesses of God; because we have
testified of God that he raised up Christ: whom he raised not
up, if so be that the dead rise not. For if the dead rise not,
then is not Christ raised: and if Christ be not raised, your faith
is vain, ye are yet in your sins. Then they also which are
fallen asleep in Christ are perished." A moment's reflection
will justify the conclusions which the apostle deduces from
the supposition that Christ had *not* risen.

Our dear Lord endured the "curse of the law"; a part of
that curse was *death*—death legal, death temporal, death eternal. He was "made a curse for us," and died. So long as He
remained imprisoned in the grave, "death had dominion over
him." We would have looked in vain to His obedience and
sufferings for the proof of the all-sufficiency and acceptable-
ness of His satisfaction, as long as the iron sceptre of the king
of terrors held Him in subjection. O what a momentous period
were the three days that intervened between the giving up the
ghost upon the cross, and the bursting of the tomb! The salvation of the whole church hung upon it. All who had already "fallen asleep" in Him, and all whom it was the purpose of God yet to call, were deeply interested in this one fact.
But on the third day the destroyed temple was raised again;
death had no more dominion over Him, its sting was extracted,
its sceptre was broken, the curse was rolled away, and the redemption of the church was complete. "He was delivered
for our offences, and *rose again for our justification*."

Let the Christian reader fully believe this one truth, that
Jesus is alive again, and it will afford to his soul greater con-
firmation of the veracity of God's character, of the truth of
His Word, and of the perfection and all-sufficiency of Christ's

work, than all other truths beside. Is Jesus alive at the right hand of God? Then the debt is paid, and justice is satisfied. Is Jesus alive at the right hand of God? Then the Father is well pleased in the work of His Son, and He " rests in His love, and rejoices over His church with singing." Is Jesus alive? Then every promise shall be fulfilled, and all the blessings of the everlasting covenant shall be freely bestowed, and I, a poor worthless sinner, yet resting upon His atoning work, shall live also. May the Holy Ghost lead you into the full belief—the belief of the heart as well as of the judgment—of this glorious truth. It is the keystone of the temple. Press it as you will, the more you lean upon it, the stronger you will find it; the more you rest upon it, the firmer will grow your hope. Only receive it in *simple faith*, Jesus is alive— alive for *you*; all you want in this vale of tears is *here*; all your temporal mercies are secured to you here; all your spiritual blessings are laid up for you here. Such is the great charter, such are the immense, untold blessings it contains, that, come how you will, come when you will, and " ask what you will, it shall be granted you of the Father," because Jesus is at His right hand. Well may we take up the dauntless challenge of the apostle, " Who is he that condemneth? It is Christ that died; *yea rather, that is risen again*, who is even at the right hand of God, who also maketh intercession for us." Your salvation is complete, your heaven secure, and all victory, happiness and glory bound up in this one great fact. Then may we not again exclaim with Peter, " Blessed be the God and Father of our Lord Jesus Christ, which according to his abundant mercy hath begotten us again unto a lively hope *by the resurrection of Jesus Christ from the dead* "?

Thus have we briefly traced the successive steps which God took to prepare the way for the permanent indwelling of the Spirit in the believer. Through the incarnation, obedience, death, and resurrection of Christ, a way was opened by which God could again dwell with man, could resume His abode in the very temple that sin had destroyed, and show forth the riches and glory of His grace far more illustriously than when this temple stood in its original perfection and grandeur. Here was the *foundation* of every successive temple that grace was about to raise. "Thus saith the Lord God, Behold, I lay in Zion for a foundation a stone, a tried stone, a precious corner-stone, a sure foundation." "Other foundation can no man lay than that is laid, which is Jesus Christ." On the dignity of His *person*, finished *righteousness*, perfect *atonement*, all-sufficient *grace* and inviolable *faithfulness*, believers, "as lively stones, are built up a spiritual house" (1 Pet. 4. 5), for the ever-lasting indwelling of God the Holy Ghost.

In passing now more specifically to the consideration of the indwelling of the Spirit, we proceed to adduce the testimony He Himself has borne to the doctrine. In the following passages the truth is unfolded. Looking into the Old Testament, sha-dowy as the period was in which that part of the inspired Word was written, we yet find clear intimation of the doc-trine before us. Ezek. 36. 27: "And I will put *my Spirit within you*." Ezek. 37. 14: "And I shall put *my Spirit in you*, and ye shall live." In the New Testament the doctrine opens upon our view with increasing power and brightness. Our Lord's own words are familiar. John 14. 16, 17: "And I will pray the Father, and he shall give you another Comforter, that he may abide with you for ever; even the Spirit of truth; whom the world cannot receive, because it seeth him not, neither knoweth him: but ye know him, for he dwelleth with you, and *shall be in you*." Rom. 8. 9: "But ye are not in the flesh, but in the Spirit, if so be that *the Spirit of God dwell in you*." Ver. 11: "But if the Spirit of him that raised up Jesus from the dead *dwell in you*," etc. 1 Cor. 3. 16: "Know ye not that ye are the temple of God, and that *the Spirit of God dwelleth in you*?" 1 Cor. 6. 19: "What? know ye not that your body *is the temple of the Holy Ghost which is in you*?" 2 Cor. 6. 16: "And what agreement hath the temple of God with idols? for ye are the temple of the living God; as God hath said, *I will dwell in them*," etc. Eph. 2. 22: "In whom ye also are builded together for *an habitation of God through the Spirit*." We will not multiply quotations; it is sufficiently clear that the indwelling of the Spirit is a revealed doctrine of Scripture. We proceed to develop it.

When does the Holy Spirit enter a soul? We reply, *at the moment of its regeneration*. This is His first gracious act. Previous to this, all is dark, desolate and dead, as we have in other places fully shown. What pen is adequate to describe the moral desolation, the fearful dilapidation of the soul of man, before the Spirit enters, bringing in His train, life, light and order? One brief sentence of Divine truth will more correctly and vividly describe it than the most elaborate human production. " Sensual, having not the Spirit." But the Spirit enters. He comes, in accordance with the eternal purpose, in harmony with the covenant of grace, borne on the wings of His own love, and travelling in the greatness of His own strength. What a triumphal entry, when He takes possession of the temple, already purchased by the Saviour's blood! At His approach, darkness, enmity, pollution and death retire, and are succeeded by light, love, holiness and life. It is true that He meets with fierce opposition from within, for " the strong man armed keepeth his palace," and " his goods are in peace "; but " a stronger than he comes," and puts to flight all opposition, bends the will, subdues the enmity, dissolves the heart and implants the sweet response, " Come in, thou blessed of the Lord, why standest Thou without? Enter, and take full possession for Thyself. Long have I closed my heart against Thee, too long have I resisted all Thine importunities. But now Thou hast conquered and prevailed; come in, blessed Spirit, and seal me for Thine own." O blissful moment, when the Spirit *enters*, convincing of sin, breaking the heart with godly sorrow, laying the soul low in the dust in the spirit of self-abasement and self-condemnation before God, then leading it to the atoning blood of Jesus and speaking pardon and peace to the conscience.

The Spirit dwells in the believer *as a manifestation of the Divine glory*. The temple that Solomon built was one of great magnificence and splendour. But it was an *earthly* glory; and although He who " dwelleth not in temples made with hands " condescended to reveal Himself in it, yet it possessed no glory in comparison with the glory that was to exist in the new spiritual temple which the Holy Ghost was to erect and in-

D

habit. Speaking of the legal dispensation, with which the temple prepared by David and built by Solomon was designed to harmonise, the apostle argues that it possessed no glory in comparison with the Gospel economy. And why? Because there was *less of the Spirit* in the former than in the present dispensation. It was the *enlarged manifestation of the Spirit*, especially His *indwelling of the saints*, which constituted the peculiar and far-surpassing glory of the new economy. " How shall not (says he) the ministration of the Spirit be rather glorious? For if the ministration of condemnation be glory, much more doth the ministration of righteousness exceed in glory. For even that which was made glorious had no glory in this respect, by reason of the glory that excelleth."

The superior glory of the new dispensation then is that it is more *spiritual*; there is a more enlarged and rich effusion of the quickening, sanctifying and sealing influences of the Holy Spirit; there is more of Christ, more of the holy liberty of adoption, a more simple, spiritual and child-like approach to God. But especially does *the indwelling of the Spirit in the saints* form a distinguished feature of the new economy. Here is an especial manifestation of the Divine glory. That the Spirit should, on the broad basis of Immanuel's finished atoning work, call a poor sinner by grace, regenerate, sanctify and then take possession of him for ever, dwell in him, witness in him, work in him and make him meet for the inheritance of the saints in light—this is a marvellous display of the Divine glory. The electing love, infinite wisdom and omnipotent power of God are glorified; the atoning work, all-sufficient grace and unspeakable compassion of Jesus are glorified; the irresistible power, infinite patience and efficacious work of the Spirit are glorified in the soul that becomes " an habitation of God through the Spirit." We even dare assert that the conversion of a soul, the sustaining of the work wrought in that soul, the keeping of the believer through a long life of holy, upright and close walk with God, and the bringing of him safe to eternal happiness, are greater displays of the mighty power of God and more glorify Him than the creation of ten thousand worlds like ours.

The Spirit dwells in the believer as *the everliving Spirit of all grace and comfort.* All that is really holy and gracious in a child of God is found in the work of the indwelling Spirit. All the holy breathings and desires of the soul, all the longings for God and for conformity to His will and image, all that is lovely and like Jesus in the saint, are the result of this gracious act of the eternal Spirit. The Lord Jesus Himself would direct us to this truth. John 4. 14: "Whosoever drinketh of the water that I shall give him shall never thirst; but the water that I shall give him shall be in him a well of water springing up into everlasting life." That this well of water is the indwelling of the Spirit, seems clear from the 10th verse: "Jesus answered and said unto her, If thou knewest the gift of God," etc.; that "gift of God" was the Holy Ghost, alluded to again still more emphatically in ch. 7. 38, 39: "He that believeth on me, as the scripture hath said, out of his belly shall flow rivers of living water. (But this spake he of the Spirit, which they that believe on him should receive: for the Holy Ghost was not yet given; because that Jesus was not yet glorified.")

Here is a gracious truth. The Spirit in every believer is a deep and living well of all spiritual blessings. He dwells in the soul "not like a stagnant pool, but like an ever-living fountain that plays at all seasons of the year, in heat and cold, and in all external circumstances of weather, whether foul or fair, wet or dry." Nature could not produce that which the indwelling Spirit accomplishes in the saints of God. The hungering and the thirsting for righteousness, the rising of the heart in filial love to God, the sweet submission to His sovereign will, the longing for more knowledge of Christ, the constant struggling with the law of sin, the mourning over the indwelling principle of sin; all this is above and far beyond nature. It is the fruit, the precious fruit, of the indwelling Spirit.

It may be, reader, that your heart is often anxious to know in what way you may distinguish between nature and grace, how you may clearly discern between that which is legal and that which is spiritual, between that which is the work of

man, and that which is the work of God. In this way you
may trace the vast difference—that which at first came *from*
God, returns *to* God again. It rises to the source whence it
descended. Divine grace in a sinner's heart is a springing well
—" a well of water *springing up* into eternal life." Did *nature*
ever teach a soul the plague of its own heart? Never! Did
nature ever lay the soul in the dust before God, mourning and
weeping over sin? Never! Did *nature* ever inspire the soul
with pantings for God and thirstings for holiness? Never!
And did it ever endear the throne of grace, and make precious
to the soul the atoning blood, the justifying righteousness of
Jesus? Never! never! All this as much transcends the power
of nature as the creating of a world. Is this your real state,
reader? O look up! " Flesh and blood " did not reveal it to
you—but the eternal God has revealed it and that by the indwelling of His own blessed Spirit in your heart.

We must not overlook His indwelling *as a Spirit of holiness*.
This is His great and crowning work in a believer. It is in
vain that we look for Him as a Witness, or as a Spirit of comfort, if we slight Him as a *Sanctifier*. Although we have assigned a distinct chapter to the subject of the sanctification
of the Spirit, we would yet briefly allude to it in connection
with His indwelling of the saints. The work of *holiness* forms
a great and glorious part of His operation as the Indweller of
His people. He has come to restore, not only order, but *purity*
to the temple. He has come to restore the reign of *holiness*,
to set up the law of God in the soul, to unfold its precepts,
and to write them upon the heart, and, shedding abroad the
love of Christ, under its gentle but powerful constraint to lead
the believer to " run the way of God's commandments." He
is pre-eminently a " Spirit of holiness " in the believer. For a
more full unfolding of the manner in which the Spirit carries
forward the work of holiness in the soul, the reader is referred
to the chapter on that subject.

Nor must it be forgotten that *He dwells in the believer as
an abiding Spirit*. It is a *permanent* indwelling. Our dear
Lord laid especial stress upon this feature. When on the eve
of leaving His disciples to return to His throne, He promised

them "another Comforter," whose spiritual presence should more than make up for the loss of His bodily presence. And lest there should be any painful apprehensions as to the *time* of His dwelling with them, He assures them that the Spirit should abide with them for ever. " And I will pray the Father, and he shall give you another Comforter, *that he may abide with you for ever.*" Do not overlook this truth. Let no spiritual darkness, no workings of unbelief, no sense of indwelling sin, rob you of the comfort and consolation which a believing view of it will impart. There may be periods when you are not sensible of the indwelling of the Spirit. Clouds and darkness may be around this doctrine; there may be severe trials, gloomy providences, foreboding fears, the way rough and intricate, the sky dark and wintry, faith small, unbelief powerful, and your soul, from its low depths, led to exclaim, " All these things are against me. Will the Lord cast off for ever? and will he be favourable no more? Is his mercy clean gone for ever? doth his promise fail for evermore? Hath God forgotten to be gracious? hath he in anger shut up his tender mercies?" Oh do not forget that even then, dejected saint of God, then when all is dark within and all is desolate without, *then* the Holy Spirit, the Sanctifier and the Comforter and the Glorifier of Jesus, dwells in you, and shall be with you *for ever.* True, you may be assailed by powerful corruptions, the " consolations of God few and small" with you, and your prayer like David's, " Cast me not away from thy presence, and take not thy Holy Spirit from me"; yet He, the blessed Indweller, is there, and His still, small and soothing voice shall soon be heard amid the roaring of the tempest, hushing it to a peaceful calm. He shall " abide with you for ever." No wanderings, no neglect, no unkindness, no unworthiness, no unfaithfulness shall ever force Him from your bosom. He may withdraw His sensible presence; He may withhold His comforting influence; He may be so grieved by a careless walk as to suspend for a while His witnessing and sanctifying power, permitting indwelling corruptions for a moment to triumph; but *He restoreth the soul*; He brings it back again; He breaks the heart, then binds it up; wounds, then heals it;

fills it with godly grief, then tunes it with thanksgiving and the voice of melody. "For a small moment have I forsaken thee; but with great mercies will I gather thee." "He restoreth my soul."

I can present, in this chapter, a mere outline of the remaining operations of the Spirit as the Indweller of the saints. I regret this the less because some of those parts of His work are more fully discussed in the chapters especially assigned to them in this treatise.

As a *Spirit of adoption* He dwells in the believer. Gal 4. 6: "And because ye are sons, God hath sent forth the Spirit of his Son into your hearts, crying, Abba, Father."

As a *Witness* He is there. Rom. 8. 16: "The Spirit itself beareth witness with our spirit, that we are the children of God."

As an *earnest and pledge of future glory* He is there. Eph. I. 13, 14: "In whom also after that ye believed, ye were sealed with that Holy Spirit of promise, which is the earnest of our inheritance," etc.

As a *Teacher* He is there. John 14. 26: "The Comforter, which is the Holy Ghost, whom the Father will send in my name, he shall teach you all things." "He shall guide you into all truth."

As a *Remembrancer* He is there. Verse 26: "He shall teach you all things, and bring all things to your remembrance."

As a *Glorifier of Jesus* He is there. John 16, 14: "He shall glorify me: for he shall receive of mine, and shall show it unto you."

All these gracious operations worketh that one and self-same Spirit, dwelling in the hearts of all believers.

In reviewing this subject, the following important reflections suggest themselves to us.

How amazing the grace of God that makes the heart of a poor sinner His dwelling-place! O what grace is this! How it prostrates all high thoughts of self, how it brings down the lofty look, and lays the soul where it should ever lie, "low in a low place." "Will God in very deed dwell with man?" "I will dwell in them," says God, "and will walk in them."

Let us not forget that *it is the humble broken heart* that forms the true temple of the Holy Ghost. He only dwells here. And here He *does* dwell. It may be a temple despised by man, but God prepares and chooses it for His abode. The proud and haughty spirit of self-righteous man may overlook it as valueless; the tear that falls in silence, the sigh that is breathed in secret, the heart that mourns over sin may be thought little of by the passer by, but with God it is of " great price." He has a bottle for that tear, a record for that sigh, and that mourning is music in His ear. " For thus saith the high and lofty One that inhabiteth eternity, whose name is Holy; I dwell in the high and holy place, with him also that is of a contrite and humble spirit, to revive the spirit of the humble, and to revive the heart of the contrite ones." Isa. 57. 15. Perhaps your cry is, " Come, blessed and eternal Spirit, into my heart; make it a temple, now and for ever, for Thine abode: worthless though the offering be, yet it is all I have to present Thee; enter, with all Thy humbling, sanctifying, sealing and comforting influences, and take full possession for Thyself." O blessed cry! O sweet fruit of that loving, faithful Spirit, who already has entered (unknown and unsuspected, it may be, by you) and has planted there this desire, the sure and certain pledge of future glory! Be assured, precious soul, that this cry, feeble as it is, is an evidence of the indwelling of the Spirit. It is the first gentle springing up of the living fountain within you, and it shall continue to spring up even unto eternal life. Cherish it as you would your greatest blessing. Pray that it may be increased and strengthened more and more, and closely watch against the slightest thing which would tend to enfeeble it.

How holy should the temple of the Spirit be! Reader, are you a temple of God the Holy Ghost? Then dedicate yourself *unreservedly* to God. You are not your own. Your body, your spirit, your family, substance, time, talents, influence, all, all belong to God. He dwells in you—walks in you—rules in you, and calls you His dwelling-place. " Know ye not that your body is the temple of the Holy Ghost which is in you?" Then what a separation should there be between you and the world that lieth in wickedness! How should you guard against every unnecessary entanglement with it; how cautious and prayerful, lest, by contracting an unholy alliance with it in any form or degree, you should defile the temple of God, "which temple you are"! Oh, what heavenly wisdom, holy circumspection and ceaseless prayer do you need that you may walk with unspotted garments—that no rival should enter your heart—that no lofty views of self, no spirit of worldly conformity, no temporising policy, no known sin, no creature idolatry should enter there—that, like the heavenly temple, nothing that defileth, neither whatsoever worketh abomination, should be cherished or entertained in the abode and in the presence of the Holy Ghost; for "what agreement hath the temple of God with idols? for ye are the temple of the living God; as God hath said, I will dwell in them, and walk in them; and I will be their God, and they shall be my people."

Reader, whose temple are you? Solemn question! Does God or Satan dwell in you? Christ or Belial? Light or darkness? Either the one or the other has, at this moment, possession of you. You cannot serve two contrary masters; you cannot entertain two opposite guests. You are living either for God or for Satan. You are travelling either to heaven or to hell. Which? On your bended knees before God, decide; and may the Lord the Spirit renew you by His grace, and if renewed, make you "a vessel unto honour, sanctified and meet for the Master's use, and prepared unto every good work."

CHAPTER V

The Sanctification of the Spirit

The Necessity and the Nature of True Holiness

" Through sanctification of the Spirit."—2 Thess. 2, 13.

WE have already briefly intimated that one most important feature in the work of the indwelling Spirit is the *sanctification* of the believer. What was merely glanced at in the preceding chapter will now, by the assistance of that same Teacher who has promised to guide into all spiritual truth, be more fully unfolded. While yet upon the threshold of our subject, let it be premised that there is an *order*, as well as a *harmony*, in the operations of the Spirit, which it is highly important should be observed. An ignorance or an oversight of this has led to great and fatal perversions of the Gospel, especially that part which relates to the doctrine now under discussion. All the self-righteousness of the Pharisee, and all the self-devotion of the deluded disciple of the papal superstition, have their origin here. Now the order of the Spirit is this: *regeneration* of the heart first, *then* its *sanctification*. Reverse this, and we derange every part of His work and, as far as our individual benefit extends, render it entirely useless. Sanctification is not the first and immediate duty of an unrenewed person. Indeed, it is utterly impossible that it should be so. Sanctification has its commencement and its daily growth in a principle of *life* implanted in the soul by the eternal Spirit; and to look for holiness in an individual still *dead* in sins is to look for fruit where no seed was sown, for the actings of life where no vital principle exists. It is to expect, in the language of our Lord, to " gather grapes from thorns, and figs from thistles." The first and imperative duty of an unrenewed man is to prostrate himself in deep abasement and true repentance before God. The lofty look must be brought low, and the rebellious will must be humbled; in the posture of one overwhelmed with a sense of guilt, he must look by faith to a crucified Saviour, and draw from Him life, pardon and acceptance. It is most solemnly true that " without holiness no man shall see the Lord "; yet all attempts towards the attainment of holiness before *repentance* toward God and *faith* in the Lord Jesus Christ will but disappoint the soul that looks for it.

This work of renewal done, sanctification is a comparatively easy and a delightful task. Motives and exhortations to a life of holiness now find a ready response in the heart, already the temple of the Holy Spirit. The " incorruptible seed " sown there, germinates into the plant, and blossoms and ripens into the fruits of holiness. The well of " living water " created there springs up and pours forth its stream of life and purity, adorning and fertilising the garden of the Lord. Let us then be careful not to disturb the arrangement, and reverse the order of the blessed Spirit in His work. From lack of such care great errors have arisen, and souls have gone into eternity fearfully and fatally deceived. Especially cautious should *they* be in this matter who are appointed to the office of spiritual instruction, to whose care immortal souls are entrusted, lest, in a matter involving interests so precious and so lasting, anyone listening to their teaching should pass into eternity ignorant of the one and true method of salvation.

Let the reader prayerfully follow us while we endeavour to unfold the necessity of sanctification in the believer, its gospel nature, and the means employed by the Spirit in its production.

There exists an absolute and solemn *necessity* for sanctification in a child of God. To remind the reader of this may at first sight appear a needless work, so self-evident, and so immediate an effect of regeneration by the Spirit does it seem. And yet the advanced believer, much more the sincere inquirer after a more perfect knowledge of the will of God, needs to be perpetually reminded of the solemn necessity, for his own happiness and his Father's glory, of a daily growth in all holiness. And as the believer is, after regeneration, an *active agent* in the furtherance of this great work, and as there is a perpetual proneness, through the many infirmities of the flesh, to settle down in a state of ease and sloth in it, the importance of being reminded of this necessity will immediately appear.

The first ground on which this necessity rests is *the holiness of God*. The nature of the God whose temple he is pleads for the sanctification of the believer. We have to do with a holy God who, from the very necessity and purity of His being, can have no fellowship with sin. He must hate, He must abhor it. A stronger plea for the sanctification of the child of God can nowhere be found. Let us for a moment trace this argument as it runs like a golden thread through every part of God's Word. We see its commencement in the Old Testament. Levit. 11. 44, 45: "For I am the Lord your God: ye shall therefore sanctify yourselves, and ye shall be holy; for I am holy . . . I am the Lord that bringeth you up out of the land of Egypt, to be your God: ye shall therefore be holy, for I am holy." Levit. 19. 2: "Speak unto all the congregation of the children of Israel, and say unto them, Ye shall be holy: for I the Lord your God am holy."

And that these commandments and this standard may not seem to belong exclusively to the Old Testament saints, the apostle Peter embodies them, as of equal force and solemnity, in his writings to the saints of the New Testament. 1 Peter 1. 15, 16: "But as he which hath called you is holy, so be ye holy in all manner of conversation: because it is written, Be ye holy, for I am holy." If this motive to sanctification came clothed with such solemnity and power, and was so felt by the Jewish church, what should be its authority and influence with the church as it now exists! The increased power and solemnity of this motive is drawn from the more resplendent exhibition of God's holiness *in the cross of Christ*. The saints of the Old Testament were not favoured with such a development of the Divine purity as an argument to sanctification. But *we* possess it; so that if we continue in sin after we have believed, we are "without excuse," and God is "clear when He judgeth." The cross is God's grand demonstration of His holiness. Here has He, as it were, unveiled His great perfections, and shown what a sin-hating, holiness-loving God He is. What! Could He not pass by His dear Son? Did He give Him up to the "shame and the spitting"? Why did He not withhold his "darling from the power of the dog"? Did justice sheath its sword in the heart of Jesus? Did it smite the Shepherd? And why all this? The answer comes from Calvary, "I, the Lord, am a holy God." And then follows the precept—O how touching!—"Be ye holy, for I am holy." See how the justice of God (and what is the justice of God but His holiness in exercise?) revealed itself as a "consuming fire" on Calvary. Our dear Lord was "a whole burnt offering" for His people; and the fire that descended and consumed the sacrifice was the *holiness* of God in active and fearful exercise. Here then springs the solemn *necessity* for sanctification in the believer. The God he loves is holy, his Father is holy— and He has written out that holiness in awful letters in the cross of His well-beloved Son, "Be ye holy, for I am holy." We must study God in Christ. There we see His holiness, justice, wisdom, grace, truth, love and mercy, all unfolded in their richest glory and most benevolent exercise.

The necessity for sanctification also springs *from the work of Christ*. The Lord Jesus became incarnate, and died as much for the sanctification as for the pardon and justification of His church; as much for her deliverance from the indwelling power of sin as from the condemnatory power of sin. His work would have been but partial and incomplete if no provision had been made for the *holiness* of the believer. But He came not only to blot out sin but to rend asunder its chain, not only to remove its curse but to break its sceptre. The believer in Jesus may be but imperfectly aware how closely associated his sanctification is with the obedience and death of Christ. Indeed the very death of Christ *for* sin out of him is the death *of* sin in him; no inroads are made upon the dominion of indwelling sin, no conquests obtained, no flesh crucified, no easy-besetting sin laid aside, save only as the believer *hangs daily upon the cross.* Observe how the Holy Ghost connects the two—the death of Christ and the holiness of the believer: thus in John 17. 19: " And for their sakes," says Jesus, " I sanctify myself, that they also might be sanctified through the truth." As their High-priest to atone and purify, He set Himself apart as a holy sacrifice to the Lord God for the church's sake. " For their sakes I sanctify myself "—or set myself apart. Oh, what a motive to holiness is this, saint of God! Can you resist it? Yet again the connection is unfolded. Tit. 2. 14: " Who gave himself for us, that he might redeem us from all iniquity, and purify unto himself a peculiar people, zealous of good works." Eph. 5. 25, 26: " Husbands, love your wives, even as Christ also loved the church, and gave himself for it; that he might sanctify and cleanse it with the washing of water by the word." Thus clearly does the Holy Spirit unfold the close and beautiful relationship between the death of Christ and the death of sin.

The covenant of grace enforces the sanctification of the believer. " It is the eternal and immutable purpose of God," observes Dr. John Owen, " that all who are His in a peculiar manner, all whom He designs to bring unto blessedness in the everlasting enjoyment of Himself, shall, antecedently thereunto, be made holy." For the security and attainment of this, all provision has been made in the everlasting covenant of grace. The very *election* of the believer to eternal life provides for and secures his holiness. There could not possibly be any holiness without election, because election provides the means of its attainment. Thus clearly does the Spirit of truth unfold it. 2 Thess. 2. 13: " We are bound to give thanks alway to God for you, brethren beloved of the Lord, because God hath from the beginning chosen you to salvation *through sanctification of the Spirit* and belief of the truth." Again, Eph. 1. 4: " According as he hath chosen us in him before the foundation of the world, *that we should be holy* and without blame before him in love." Let this be clearly understood. On the ground of no foreseen holiness in the creature, did God thus purpose to save him; but seeing the indispensable necessity of sanctification in order to eternal glory—the impossibility of the one without the other—He chose us in Christ "that we should be holy."

Let not the Christian reader turn away from, or treat lightly, this precious revealed truth of God's Word—an election of a people unto holiness here and glory hereafter. The prejudice of education, early modes of thought, a preconceived system, and most of all the neglect of a close and prayerful investigation of God's Word for himself, may lead to the rejection of the doctrine. But he who first objects to it, and then renounces it, without a thorough and prayerful sifting of its scriptural claims to belief, stands on solemn ground, and his attitude may have fearful consequences. What God has revealed, "that call not thou common." What He has commanded, do not turn from, lest you be found to have turned from God Himself. *Why* it has pleased the Lord to choose a people in this way, it is not our province to inquire, nor, we believe, would it be for our happiness to know. We do not attempt to explain the doctrine, much less to *account* for it. We simply and, we trust, scripturally state it, leaving God to vindicate and bless it. He is the best defender and apologist of His own sacred truth. " Secret things belong unto the Lord our God : but those things which are revealed belong unto us and to our children for ever, that we may do all the words of this law." (Deut. 29. 29.) The *secret* thing in the doctrine of *election* is *why* God has done it; the thing which is *revealed* is that He *has* done it. Let us not then seek to be wise *above* what is written, though it is our duty, as an acute writer has remarked, to be wise *up* to what is written, leaving the more perfect knowledge of the things that are now seen as " through a glass darkly," to that period of perfect illumination when we shall " know, even as we are known." But thus much we know, that it is the eternal purpose of God, revealed and provided for in the covenant of grace, that all who are chosen, called, and justified, shall, with a view to their being glorified, be " partakers of His holiness." Heaven is a holy place, its inhabitants are a holy people, and He whose glory fills the temple is a holy God. Behold then the provision God has made for the sanctification of the believer in the everlasting covenant of grace. The foundation is laid in the death of Christ, it commences in the effectual calling of the Spirit and, by all the precious assurances of grace, wisdom and strength provided in the covenant, it is carried forward to a glorious completion.

We would only specify, as one more consideration pleading for the sanctification of the believer, *his own personal happiness*. Holiness is necessary to the *comfort* of the believer, as it is an essential element of his Christian character. Sanctification is a part of the new creation. Although not the first step the soul takes into the new world of holiness, it yet immediately follows. Regeneration is the commencement of the reign of holiness, or (to change the figure) the planting of the germ, which time and the Lord's covenant dealings cause to take deep root and to put forth its lovely and fragrant flower. In proportion as the sanctification of a believer advances, his real happiness advances with it. Holiness brings its own peculiar and high enjoyment. It is from heaven, and conveys into the heart the happiness of heaven; so that he who is most holy has most of the material of heaven in his soul. O how loudly does the *happiness* of a child of God plead for his holiness! As his soul approximates to the likeness of God, his circumstances, trying as they may be, cannot remove the fine edge of his inward and concealed enjoyments. Indeed, sanctified by the indwelling Spirit, trials only heighten those enjoyments, and are found the most effective helps to the maturing of holiness in his soul.

These are some of the grounds on which the necessity of sanctification is enforced in the Divine Word. It will now be proper to unfold its gospel *nature*.

What is true sanctification? The question is vastly more important than would at first sight appear. Unscriptural views of sanctification have been found to exist, not only among the unregenerate, but even in the church of Christ. Yet every dear child of God who honestly desires to follow the Lord fully and to live as a temple of the Holy Ghost, deeply feels the necessity of the Spirit's teaching in a matter so personal and so momentous as this. How much do we who now

write and they who read need, while contemplating this subject, the anointings of the Holy One and the eye that looks at
the blood that cleanses from all sin!

Sanctification has been defined as "the work of the Holy
Spirit whereby we are renewed in the whole man after the
image of God, and are enabled more and more to die unto sin
and live unto righteousness." Briefly and emphatically, it is
*a progressive conformity of the whole man to the Divine
nature*. Under the Levitical dispensation the term *sanctified*
had a peculiar meaning. Persons and things were said to be
sanctified which were *separated, set apart* and *offered to God*.
Thus the *furniture* of the temple was pronounced holy, or
sanctified; the ark, the altar, all the utensils of the temple and
the vestments of the priest were regarded as sanctified, because
set apart and dedicated to God. For the same reason, *persons*
were said to be *sanctified* who were solemnly consecrated to
the service.

The dispensation of ritual having passed away, the word,
by an easy and natural accommodation, has assumed a more
comprehensive and evangelical meaning; and is now employed
to set forth the advance of the believer in a conformity of heart
to the will and image of God. In explaining the nature of
sanctification, we would first of all establish from the Scripture *the spirituality of the Divine law*. There is a sense, as
we have elsewhere shown, in which the believer is *dead to
the law*. His union to Christ has delivered him from the law
as a covenant of works. "Ye are become dead to the law
by the body of Christ; that ye should be married to another,
even to him that is raised from the dead, that we should bring
forth fruit unto God." Again, "Now we are delivered from
the law, that being dead (marg. *being dead to that*) wherein
we were held; that we should serve in newness of spirit, and
not in the oldness of the letter." (Rom. 7. 4, 6.) This then is
the deadness to which the apostle refers. It is a release from
the law as a ground of acceptance. The believer is "accepted
in the Beloved"—pardoned, justified, and sanctified in Christ.
He is married to Christ—is one with Christ. As such he is
delivered from the law, under whose condemnation he once

rested: being dead to that wherein he was held, it can no longer assert its claims, or exact obedience as the condition of life. It can no longer threaten or condemn. Shut up in the faith of Jesus, and receiving pardon and justification through Him, he is beyond the power of the law as a covenant of life, and is screened from its vengeance as a source of condemnation. No single truth has the Holy Ghost more clearly written out than this. He has shown, too, that it forms the basis of sanctification in the justified believer. His release from a covenant of works and his translation into the covenant of grace, his deliverance from the law and his union to Christ, form the ground of all holy liberty, filial obedience and spiritual fruitfulness. They that are under the law are under the curse— but "there is no condemnation to them that are in Christ Jesus"—therefore the believer in Christ is not under the law.

But we come to the sense in which they "that are in Christ Jesus" have yet to do with the law. Released from it as a covenant of life, it yet remains obligatory *as a rule of obedience to Christ*. If we suppose that the law has lost all authority and use—to be entirely abrogated—we must suppose that the relation of God to His creatures as their moral Governor has also ceased—that, having laid aside all rule of obedience, He has with it abdicated the throne of the universe, and that man has ceased to be the subject of a moral government. But, far from this, the law of God remains in all its dignity, purity and force. The believer in Christ is released from it as a ground of acceptance, but not as a standard of holiness. Is it true that Christ is the standard and pattern of a believer's holiness? Undoubtedly. Then we argue that the moral law was the standard of Christ's holiness; therefore it must necessarily be the standard of the believer's. The whole life of Jesus was a conformity to the purity of the Divine law which was His standard of holiness and His pattern of obedience; therefore in following the example of Christ we are being conformed to the purity of the law "in newness of spirit, and not in the oldness of the letter."

Sanctification, then, is a growing conformity to the spirituality of the Divine law. The sincere believer acknowledges

" that the law is holy, and the commandment holy, and just, and good "; he knows " that the law is spiritual." He therefore " delights in the law of God after the inward man." Does his faith in Jesus " make void the law "? " God forbid." Instead, his faith " establishes the law," reflects its spirituality, maintains its purity, vindicates its holiness and glorifies its Divine Author. The closer then the resemblance of the believer to the spirituality of the law of God in his life, his temper, and habit of his mind, his principles, his daily walk in the world and out of the world, among the saints or as surrounded by the ungodly, the more thoroughly is the work of sanctification advancing in his soul.

In all this *there is a more simple surrender of the will to God*. The holy Robert Leighton has remarked that to say from the heart " Thy will be done " constitutes the very essence of sanctification. There is much truth in this, more than perhaps strikes the mind at the first view. Before conversion, the *will* —the governing principle of the soul—is the seat of all opposition to God. It rises against God, His government, His law, His providence, His grace, His Son; to all that appertains to God, the unrenewed will of man is hostile. Here lies the depth of man's unholiness. The will is *against* God; and so long as it refuses to obey Him, the creature must remain unholy. Now it needs no lengthy argument to show that when the will, as renewed by the Holy Ghost, is made to submit to God, the holiness of the believer must be in proportion to the degree of its submission. There could not be perfect holiness in heaven were there the slightest preponderance of the will of the creature towards itself. The angels and " the spirits of just men made perfect " are supremely holy because their wills are supremely swallowed up in the will of God. " Thy will be done on earth, *even as it is in heaven*." The will of God is supremely obeyed in heaven, and in this consist the holiness and the felicity of its glorious inhabitants.

Now in exact proportion as God's will " is done on earth " by the believer, he drinks from the pure fountain of holiness; and as he is enabled by the grace of Christ in all things to look up to God with filial love and to say, " Not my will, O my Father, but Thine be done," he attains the very *essence* of sanctification. Let us trace out this subject. It is God's revealed will that His child should be *holy*—" this is the will of God, even your sanctification." When the will of the believer rises and blends itself with God's will here, and in the spirit of sonship responds, "Lord, is it thy will that I should be holy? Then make me so in body, in soul and in spirit. Subdue all my corruptions, break the power of my lusts; bring every thought, affection, word and look into sweet obedience to Thyself; rule Thou in the midst of Thine enemies "—how truly does the work of sanctification advance in the soul!

It is the revealed will of God that His child should maintain a walk in all things pleasing to Him : " that ye might walk worthy of the Lord unto all pleasing, being fruitful in every good work, and increasing in the knowledge of God." When the believer's will fully acquiesces in this, and the heart is drawn out in earnest and agonising prayer for an upright walk, worthy of his high calling and of the Lord by whom he is called, for more fruitfulness in every good work, and for an increase of faith, love and knowledge of God, who will not say that such a soul is rapidly growing in sanctification?

It is the revealed will of God that the believer should walk as an *obedient child*: " O that thou hadst hearkened to my *commandments*! then had thy peace been as a river, and thy righteousness as the waves of the sea." And, when these are the responsive breathings of his soul: " I love thy commandments above gold, yea, above fine gold; therefore I esteem all thy precepts concerning all things to be right; and I hate every false way. I will run the way of thy commandments, when thou shalt enlarge my heart "—such a soul is maturing in holiness, and is becoming fitted "for the inheritance of the saints in light."

It is the revealed will of God that His child should meekly and silently bow to His chastening hand: " My son, despise not thou the chastening of the Lord, nor faint when thou art rebuked of him." And when the tried and afflicted believer " hears the rod, and who hath appointed it," and with a humble and filial acquiescence, justifies the wisdom and the

love and even the tenderness that sent it—surely such a soul
is a rich partaker of God's holiness. In all these particulars,
there is a surrender of the will to God, and consequently an
approximation to the holiness of His nature. The point we
are now considering is one of great importance. It involves as
much your holy and happy walk as it does the glory of God.
We put the simple questions—can there be any advance of
sanctification in the soul when the will is running counter to
the Divine will?—and can that believer walk happily when
there is a constant opposition in his mind to all the dealings
of his God and Father? O no! Holiness and happiness are
closely allied; and both are the offspring of a humble, filial,
and complete surrender of the will in all things to God. Such
an attainment in holiness is not soon or easily gained. Far
from it. In many, it is the work of years; in all, of painful
discipline. It is not on the high mount of joy, but in the low
valley of humiliation, that this precious and holy surrender
is learned. It is not in the summer day—when all things smile
and wear a sunny aspect—*then* it were easy to say, " Thy will
be done "; but when a cloudy and a wintry sky looks down
upon you, when the chill blast of adversity blows, when
health fails, when friends die, when wealth departs, when the
heart's fondest endearments are yielded, when the *Isaac* is
called for, when the world turns its back—when all is gone
and you are like a tree of the desert, over which the tempest
has swept, stripping it of every branch—when you are brought
so low that it would seem to you that you could not be any
lower—*then* to look up with filial love and exclaim, " My
Father, Thy will be done!"—oh, this is holiness, this is happiness indeed. It may be that God, your God and Father, is deal-
ing in this way with you now. Has he taken from you *health*?
Has he asked for the surrender of your *Isaac*? Have *riches*
taken to themselves wings? Does the world frown? Ah!
little do you realise how God is now about to unfold to you the
depths of His love, and to cause your will sweetly, and filially,
and entirely to flow into His. Let me repeat the observation
—a higher degree of sanctification there cannot be than a will
entirely swallowed up in God's. Earnestly pray for it, dili-

gently seek it. Be jealous of the slightest opposition of your mind, watch against the least rebellion of the will, wrestle for an entire surrender—to be where, and to be what, your covenant God and Father would have you; and so shall you be made a partaker of His holiness.

Furthermore, sanctification includes a *growing resemblance to the likeness of Christ*. How beautifully and explicitly has the Holy Ghost unfolded this in His Word! This was the exhortation of our dear Lord, "Learn of me, for I am meek and lowly in heart"; and throughout the writings of His apostles the same truth is exhibited: "Whom he did foreknow, he also did predestinate to be *conformed to the image of his Son*." Rom. 8. 29. "Speaking the truth in love, may *grow up into him in all things*, which is the head, even Christ." Eph. 4. 15. Here is the glorious pattern of a child of God. Sanctification is a conformity to the image and the example of Christ. The more the believer is growing *like Jesus*, the more he is growing in holiness. And on the contrary, the less resemblance there is to Christ in his principles, in the habit of his mind, in his spirit, temper, daily walk, in every action and in every look, the less is he advancing in the great work of holiness. O how many who profess His dear name, and who are expecting to be with Him for ever, never pause to consider what resemblance they bear to Him *now*! Were they to deal faithfully with conscience in the much-neglected duty of *self-examination*, were they to bring themselves to this great standard—how far below it would they be found to have come! How much in their principles, in their governing motives, in their temper, spirit, and daily conduct, how much in their walk in the world, in their deportment in the church, and in their more concealed conduct in their families, would be discovered that was *unlike Christ*! How much that was "from *beneath*," how little that was "from *above*"—how much of the "image of the *earthy*," how little of the "image of the *heavenly*"! But, look at the image of our dear Lord—how lowly, how holy it is! Look at His poverty of spirit, lowliness of heart, humility of deportment, tenderness, gentleness, forgiveness of injuries, self-denial, prayerfulness, zeal for His

Father's glory, yearnings for the salvation of men. O to be like Jesus!—to grow up into Him in all things! *This* is to "walk worthy of the Lord unto all pleasing"; *this* is to realise "the will of God, even our sanctification." Let it not then be forgotten that an advancing believer is one growing in a resemblance and conformity to the image and example of Christ.

We must include, though in general terms, as involved in the growing sanctification of the believer, an increasingly tender conscience, a soft and gentle walk, deepening views of sin, looking at it more directly in the light of the cross, mourning over, confessing, hating, and crucifying it *there*. Nor must we omit a more complete investiture of the Christian with the graces of the Spirit; the *active* graces—faith, love, zeal, self-denial; the *passive* graces—meekness, long-suffering, gentleness, peace. There are some, and not a few cases, in which all of these features distinguish a believer advancing in sanctification.

Having thus briefly considered the nature of sanctification, we now proceed to the main design of this chapter which was to show *the agency of the Holy Spirit in its production.*

The work of sanctification is pre-eminently the product of the Spirit. He is the great Sanctifier of the soul. We have shown that the implantation of the germ of holiness in regeneration is of Him. For let it ever be borne in mind that a renewed soul has within it the "incorruptible seed" of holiness. Although its growth in many instances may be slow and scarcely perceptible, although during a long period of his journey the believer may be the subject of strong corruptions and clinging infirmities, which, in a degree, act like frosts upon the tender scion, checking its advance to maturity—yet *the seed is there.* Indwelling sin cannot destroy it, the frosts cannot kill it, it is "incorruptible" and therefore cannot be corrupted. In process of time, under the tender and faithful culture of the eternal Spirit, it shall deepen and expand its roots, and put forth its branches and its boughs, and then shall appear the fruit, "first the blade, then the ear, after that the full corn in the ear". It will vary in its degree of fruitfulness among the saints, in "some thirty, some sixty, some an hundredfold," but in all it will be of the same nature and the product of the same Spirit.

It has been the constant effort of Satan to divert men from the great point we are now considering. In two ways has he proved successful. First, in setting them upon the work of mortification of sin *before regeneration*; and second, in setting them upon the same work after conversion, *in their own strength*. With regard to the first, we have shown at some length that sanctification is not the work of an unbeliever; that, although it is solemnly true that "without holiness no man shall see the Lord," yet the attainment of holiness is an utter impossibility so long as the heart remains a stranger to the regenerating operations of the Holy Spirit. *Repentance* and *faith* are the first necessities in order of time for an unconverted man. With regard to the second effort of Satan to deceive the soul, it is equally ruinous to all true mortification of sin. No child of God can accomplish this mighty work in his own strength. Here lies the secret, be assured, of all our failure and disappointment in the work. Forgetting that he who would prove victorious in this warfare must first learn the lesson of his own weakness and insufficiency, and, thus schooled, must go forth in the "strength that is in Christ Jesus," and in the "power of His might," taking the shield of faith, and the helmet of salvation, and the sword of the Spirit—forgetting this important truth, we march to the overthrow of our giant corruptions in our own fancied wisdom and power; and the result always has been, and with the same means ever will be, our complete discomfiture. Oh! when shall we learn that we are nothing—that we have "no might" —and that our feeblest enemy will triumph if his overthrow be attempted in our own insufficiency?

The Holy Spirit is the efficient cause of all holiness in the believer. If we look into the prophecy of Ezekiel, we find clear intimations of the promise of the Spirit to this effect. There God unfolds what may be regarded as the foundation of all sanctification—the removal of the stony heart and the implanting of a new spirit. Ezek. 11. 19: "I will give them one heart, and I will put a new spirit within you." Ezek. 36. 26: "A new heart also will I give you, and a new spirit will I put within you." Let us see the doctrine as more clearly unfolded in the writings of the apostles. Rom. 8. 9: "Ye are not in the flesh, but in the Spirit, if so be that the Spirit of God dwell in you. Now if any man have not the Spirit of Christ, he is none of his. And if Christ be in you, the body is dead because of sin; but the Spirit is life because of righteousness." 1 Cor. 6. 11: "And such were some of you: but ye are washed, but ye are sanctified, but ye are justified in the name of the Lord Jesus, and *by the Spirit of our God*." 2 Thess. 2. 13: "But we are bound to give thanks alway to God for you, brethren beloved of the Lord, because God hath from the beginning chosen you to salvation *through sanctification of the Spirit*, and belief of the truth." 1 Pet. 1. 2: "Elect according to the foreknowledge of God the Father, *through sanctification of the Spirit*." We are far from excluding the Father and the Son from any part in this great work—we believe They are deeply interested in it, as the Divine Word shows in Jude 1: "Them that are sanctified by God the Father." 1 Cor. 1. 2: "Them that are sanctified in Christ Jesus." But the Holy Spirit is the special and immediate Agent to whom the work of sanctifying the believer is assigned. Let us now attempt to show *in what way* He sanctifies the believer.

First, *by leading to a deeper acquaintance with the existence and power of indwelling sin*. Perhaps the first impression of the reader is, how can this be? How does the breaking up of the deep fountain of inbred sin lead to the quieting of its dark and turbulent waves? But the Holy Spirit works in a way contrary to the dictates of our poor reason—in a way often that we never should have conceived, and by methods we should never have selected. This is one method of His operation in subduing our iniquities, and in making us partakers of the Divine holiness. The knowledge of indwelling sin, its existence and power, is often exceedingly defective at conversion, and this ignorance may continue for years after. We just see sin enough to alarm the conscience, awaken conviction and take us to Christ. As a thing against God, we hate it, mourn over it and seek its pardon through the atoning blood. This is followed by a sweet and lively sense of its blotting out and a growing desire after Divine conformity. But, oh, the *unknown depths of sin!*—these we have never explored. What infinite wisdom and love are seen in hiding these depths at first from our knowledge! Were the Lord fully to have revealed the hidden evils of the heart at the period when grace was yet in the bud, and faith was feeble, and our views of the Lord Jesus dim, and the " new creature " yet in its infancy, deep and dark despair must have gathered around the soul. With perhaps just knowledge enough of Christ to go to Him as a Saviour, with just faith enough to touch the hem of His garment, the eternal Spirit first disclosed to us the existence and the guilt of sin; a *full* disclosure might have shut us up in hopeless despair. As believers it is sweet to remember the tender love of God in our espousals, to trace the gentleness of His first dealings with us in conversion, and to bear in mind that what He was *then*, He is at *this moment*.

But trace the work of the Spirit in the after days of our experience. He comes, in accordance with the design of the covenant of grace, to sanctify, having called and quickened us. He is about to enlarge the " kingdom of God within " us, to stamp more deeply and bring out more vividly and broadly on the soul the varied lineaments of the Divine image. He is about to purify the temple more thoroughly, to take a fresh possession for God, to expel every rival that, by slow and imperceptible degrees, may have insinuated itself there; in a word, He is about to *sanctify* us. And how does He commence the work? By leading us into the chamber of imagery, by disclosing the depths of indwelling sin. Sin whose existence we had never imagined, He shows to have its principal dwelling in the heart. Iniquity that we had never thought of, He reveals as lurking in secret ambush within. O what darkness, what evil, and what baneful principles are found to have existed for so long, where we thought all was light, holiness and rectitude! We start, we shudder, and we shrink away, aghast at the discovery. " What!" says the alarmed soul, " does all this evil dwell in *me*? Have I carried about with

me for so long these sinful desires? Have I dwelling in me
the seeds of such deep and dark depravity? Wonder of wonders is it, that the flood has not long since carried me away
—that these deep evils have not broken out, to the wounding
of my peace, and to the dishonouring of my God and Saviour."
Thus made acquainted with his own heart, almost a stranger
to him before, the Holy Spirit awakens in his soul an ardent
desire for *holiness*. In view of such a discovery, whither can
he fly but to the throne of grace? Thither, then, he goes—
weeping, mourning, confessing—and his prayer is, "Lord, subdue these evils of my heart—I am overwhelmed with astonishment. 'I lie down in shame, and my confusion covereth
me,' that I should have harboured so long these treacherous
foes against Thee, Thou God of holiness and love. 'Save me,
O God; for the waters are come in unto my soul. I sink in
deep mire, where there is no standing: I am come into deep
waters, where the floods overflow me.' 'Search me, O God,
and know my heart; try me, and know my thoughts; and see
if there be any wicked way in me, and lead me in the way
everlasting.'" Now the Spirit deepens and strengthens this
desire for sanctification; the believer is set upon earnestly seeking holiness of heart; he sees such an iniquity in sin as he
never saw before, and seeing it, he abhors it, and abhorring it,
he takes it to the Spirit of holiness, that He might overcome
and subdue it. Thus, in leading the believer into a deeper
acquaintance with the existence and power of indwelling sin,
does the blessed Spirit sanctify the soul, by making it the occasion of stirring up its desires for holiness. So do not be cast
down at the discovery of the hidden evil of your heart. Sweet
is the evidence it affords to the fact that the Holy Spirit is
working there. Whatsoever be the sin that is brought to light
—pride, deceit, carnality, inordinate affection, evil thoughts,
unbelief, impatience, whatsoever it be—He is revealing it to
you, not unnecessarily to wound and grieve you—O no, he is
a loving and a gentle Spirit—but to beget this desire in your
heart, "Lord, conform me to Thine image—make me holy as
Thou art holy."

Another process by which the Spirit sanctifies, is *by deepen-*

ing and strengthening the Divine life in the soul. There is, in every believer, a spiritual life. This life is from God. He is therefore said to be a " partaker of the Divine nature." This new and Divine life is, from its very nature, holy, and therefore opposed to the flesh. The flesh and the Spirit are ever hostile the one to the other, " for the flesh lusteth against the Spirit, and the Spirit against the flesh: and these are contrary the one to the other." Paul, referring to his own experience, corroborates this statement. " I see another law in my members, warring against the law of my mind, and bringing me into captivity to the law of sin which is in my members." Now the advance of the believer in true sanctification is just in proportion to the state of the Divine life within him. If it be low and declining, feeble and drooping, then the flesh gains the ascendancy and the root of sin is strengthened. If, on the contrary, the life of God in the soul is deepening and expanding, healthy and vigorous; if the " kingdom of God within," which is the new creation, is filling up every avenue of the mind, extending its conquests, and bringing every thought and affection into captivity to Christ; then the great work of sanctification is advancing, and " the law of the mind " is prevailing against " the law of sin."

There is an idea, fatal to all true sanctification of sin, which some believers, especially those who are young in experience, are prone to entertain, that nothing is to be done in the soul after a man has believed, that the work of conversion having taken place, all is accomplished. So far from this being the case, he has but just entered upon the work of sanctification, just started in the race, just buckled on the armour. The conflict can hardly be said to have begun in conversion; and therefore to rest indolently with the idea that the soul has nothing more to do than to accept of Christ as his salvation—that there are no corruptions to subdue, no sinful habits to cut off, no long-existing and deeply-embedded sins to mortify, root and branch, and no high and yet higher degrees in holiness to attain—is to form a most contracted view of the Christian life, such a view as, if persisted in, must necessarily prove detrimental to the spiritual advance of the believer.

The work of sanctification is a great and a daily work. It commences at the very moment of our translation into the kingdom of Christ on earth, and does not cease until the moment of our translation into the kingdom of God in heaven. The notion, so fondly cherished by some, of perfect sinlessness here, is as fatal to true sanctification as it is contrary to God's Word. They know but little of their own heart, who do not know, that sin (to borrow the language of John Owen), " not only still abides in us, but is still acting, still labouring to bring forth the deeds of the flesh." They know little who do not know that in their " flesh there dwelleth no good thing," that " that which is born of the flesh is flesh," and will retain its fleshly nature and propensities to the very last. Let us not exult " as though we had already attained, or were already perfect "; let us not be " ignorant of Satan's devices," one of which is to build us up in the belief that, in the present life, a man may cease from the work of mortification. The Lord keep the reader from cherishing so erroneous an idea. The work of sanctification is the work of a man's life. " When sin lets us alone (as has been remarked) we may let sin alone." But when is the day, indeed, when is the hour, that sin does not strive for the mastery, and in which the believer can say that he has completely slain his enemy? He may, " through the Spirit, mortify the deeds of the body," and if he does, " he shall live "; but as the heart is the natural and luxuriant soil of every noxious weed of sin, and as another springs up as soon as one is cut down, indeed as the *same root* appears again above the surface with new life and vigour, it requires a ceaseless care and vigilance, a perpetual mortification of sin in the body, until we throw off this cumbrous clay and go where sin is known no more.

In this way does the Spirit deepen the holiness of the child of God. He strengthens the Divine life within him; He invigorates the principle of holiness; waters, and revives, and expands the germ; infuses new life into His own blessed work; gives a new spring to faith, a new impulse to obedience, enlarges the heart with the love of Christ, and excites such a thirsting for holiness as none but God Himself can satisfy.

We would not omit to notice *the influence of sanctified afflictions, which, through the eternal Spirit, are a powerful means of sanctification to the soul.* " It is good for me that I have been afflicted," has been the exclamation and the testimony of many of the Lord's covenant and tried people. It is often difficult at the time to justify the wisdom and the goodness of God in His dealings with His saints. David found it so, when he saw with envy the prosperity of the wicked. Job found it so, when in the hour and depth of his afflictions, he exclaimed, "Thou art become cruel to me: with thy strong hand thou opposest thyself against me." Jeremiah found it so, when in his affliction he said, "He hath hedged me about, that I cannot get out: he hath made my chain heavy." And yet where is the furnace-tried, tempest-tossed believer that has not had to say, "In very faithfulness hath he afflicted me"? During the pressure of the trial, at the moment when the storm was the heaviest, he may have thought, "all these things are against me"; but soon he has been led to justify the wisdom, and the love, and the faithfulness, and the tenderness of his covenant God and Father in His dealings, and to sing, in sweeter notes than ever,

> " 'Tis my happiness *below*
> *Not to live without the cross,*
> *But the Saviour's power to know,*
> *Sanctifying every loss.*"

(Cowper.)

The furnace is a needed process of sanctification. If not, why has God so ordered it? If not, why is it that so many of His people are " chosen in the furnace of affliction "? Why do all, more or less, pass through it? *The furnace is needed.* It is needed to " purify the sons of Levi, and purge them as gold and silver, that they may offer unto the Lord an offering in righteousness." It is needed to consume the dross and the tin which adhere so closely to the precious ore, to burn up the chaff that mingles with the precious grain, to purify the heart, to refine the affections, to chasten the soul, to wean it from a poor, empty world, to draw it from the creature, and to centre it in God. O the blessed effects of this sanctified process! Who can fully unfold them? That must be blessed indeed which makes sin more exceedingly sinful, which weans and draws away from earth, which endears Jesus and His precious blood and righteousness, and which makes the soul a "partaker of His holiness." This is the blessed tendency of the sanctified discipline of the covenant. In this way does the Holy Spirit often sanctify the child of God.

Are *you* a child of affliction? Ah! how many whose eye falls on this question shall say, "I am the man that hath seen affliction!" So too was your Lord and Master, and so too have been the most holy and eminent of His disciples. Then "think it not strange concerning the fiery trial which is to try you, as though some strange thing happened unto you; but rejoice, inasmuch as ye are partakers of Christ's sufferings; that, when his glory shall be revealed, ye may be glad also with exceeding joy." This is the path along which all the Lord's covenant people are led, and in this path, thorny though it be, they pluck some of their choicest flowers, and find some of their sweetest fruits. I am not addressing myself to those who are strangers to sanctified sorrow, whose voyage so far has been over a smooth and summer sea, whose heart's affections have never been sundered, whose budding hopes have never been blighted, whose spring blossoms have never fallen just when the fruit was beginning to appear, or whose sturdy oaks around which they fondly and closely clung have never been stricken at their side; to such, I speak a mystery when I speak of the peculiar and costly *blessings* of sanctified affliction. It is not so with the experienced child of God, the "man that hath seen affliction by the rod of His wrath." He is a witness to the truth of what I say. From this mine, he will tell you, he has dug his richest ore. In this field he has found his sweetest fruit. The knowledge of *God* to which he has here attained—His tender, loving and wise dealings with His people, His glorious character and perfections, His unchangeable love and faithfulness; the knowledge of *Christ*—His all-sufficiency and fulness, His sympathy and love; the knowledge of *himself*—his poverty, vileness and unworthi-

ness: O where, and in what other school, could these high
attainments have been made but in the low valley of humiliation, and beneath the discipline of the covenant of grace?
Thus does the Spirit sanctify the soul through the medium of
God's afflictive dispensations; thus they deepen the work of
grace in the heart—awaken the soul from its spiritual drowsi-
ness—empty, humble, and lay it low—thus they lead to
prayer, to self-examination, and afresh to the atoning blood;
in this way, and by these means, the believer advances in
holiness " through sanctification of the Spirit."

Again, it is *by simple, close, and searching views of the cross
of Christ* that the Spirit most effectually sanctifies the believer.
This is the true and great method of gospel sanctification. Here
lies the secret of all real holiness, and, may I not add, of all real
happiness? For if we separate happiness from holiness, we
separate that which, in the covenant of grace, God has wisely
and indissolubly united. The experience of the true believer
must testify to this. We are only happy as we are holy—as the
body of sin is daily crucified, as the power of the indwelling
principle of sin is weakened, and as the outward deportment
more beautifully and closely corresponds to the example of
Jesus. Let us not then look for a *happy* walk apart from a
holy one. Trials we may have; indeed if we are the Lord's
covenant ones, we *shall* have them, for He Himself has said,
" in the world ye *shall* have tribulation "; disappointments we
may meet with—broken cisterns, thorny roads, wintry skies;
but if we are walking in fellowship with God, walking in the
light, growing up into Christ in all things, the Spirit of adoption dwelling in us, and leading to a filial and unreserved surrender—oh, there is happiness unspeakable, even though in
the very depth of outward trial. A holy walk is a happy
walk. This is God's order; it is His appointment, and therefore
must be wise and good.

The Spirit especially and effectually sanctifies by unfolding
the cross of Jesus. We desire to enlarge upon this point, not
only because He Himself presents it in His Word as one of
vast importance, but from the sober conviction of our judgment that there is no great advance in holiness without a

growing knowledge of Christ as the sanctification of the believer. A reference to God's Word, will place this truth in its
proper light. Matt. 1. 21 : "And thou shalt call his name
Jesus : for he shall save his people from their sins." Not only
shall He save them from the guilt and condemnation of sin,
but also from the indwelling power or reign of sin, so that
"sin shall not have dominion over" them. We shall presently show more fully how, in His sacerdotal office, He
accomplishes this.

Again, 1 Cor. 1. 2 : "Unto the church of God which is at
Corinth, to them that are sanctified in Christ Jesus." But the
most striking allusion to this important truth is found in the
30th verse, where the Lord Jesus is especially spoken of as
made of God the sanctification of His people : "But of him
are ye in Christ Jesus, who of God is made unto us wisdom,
and righteousness, and *sanctification*, and redemption." Now
it is essential to a right reception of the subject that we should
know in what points of view Christ is made our sanctification; so that believing in Him and receiving Him as such, we
may "grow up into Him in all things."

In the first place, *the atoning work of Christ lays the
foundation of sanctification.* He opens a way by which God,
so to speak, can treat with the soul in the great business of
its holiness. Only upon the broad basis of His law honoured,
His holiness secured, and His justice satisfied, can God, in the
way of mercy, have communication with the sinner. Here
we see the great glory of Jesus as the God-Man Mediator. His
atoning work opens a channel through which God, without
compromising a single perfection of His nature, can communicate the saving and sanctifying power of His grace to
the soul. The obedience and bloodshedding of our adorable
Lord, are ever, in the Divine Word, connected with the sanctification of the church. A few examples will suffice to show
this.

Speaking of the legal, but imperfect sanctification by the
sacrifices under the law, the apostle supplies an argument in
favour of the superior sanctification by the blood of Christ.
Heb. 9. 13, 14 : "For if the blood of bulls and of goats, and

the ashes of an heifer sprinkling the unclean, sanctifieth to the purifying of the flesh, how much more shall the blood of Christ, who through the eternal Spirit offered himself without spot to God, purge your conscience from dead works to serve the living God?"

Again, in Rom. 6. 3-6, the following phrases occur: "Planted in the likeness of his death"—"our old man crucified with him"—"the body of sin destroyed"—"that *henceforth* we should not serve sin." Let the reader also consult the following passages: Rom. 5. 9; 1 Pet. 3. 18; Col. 1. 14; Heb. 2. 14, 15; 1 John 4. 10. Thus does the atoning blood of Jesus lay the foundation of all future degrees of sanctification. The cross of Christ is, so to speak, the starting point of the soul in this glorious career of holiness, and the goal to which it again returns. *By* it, the body of sin is wounded, and wounded fatally; *from* it, pardon, and peace, and holiness flow; and *through* it, the soul daily rises to God in a holy surrender of itself to His service. Let no man dream of true mortification of sin, of real sanctification of heart, who does not deal constantly, closely and believingly with the atoning blood of Jesus. The Holy Spirit brings the cross into the soul and lays it upon the heart to be the death of sin. "I am crucified with Christ." "That I may know him, and the power of his resurrection, and the fellowship of his sufferings, being made conformable unto his death." "I bear in my body the marks of the Lord Jesus"—and see how the cross lifted him above the world and deadened him to it—"God forbid that I should glory, save in the cross of our Lord Jesus Christ, by whom the world is crucified unto me, and I unto the world." Thus did Paul breathe after and attain unto holiness.

The intercession of our Lord Jesus pleads for and secures the sanctification of the believer. In this sense it may be said that He is "made of God unto us sanctification." The Christian reader may be but imperfectly aware how closely connected is every spiritual grace and blessing that he receives with the advocacy of Jesus at the right hand of God. (The Lord increase our faith in this great and sanctifying truth!) While yet upon earth, our dear Lord commenced that work

E

of intercession for the sanctification of the church, which He ascended up on high more fully to carry on. This was the burden of His prayer, and it forms, as John Owen observes, "the blessed spring of our holiness"—"Sanctify them through thy truth." And not only would He leave it, as it were, as a model of the intercession of His exalted priesthood, but, for our encouragement, He would provide an evidence of its success. To Peter, about to pass through a severe temptation, He says, "I have prayed for thee, that thy faith fail not." Nor did his faith fail. It was sifted, it was severely shaken, it was powerfully tried, but *it failed not*; not a particle of the pure gold was lost in the refining, not a grain of the pure wheat in the sifting: and why?—because Jesus had interceded, and His intercession was all-prevailing. O the vast and costly blessings that flow into the soul from the intercession of Christ! Never shall we know the full extent of this, until we pass within the veil. We shall then know the secret of our spiritual life—of all our supports, consolations and victories; why it was that the spark in the ocean was not quite extinguished, why the vessel in the storm and amid the breakers did not quite become a wreck; why, when temptations assailed, and crosses pressed, and afflictions overwhelmed, and unbelief prevailed, that our faith still did not fail, and our bark was not driven from its moorings, and that "out of the depths" we were enabled to cry, "Thanks be unto God, who always causeth us to triumph in Christ." The secret will then disclose itself—*the intercession of Jesus our great High Priest*.

How sweet and consoling to the believer is this view of our exalted Immanuel in the hour of bereavement, when confined to his chamber of solitude, or languishing upon his bed of "pining sickness." Too deeply absorbed in sorrow, it may be, to give utterance to his anguished spirit in prayer—his bodily frame so weakened by disease, and racked by pain, as to render the mind unfit for close and connected spiritual thought—O how sweet is *then* the intercession of Jesus; how sweet to know that, in the hour of the soul's extremity when human sympathy and power are exhausted, "Jesus has

entered into heaven, *now* to appear in the presence of God"
for His suffering child. And when all utterance has failed on
earth; when the heart is broken and the lips are sealed, *then*
to look up and see our elder Brother, the Brother born for our
adversity, the exalted High Priest waving the golden censer
before the throne, while the cloud of His atoning merit goes
up before the mercy-seat, bearing as it ascends, the person,
the name, the circumstances and the wants of the sufferer
below—precious gospel, that opens to the eye of faith so
sweet a prospect as this! When you cannot think of Him,
afflicted soul, He is thinking of you; when you cannot pray *to*
Him, He is praying *for* you, for "He ever liveth to make
intercession."

But our Lord Jesus is the sanctification of the believer in
still another and blessed sense. *View Him as the Head of all
mediatorial fulness to His people.* "It pleased the Father
that in him should all fulness dwell." "And of his fulness
have all we received, and grace for grace." Here is sanctification for the believer who is mourning over the existence and
power of indwelling sin, feeling it to be his greatest burden
and the cause of his deepest sorrow. In the growing discovery
of the hidden evil—each successive view, it may be, deeper
and darker than the former—where is he to look but unto
Jesus? Where can he fly, but to His cross? Hemmed in on
every side by a host of spiritual Philistines, no avenue of
escape presenting itself, the eternal Spirit leads the soul to a
simple view of Jesus, opens to him the vast treasury of His
grace, and the free welcome to all comers. And what does
he find in that fulness? All that he wants to pardon sin, to
hide deformity, to overcome unbelief, and break the power of
strong corruption; he finds that there is enough in Christ to
make him holy, that, in simply taking his sins to Jesus, they
are pardoned; in taking his strong infirmities, they are subdued; in taking his wants, they are supplied; in a word, he
finds Christ to be his "wisdom and righteousness, sanctification and redemption."

We close this chapter with a few remarks in the way of
caution, direction and encouragement in this great work.

Do not mistake the nature of true sanctification. It is an internal and radical work. It has its seat in the *heart*. A mere external mortification of sinful habits does not come up to the standard of gospel sanctification. True, this is included in real holiness, yet it may exist without a holy heart. A man may cut off outward sins, and leave the *principle* of all sin yet remaining in its unsubdued power. We may visit a forest, and level a tall cedar to the earth; yet, if we leave the root deeply embedded in the soil, the vital principle yet remaining in all its vigour, what marvel if, in course of time, that root shall again shoot forth, and branch out as before? True sanctification is a daily mortification of the *root* of sin in the heart—the continual destruction of the *principle*. The Word of God bears us out in this; Gal. 5. 24: "And they that are Christ's have crucified the flesh with the affections and lusts." Rom. 6. 6: "Knowing this, that our old man is crucified with him, that the body of sin might be destroyed, that henceforth we should not serve sin." Do not rest short of this. Would you be holy as God is holy, and happy as the saints in glory are happy?—then must you reach after this and rest not until you attain it.

Again we would urge—*seek high attainments in holiness.* Do not be satisfied with a low measure of grace, with a stunted religion, with just enough Christianity to admit you into heaven. O how many are thus content, satisfied to leave the great question of their acceptance to be decided in another world, and not in this, resting upon some slight evidence, in itself faint and equivocal, perhaps a former experience, some impressions or sensations or transient joys long since passed away; and thus they are content to live, and thus content to die. You should not be satisfied with anything short of a *present* Christ, received, enjoyed and lived upon. Forget the things that are behind, reach forth unto higher attainments in sanctification, seek to have the daily witness, daily communion with God; and for your own sake, for the sake of others, and for Christ's sake, " give all diligence to make your calling and election sure."

Beware of self-dependence in this work. Remember the

words that Jesus once spake to His disciples, and now speaks to you, "Without me ye can do nothing." Self-trust, self-complacency, self-boasting, all must be crucified; and, strong only in the strength that is in Christ Jesus, must the believer gird himself to the work. Our wisdom is to go in our weakness and folly to Jesus. In this lies the great secret of our victory: "When I am weak, then am I strong": "My grace is sufficient for thee": "I can do all things through Christ which strengtheneth me."

Do not forget that *the truth of God is the great instrument of sanctification.* "Sanctify them through thy *truth*: thy word is truth." There is that in the truth of God, which, when brought into the soul by the power of the Holy Ghost, always sanctifies. It is *holy* truth; it unfolds a holy God, reveals a holy law, exhibits a holy sacrifice, and enforces by the most holy motives the sanctity of the most holy precepts. In proportion as the renewed mind is brought into a close and constant contact with God's truth, it grows nearer to its spirit. Let then "the word of Christ dwell richly in you in all wisdom" and spiritual understanding. Be close, diligent and prayerful students of the Word of God. Do not separate the doctrine from the precept, nor the precept from the promise; every part is essential to the sanctification of the believer; to secure this great end, the doctrine, the precept and the promise must be alike received, and brought into active, holy exercise.

Deal much and closely with the atoning blood of Jesus. There is no victory over the indwelling *power* of sin, and there is no pardon for the *guilt* of sin, but as the soul deals with the blood of Christ. The great object of our dear Lord's death was to destroy the works of the devil. *Sin* is the great work of Satan. To overcome this, to break its power, subdue its dominion, repair its ruins and release from its condemnation, the blessed Son of God suffered the ignominious death of the cross. All that bitter agony which He endured, all that mental suffering, the sorrow of His soul in the garden, the sufferings of His body on the cross—all was for sin. "He gave himself for us, that he might redeem us from all iniquity, and purify unto himself a peculiar people, zealous of good works." Tit. 2. 14. "He gave himself for the church, that he might sanctify and cleanse it and that he might present it to himself a glorious church, not having spot or wrinkle or any such thing, but that it should be holy and without blemish." Eph. 5. 25-27. See, then, the close and beautiful connection between the death of Christ and the death of sin. All true sanctification comes through the cross. Reader, seek it there. The cross brought into your soul by the eternal Spirit, will be the death of your sins. Go to the cross—oh, go to the cross of Jesus. In simplicity of faith, go—with the strong corruption, go—with the burden of guilt, go—*go to the cross*. You will find nothing but love there, nothing but welcome there, nothing but purity there. The precious blood of Jesus "cleanseth from all sin." And while you are kept low beneath the cross, your enemy dares not approach you, sin shall not have dominion over you, nor shall Satan your accuser condemn you.

Deal much and closely with the fulness of grace that is in Jesus. All this grace in Christ is for the sanctification of the believer. "It pleased the Father that in Him should all fulness dwell," for the necessities of His people; and what necessities so great and urgent as those which spring from indwelling sin? Take the corruption, whatever be its nature, directly and simply to Jesus: the very act of taking it to Him weakens its power; indeed it is half way to victory. The blessed state of mind—the holy impulse that leads you to your secret place, there to fall prostrate before the Lord in lowliness of spirit, brokenness of heart and humble confession of sin, with the hand of faith on the head of Jesus the atoning Sacrifice— is a mighty achievement of the indwelling Spirit over the power of indwelling sin. Learn to take the guilt as it comes, and the corruption as it rises, *directly* and *simply* to Jesus. Do not allow the guilt of sin to remain long upon the conscience. The moment there is the slightest consciousness of a wound received, take it to the blood of Christ. The moment a mist dims the eye of faith, so that you cannot see clearly the smile of your Father's countenance, take it that instant to the blood of atonement. Let there be no distance between God and your soul. *Sin separates.* But sin immediately confessed, mourned over and forsaken, brings God and the soul together in sweet, close and holy fellowship. O the oneness of God and the believer in a sin-pardoning Christ! Who can know it? Only one who has experienced it. To cherish, then, the abiding sense of this holy, loving oneness, the believer (to use the figure of the tabernacle) must wash daily in the brazen laver that is outside—then, entering in within the veil, he may " draw near " the mercy-seat and ask what he will of Him who dwells between the cherubim. " Having therefore, brethren, boldness to enter into the holiest by the blood of Jesus, by a new and living way, which he hath consecrated for us, through the veil, that is to say, his flesh; and having an high priest over the house of God; let us draw near with a true heart in full assurance of faith, having our hearts sprinkled from an evil conscience, and our bodies washed with pure water." Heb. 10. 19-22.

Thank God for the smallest victory gained. Praise Him for any evidence that sin has not entire dominion. Every fresh triumph achieved over some strong and besetting weakness is a glorious battle won. No victory that ever flushed the cheek of an Alexander or a Cæsar can be compared with his, who, in the grace that is in Christ Jesus, overcomes a single corruption. If " he that ruleth his spirit is better than he that taketh a city," then he who masters one corruption of his nature has more real glory than the greatest earthly conqueror that ever lived. O how God is glorified, how Jesus is honoured and how the Spirit is magnified in the slaying of one spiritual enemy at the foot of the cross! Cheer up, precious soul! You have every encouragement to persevere in the great business of sanctification. True, it is a hard fight; true, it is a severe and painful contest, but the victory is yours! The " Captain of your salvation " has fought and conquered for you, and now sits upon His throne of glory, cheering you on, and supplying you with all needed strength for the warfare in which you are engaged. Then " fight the good fight of faith," " quit you like men," " be strong in the grace that is in Christ Jesus," for you shall at length "overcome through the blood of the Lamb" and be "more than conquerors through Him that hath loved us." Here, beneath the cross, would I breathe for you the desire and the prayer once offered by the apostle of the Gentiles in behalf of the church of the Thessalonians, "And the very God of peace sanctify you wholly; and I pray God your whole spirit and soul and body be preserved blameless unto the coming of our Lord Jesus Christ." Amen and Amen.

CHAPTER VI

The Sealing of the Spirit

THE BELIEVER AN EPISTLE

" Ye are our epistle."—2 Cor. 3. 2.

" In whom also after that ye believed, ye were sealed with that Holy Spirit of promise."—Eph. 1. 13.

WHAT an inestimable gift is God the Holy Ghost, and how vast is His work! Each successive step we take in unfolding it does but more deeply convince us of this. New rays of light are reflected, new aspects of importance present themselves, and new features of interest and beauty are brought to view, as we pursue our research into this essential and important department of Divine truth. The more thoroughly and prayerfully we are led to investigate the operations of the Spirit upon the soul, especially if we watch closely His work in our own hearts, the more powerfully will the conviction press itself upon the mind that all real advance in Divine knowledge, in righteousness, joy and peace, is inseparably connected with His indwelling and sanctifying power. In the previous chapter, we endeavoured to unfold this. We have seen Him as the Author and Finisher of holiness in the soul—beginning the great work, carrying it forward, strengthening it when feeble, reviving it when drooping, and thus preparing the believer for the " inheritance of the saints in light." Closely connected with this part of His work is His *sealing* operation. As various opinions have been held regarding the nature of the Spirit's sealing, as it is a subject of a highly spiritual and practical tendency and (to an inquirer after a more perfect knowledge of the truth) of much importance, we enter upon the discussion of the subject the more readily, and, we trust, with earnest prayer for Divine assistance in unfolding it.

What do we understand by the sealing of the Spirit? What does the Word of God teach upon the subject? There are various passages in which the same figure is employed, but which do not convey the idea we ascribe to His present operation. For example, there is a sealing spoken of in 2 Tim. 2. 19: " Nevertheless the foundation of God standeth sure, having this *seal*, The Lord knoweth them that are his." We think it clear that the seal here alluded to has respect to the Father's sealing His people in election with the seal of His foreknowledge, which, of course, is an operation anterior to the existence of faith in the soul, and is within Himself, and not upon them. It is, so to speak, His secret designation of His people, known especially and only to Himself.

There is also a sealing spoken of in the Song of Solomon 8. 6: " Set me as a *seal* upon thine heart, as a *seal* upon thine arm : for love is strong as death." It is equally clear that this cannot refer to the work of the Spirit, but must refer to Christ's strong and unchangeable love to His people. They are set as a seal upon His *heart*, the dwelling-place of love, and upon His *arm*, the instrument of power; unchangeable *love* and omnipotent *power* are pledged to their eternal security. As a seal set upon His heart and worn upon His arm, they are precious to, and valued by, Him.

Nor are we to interpret the sealing under consideration to mean the extraordinary gifts of the Spirit; for it is a remarkable fact, already alluded to—and it speaks solemnly to those who are forming a higher estimate of gifts than of graces— that the Corinthian church, the most distinguished for its possession of the gifts of the Spirit, was at the same time most remarkable for its lack of the sanctifying graces of the Spirit. It was the most gifted, but at the same time least holy community gathered and planted by the apostles.

The question still recurs—what are we to understand by the sealing of the Spirit? It is that act of the Holy Spirit by which the work of grace is *deepened* in the heart of the believer, so that he has an *increasing* and *abiding* conviction of his acceptance in Jesus, and his adoption into the family of God. It is a clearer and more undoubted manifestation of Christ to the soul, a larger degree of the sanctifying, witnessing and anointing influences of the Holy Ghost, evidencing itself in a growing holiness of character. Let us not be misunderstood. We are not speaking of some peculiar and sudden impulse on the mind, of some immediate suggestion or revelation to the soul, some vision of the night, or voice in the air.[1] No: we speak of a growth in a knowledge of Christ, in sanctification of heart, in holiness of life, in an increasing and abiding moral certainty of the believer's " calling and election." " In whom also after that ye believed, ye were sealed with that Holy Spirit of promise." The Holy Spirit is both the seal and the sealer; even as Jesus was both the sacrifice and the priest. He deepens the work of grace in the heart; He witnesses to the believer that he is born of God; He seals the soul to the day of redemption, and by His indwelling and anointing influences enables him to say, " I know whom I have believed—He hath loved me and given Himself for me."

With this brief and simple definition of the nature of the sealing of the Spirit, we proceed to unfold the manner in which it is effected.

It is sometimes a *sudden* work of the Spirit. A soul may be so deeply sealed in conversion, may receive such a vivid impression of Divine grace, such an enlarged communication of the Divine Spirit, as it never afterwards loses. It is sealed " unto the day of redemption "; and that too, in the most simple way. In the hearing of a single sermon, the reading of a single chapter of God's Word, some promise brought with the power of the Holy Ghost and sealed upon the heart, in a moment the soul is brought into the full assurance of under-

---

[1] We would suggest to those afflicted with this or a like infirmity, that Jonathan Edwards on *The Religious Affections*, has been signally honoured of the Spirit in exploding sentiments so contrary to the Word of God, and so disastrous in their influence upon the mind. It should be read with much prayer, and " looking unto Jesus."

(This work will be found in Vol. III of *The Select Works of Jonathan Edwards* now being published by the Banner of Truth Trust.)

standing and of faith. Take, for example, that one precious
promise which the Spirit has sealed, never to be effaced, upon
many a poor sinner's softened heart: " him that cometh unto
Me I will in no wise cast out." O what a sealing is this! God
speaking to a poor, distressed, and disconsolate soul, assuring
it of a cordial welcome and of a free pardon—that though no
tongue can express its vileness and poverty, and no imagination conceive its deep sorrow, yet, coming to Jesus just as it
is, it shall in no wise be cast out! Is not *this* an impression
of the seal in the hands of the great Sealer, which is unto the
day of redemption?

Sometimes it takes place as the Holy Spirit unfolds to the
anxious soul the great truth that Christ is the Saviour of a
sinner. You have been long waiting for some offering, some
gift, some price with which to come; long lingering on the
margin of the fountain, waiting for some preparation to enter
—in other words (for it amounts to this), waiting to feel less
vile, less unworthy, in order that you may be more welcome.
And now, the blessed Spirit opens to your mind that great
and precious truth, that " Christ died for the *ungodly*," that
He is the mighty and the willing Saviour of a *sinner*; that no
gift, no price, is asked; no previous fitness or self-preparation
is necessary; that the more vile and unworthy, the more fit
and the more welcome. O what an impression of the seal is
this upon a wounded heart! When the glorious announcement is brought home to the soul—a full and free pardon for
a poor sinner—the blood of Jesus cleansing from sin—is it
any marvel that no change of time or circumstance can
obliterate the impression or the remembrance of that moment
from the mind? It was a *sealing* of pardon upon a heart
which God had made soft, and which was the sure prelude to,
indeed the beginning of, eternal glory.

But in most cases the sealing of the Spirit is a more *gradual*
work. It is a work of time. The soul is placed in the school
of deep experience and is led on step by step, stage by stage.
The knowledge of self and of Christ increases, deeper views
of indwelling sin are discovered, the heart's treachery is more
acutely felt, the devices of Satan are better known, the mystery

of God's gracious and providential dealings with His children is more clearly unfolded and better understood. And all this, it may be, is arrived at through a process—the deep, painful, yet sanctified discipline of the covenant—so that years may elapse before a child of the covenant attains to the full sealing of the Spirit. And yet, blessed be God, the work of regeneration is so perfect in itself, the blotting out of all a believer's sins so complete, and his justification so entire, that a saint of God dying in the first stages of the Divine life is safe for ever. May we not refer to the thief upon the cross as an example illustrating and confirming this?

There are, then, degrees, or progressive stages of the Spirit's sealing. The first impression is made in regeneration. This is often faint, and in numerous cases, scarcely perceptible. Especially is it so in ordinary conversions. We mean by ordinary conversions those that occur under the common influences of the Spirit, in the use of the stated means of grace. Where the Holy Spirit descends in an especial and extraordinary manner (as the history of the American churches and, more recently, of many in our own land testifies that He sometimes does), conversions assume a more marked character and type. They are clearer, more perceptible, and undoubted. The work is of a deeper kind, views of sin are more pungent, the law-work of the soul more thorough, and, when the soul emerges from its gloomy night of conviction into the glorious light of pardon, it seems more like the "perfect day" of God's forgiveness. There is, in a work of grace transpiring during an especial outpouring of the Holy Spirit, a deeper impression of the seal of the Spirit upon the heart, a clearer and more manifest sense of pardon and acceptance, than in the normal conversions of ordinary times. Nor is this difficult to account for. *There is a greater and richer manifestation of the Holy Spirit.* This is the grand secret. He gives more of Himself. He imparts more of His anointing influences; and the larger the degree we possess of the quickening, sanctifying influences of the Spirit, the more in proportion do we know of His sealing operation. How this thought should awaken the desire, and impart power and fervency to the prayer, for a more enlarged communication of the Holy Ghost! Ceaseless should be the cry, "Lord, fill me with the Spirit!" But, as we have remarked, in conversions occurring under the more ordinary instrumentalities, the first impression of the seal of the Spirit is often but little beneath the surface. The work of grace is feeble. It may be compared to the faint outline of a picture : the design is there, the idea of the artist is seen, but the fulness of its parts, the colouring, the light and shade, are wanting to the perfection of the whole. It may be compared, also, to the first streak of morning light, before it deepens into "perfect day," or to the gentle rising of the rivulet, ere it widens into the "broad river." Its beginnings are feeble, and yet real. The light is not less light because it is but a faint and struggling ray, nor is the rivulet less a rivulet because its issues are feeble and almost unseen. Grace loses nothing of the greatness and glory of its character in the smallness of its degree. An infant loses nothing of its identity with its species because it is not a "perfect man," nor does the father disown it as his child because it is the smallest and the feeblest of his family. O no—feeble grace is still Divine grace; and he who touches but the hem, is as much saved, and shall be as surely glorified, as he whose faith removes the mountain and casts it into the sea. The first impression is as much the work of the Spirit as any deeper one in after years. Let not the weak believer overlook or undervalue what God has done for him. That feeble light, that little strength, that faint and flickering ray, that touching but the hem—oh, it is the blessed product of God the eternal Spirit. Nature never taught you your sinfulness, your worthlessness, your vileness, your nothingness; "flesh and blood" never revealed to you the absolute necessity of a better righteousness than your own, nor led you to Jesus, as your "wisdom and righteousness, sanctification and redemption." Then "give glory to the Lord your God" for what He has done. Praise, O *praise* Him for the work He has wrought in you. Tell to others the wonders of His love, His grace and His power. Confess his name before angels and men. Be very diligent in seeking large and yet larger supplies of that "river that maketh glad the city of God." "In whom also, after that ye believed, ye were sealed with that Holy Spirit of promise."

But a yet deeper impression of the seal is made, when the believer is led more fully into the realisation of his *sonship*, when he attains to the blessed sense of the "adoption of children." Although it is most true that the moment a sinner believes in Jesus, he becomes actually an "heir of God, and a joint heir with Christ," and enters into the family as an adopted child, yet the clear and undoubted sense of this vast mercy may not be *sealed* upon his heart until later years. He may long have walked without the sweet sense of God's adopting love in his heart; the frame of his spirit and the language of his soul in prayer may have been more akin to that of the "son of the bond-woman" than the "son of the free-woman." He may have known but little of the "free spirit," the spirit of an adopted child, and may seldom have gone to God as a kind, loving, tender and faithful *Father*. But now the Divine Sealer—the eternal Spirit of God—enters afresh, and impresses deeply upon his soul the unutterably sweet and abiding sense of his adoption. O what an impression is then left upon his heart, when all his legal fears are calmed, when all his slavish moanings are hushed, when all his bondage spirit is gone, and when under the drawings of filial love, he approaches the throne of grace and cries, "My Father!"—and his Father responds, "My child!" "Thou shalt call me, My Father; and shalt not turn away from me." Jer. 3. 19. "In whom also, after that ye believed, ye were sealed with that Holy Spirit of promise."

In the process of *sanctified affliction*, the soul often receives a fresh and a deep impress of the seal of the Spirit. The furnace works wonders for a believer. O that he should ever wish to be exampt from it! Indeed, it may be remarked that real grace is inseparable from a state of trial. Where there is real faith, the Lord will try it. Where there is the true ore, the Refiner will prove it in the furnace. There is not a grace of the Spirit but, more or less, and at one time or another, Jesus tries that grace. "The Lord trieth the righteous." He tries their principles, tries their graces, tries their obedience, proves His own work, brings out the new man in all its muscular fulness, develops the nature and character of His work and shows it to be His mighty product, and in all respects worthy of Himself. Much, then, as we would wish at times, exemption from a state of trial, anxious for the more smooth and easy path, yet, if we are really born of God, and His grace has truly made us one of His family, like them we have been " chosen in the furnace of affliction," and with them in the furnace we are brought into the possession of some of the most costly blessings of our lives.

Real grace, then, is tried grace. And note how, in the process of its trial, the blessed and eternal Spirit more deeply seals the believer. The hour of affliction is the hour of *softening*. Job bore this testimony : " He maketh my heart soft." The hardness of the heart yields, the callousness of the spirit gives way, the affections become tender, conscience is more susceptible. It is the season of holy abstraction, meditation and prayer, of withdrawal from the world and from creature delights, while the soul is more closely shut in with God. The heart, now emptied, humbled and softened, is prepared for the seal of the Spirit; and what an impression is then made, what discoveries of God's love to the soul, what enlarged views of the personal glory of Christ, of the infinite perfection of His work, of the preciousness of the atoning sacrifice, of the hatefulness of sin, and of the beauty of holiness! His own personal interest in this great work of Christ is made more clear and certain to his soul. The Spirit bears fresh witness to his acceptance, and seals him anew with the adopting love of God. It was the psalmist's wisdom to acknowledge, " It is good for me that I have been afflicted." Let it not then be forgotten that an *afflicting* time is often a *sealing* time.

We would remark in this connection that the sealing of the Spirit does not always imply a *rejoicing* state. It is not necessarily accompanied by great spiritual joy. While we cannot forget that it is the believer's privilege to be " always rejoicing," " rejoicing evermore," and that a state of spiritual joy is as much a holy as it is a happy state, yet we cannot suppose that the " sealed " are always in possession of this " fruit of the Spirit." It is perhaps more a state of *rest* in God, a state of holy quietude and peace, which, in many cases, seldom rises to that of joy. There is an unclouded hope, a firm and unshaken resting on the finished work, a humble reliance on the stability of the covenant and on the immutability of God's love, which is never moved even when there is no sensible enjoyment and when comfort seems to die. It is a state corresponding to that which David thus expresses : " Although my house be not so with God; yet he hath made with me an everlasting covenant, ordered in all things, and sure : for this is all my salvation, and all my desire, although he make it not to grow." Perhaps it is more akin to Job's frame of soul when he exclaimed, " Though he slay me, yet will I trust in him." A sense of comfort may be withdrawn, joy may be absent, the Sun of righteousness casting but a faint twilight over the soul, and yet, such is the power of faith grasping the cross of Christ, such is the firm resting of the soul upon the stability of the covenant, upon what God is, and upon what He has promised, that, without one note of joy, or one ray of light, the believer can yet say, " I know whom I have believed." And why, we ask, this strong and vigorous reliance? Why this buoying up of the soul in the absence of sensible comfort? We reply that it is *because that soul has attained unto the sealing of the Spirit.* This forms the great secret.

This conducts us to another reflection. The *believer will never lose the sealing of the Spirit.* The impression of God's pardoning love made upon the heart by the Holy Ghost is never entirely effaced. We do not say that there are no moments when the " consolations of God are small " with the believer, when he shall have no severe " fightings within and fears without," when the experience of the church shall be his, " I opened to my beloved : but my beloved had withdrawn himself, and was gone : my soul failed when he spake : I sought him, but I could not find him; I called him, but he gave me no answer "—all this he may experience, and still not lose the sealing of the Spirit. In the midst of it all, even in the lowest depth, there shall be the abiding conviction of an interest in God's love which sustains, animates and comforts. It will be seen, by reverting to the state of the church alluded to above, that although there was the consciousness of her Beloved's withdrawal—though He was gone, and she *sought* Him but could not find Him, *called* Him but He gave her no answer—yet not for one moment did she lose the impression that *He still was her Beloved*. Here was the glorious triumph of faith in the hour when all was loneliness, desolation and joylessness. Here was the sealing of the Spirit which never left her, even though her "Beloved had gone." And while not a beam of His beauty glanced upon her soul, nor a note of His voice fell upon her ear, she still could look up and exclaim, "I am my Beloved's, and my Beloved is mine." O mighty power of faith that can anchor the soul firm on Jesus in the darkest and wildest tempest! And this, reader, is indeed the sealing of the Spirit. It is the Holy Ghost so deeply impressing on the heart a sense of pardoning love, so firmly establishing it in the faithfulness of God, in the finished work of Christ, in the stability of the covenant, and in the soul's adoption into the one family, that in the gloomiest hour, and under the most trying dispensation, there is that which keeps the soul steady to its centre—JEHOVAH JESUS. And even should his sun go down behind a mist, he has the sustaining assurance that it will rise upon another world, in peerless, cloudless splendour. O yes! the sealing of the Spirit is a permanent, abiding impression. It is "unto the day of redemption"—the day when there shall be no more conflict, no more darkness, no more sin. It is not to the day of pardon, for he cannot be more entirely pardoned than he is; it is not to the day of acceptance, for he cannot be more fully accepted than now. No, it is to the glorious "day of redemption," the day of complete emancipation longed for by the sons of God, and even sighed for by the "whole creation": "and not only they, but ourselves also, which have the first-fruits of the Spirit, even we ourselves groan within ourselves, waiting for the adoption, to wit, the redemption of our body." O shout for joy, you who are sealed of the Lord! Tried and afflicted, tossed with tempest, and not comforted, you who find the world to be but a wilderness, a vale of tears—the path rougher and rougher, narrower and narrower—lift up your heads with joy; the hour of "your redemption draweth nigh," and the "days of your mourning shall be ended." And this is your security: a faithful covenant-keeping God, "who hath also sealed us, and given the earnest of the Spirit in our hearts."

In closing this chapter, we would remark in the first place that *it is the duty and the privilege of every believer diligently and prayerfully to seek the sealing of the Spirit.* He rests short of his great privilege if he slights or undervalues this blessing. Do not be satisfied with the impression which you received in conversion. In other words, do not rest content with a *past experience.* Many are satisfied with a mere hope that they once passed from death unto life, and with this feeble and (in many cases) doubtful evidence, they are content to pass all their days and to go down to the grave. Ah, reader, if you are really converted, and your soul is in a healthy, growing, spiritual state, you will want more than this. And especially, too, if you are led into deeper self-knowledge, into a more intimate acquaintance with the roughness of the rough way and the straitness of the strait path, you will want a *present* Christ to *lean* upon and to *live* upon. Past experience will not do for you, save only as it confirms your soul in the faithfulness of God. "Forgetting those things that are behind," you will *seek* a *present* pardon, a *present* sense of acceptance; and the daily question, as you near your eternal home, will be, "How do I *now* stand with God? Is Jesus precious to my soul *now?* Is He my *daily* food? What do I experience of *daily* visits from and to Him? Do I more and more see my own vileness, emptiness and poverty, and His righteousness, grace and fulness? And should the summons come *now,* am I ready to depart and to be with Christ?" As you value a happy and a holy walk, as you would be jealous for the honour and glory of the Lord, as you wish to be the "salt of the earth," the "light of the world," and to be a savour of Christ in every place—O seek the sealing of the Spirit. Do not rest short of it, reach after it, press towards it:

it is your duty. O that the duty may be your privilege : *then* shall you exclaim with an unfaltering tongue, " Abba, Father " —" my Lord and my God !"

Again, I remark, *this blessing is only found in the way of God's appointment.* He has ordained that *prayer* should be the great channel through which His covenant blessings should flow into the soul. If it is your anxious desire to attain to this blessing, I would quote for your direction a remark of that eminent servant of Christ, Dr. Thomas Goodwin : " Be sure of this," says he, " that, before God ever communicates any good to a soul, He puts that soul in a state of holiness to receive it." To confirm and illustrate this thought, let me ask —what was the state of the apostles when the Holy Spirit descended upon them in His witnessing, anointing and sealing influences? It is described in these words—" these all continued with one accord in prayer and supplication, with the women, and Mary the mother of Jesus, and with his brethren." Acts 1. 14. What is the important lesson thus taught us? That God would have His child in a waiting, seeking, supplicating posture; and in this holy state prepared to receive the high attainment we plead for. Do you earnestly desire the sealing of the Spirit? " Ask, and ye shall receive; seek, and ye shall find." As surely as you petition for it—sincerely, humbly, believingly, seeking it in the name of Jesus—through the Cross of Christ, you *shall* have it. The Lord the Spirit is ready to impart it to you. It is the fresh gift of His love, without respect to any worth or worthiness on the part of the soul that receives it. It is a gift of grace for the poor, the dependent, the unworthy, those who are little in their own eyes, and little in the eyes of others; and if this is your conscious state, then is it for *you*. And O, the blessed *results*! Who can describe them? Sealed! How will all your legal fears and unbelieving doubts in a moment vanish away; your soul, so long fettered and imprisoned, shall now go free; the cross you have so long looked at, not daring to bow your shoulder to it, shall now be taken up with a cheerful mind; Christ's yoke, so long resisted, will now be easy, and His burden, so long refused, will now be light; and, with a heart enlarged

with the love of Jesus, you will "run the way of His commandments," esteeming His precepts better than life. Prayer,
importunate prayer, will bring the blessing we plead for into
your soul. Seek it with your whole heart, seek it diligently,
perseveringly. Seek it by day and by night, seek it in all the
means of grace, in every way of God's appointment; especially seek it in the name of Jesus, as the purchased blessing of
His atoning blood. "Ask what you will in My name," are
His own encouraging words, "and it shall be granted unto
you." Then ask for the sealing of the Spirit. Ask nothing less :
more you do not want. Feel that you have not "attained"
until you possess it, that you have not "apprehended that for
which also you are apprehended of Christ Jesus" until you
have "received the Holy Ghost" as a Sealer.

It is, and has long been, the solemn conviction of the writer,
that much of the spiritual darkness—the lack of spiritual consolation, the stunted piety, the harassing doubts and fears, the
imperfect apprehensions of Jesus, the feeble faith, the sickly
drooping state of the soul, the uncertainty of their full acceptance in Christ which mark so many of the professing people
of God in this our day—may be traced to the absence of a
deep sealing of the Spirit. Resting satisfied with the faint impression in conversion, with the dim views they then had of
Christ, and the feeble apprehension of their acceptance and
adoption, is it any marvel that all their life-time they should
be in bondage, through slavish doubts and fears? Fears that
they should never attain to the "stature of perfect men in
Christ Jesus," that they should never rise to the humble boldness, the unwavering confidence, the blest assurance and the
holy dignity of the sons of God? O no! They *rest short* of
this blessing. They stay at the door of the ark; they remain
upon the border of the goodly land, and not entering fully in,
they experience the effects which we have described. But the
richest ore lies buried the deepest; the sweetest fruit is on the
higher branches; the strongest light is near the sun. In other
words, if we desire more knowledge of Christ, of our full
pardon and complete acceptance, if we desire the earnest of
our inheritance, and even now would taste the "grapes of

Eshcol," we must be "reaching forth unto those things that are before." We must "press toward the mark," and not rest until our rest is found in a clear, unclouded, immovable and holy assurance of our being in Christ; and this is only experienced in the sealing of the Spirit. Again, we say, with all the earnestness which a growing sense of the vastness of the blessing inspires, *seek to be sealed of the Spirit.* Seek the "earnest of the Spirit"; seek to be "filled with the Spirit"; seek the "anointing of the Spirit"; seek the "Spirit of adoption." Do not say that it is too immense a blessing, too high an attainment for one so small, so feeble, so obscure, so unworthy as you. O do not thus malign the grace of God. All His blessings are the bestowments of grace; and grace means free favour to the most unworthy. Anyone who reads this page may, under the blessed sealing of the Spirit, look up through Jesus to God as a Father. Low views of self, deep consciousness of vileness, poverty of state or of spirit, are no objections with God, but rather strong arguments that prevail with Him to give you the blessing. Only *ask*, only *believe*, only *persevere*, and you shall obtain it. It is in the heart of the Spirit to seal "unto the day of redemption" all who believe in Jesus. May it be in the heart of the reader to desire the blessing, seeing that it is so freely and richly offered.

Reader, whose superscription do you bear? It may be your reply is—"I want Christ; I secretly long for Him; I desire Him above all beside." Is it so? Then take courage, and *go to Jesus.* Go to Him simply, go to Him unhesitatingly, go to Him immediately. That desire is *from* Him, let it lead you *to* Him. That secret longing is the work of the Spirit; and having begotten it there, do you think that He will not honour it and welcome you when you come? Try Him. Bring Him to the touch-stone of His own truth. "Prove me now herewith" is His gracious invitation. Take His promise, "Him that cometh unto Me I will in no wise cast out"; plead it in wrestlings at the mercy-seat, and see if He will not "open the windows of heaven, and pour you out a blessing, that there shall not be room enough to receive it." Go to Him just as you are. If you cannot take to Him a *pure* heart, take an *impure* one; if you cannot take to Him a *broken* heart, take a *whole* one; if you cannot take to Him a *soft* heart, take a *hard* one—*only go to Him.* The very act of going will be blessed to you. And oh, such is the strength of His love, such is His yearning compassion and melting tenderness of heart for poor sinners, such is His ability and willingness to save, that He will no more cast you out than deny His own existence. Precious Lord Jesus! set us as a seal upon Thine heart, and by Thy Spirit, seal Thyself upon our hearts; and give us, unworthy though we are, a place among " them which are sealed."

CHAPTER VII

The Witness of the Spirit

JESUS THE TRUE GOD, AND HIS WORK ALL-SUFFICIENT

" He that believeth on the Son of God, hath the witness in himself."
—1 John 5. 10.

WE have now looked at the work of the Spirit in some of its solemn and important aspects. We have considered His quickening, indwelling, sanctifying and sealing offices; and the spiritual eye will not have failed to discover the intimate and beautiful relation of each of these separate parts of His work to the others, and of all of them to the perfection and symmetry of His work as a whole. One important point at least must have been established in the mind, and that is the equality of the personal glory of the Spirit with the first and second Persons of the adorable Trinity. The work ascribed to Him in the preceding pages, and proved from Scripture to belong especially to Him, can only be predicated of a Divine Being. On this essential doctrine of Divine truth, we cannot too frequently nor too strongly insist. With regard to our *real belief* in it, we cannot institute too rigid an examination. It is to be feared that the principles of many professing Christians need sifting on this point. We profess a belief in His distinct personality in the Godhead—do we *worship* the Holy Spirit as such? We acknowledge His supreme divinity—do we render to him *Divine honour* by reposing in Him our faith, hope and love? We admit as an article of our creed that He sustains an equal part in our salvation with the Father and the Son—do we render to Him *equal praise* and *glory?* On these important points, may there not exist a painful want of harmony between our professed belief and its corresponding practice? And we would humbly suggest the consideration—may not the small measure of the anointing, sanctifying and sealing influence of the Spirit, which many professing Christians appear to possess, be mainly attributed, as a cause, to the low views they entertain of the personal dignity of the Spirit? Can any believer expect a growth of spirituality, an increase of vital godliness in his soul, while he secretly, and it may be unsuspectingly, cherishes opinions derogatory to the personal glory of the Holy Ghost? Never! His gracious and all-important work is inseparably connected with the glory of His person. His deity imparts to His work its efficacy—and His personality, its adaptation to our peculiar circumstances. And may we never look for the unction that anoints, for the light that instructs, for the seal that testifies, or the influence that sanctifies, while we secretly or openly whittle away His personal glory and refuse Him the honour, the praise and the worship that are His just and proper due. The force of these remarks will be felt as we advance in the discussion of the subject immediately before us.

The *witness of the Spirit* is a highly important and blessed part of His great work. Hence we find repeated and marked allusions to it in the Word of God. The following are sufficient to prove it a doctrine of revelation. John 15. 26: "He (the Spirit) shall testify of me." Heb. 10. 15: "Whereof the Holy Ghost also is a witness to us." 1 John 5. 6: "And it is the Spirit that beareth witness." Rom. 8. 16: "The Spirit itself beareth witness with our spirit."

In view of what has been advanced touching the personal character of the Spirit, it will be the less necessary that we enlarge at length upon His *qualifications as a Witness*. Of His perfect competence for this office, there can be no question. Is it essential to a competent witness, that he should be of *sound mind*, and capable of judging of the facts to which he testifies? In a pre-eminent degree does this belong to the Holy Spirit. Thus, in the language of prophecy, is he spoken of: "And the Spirit of the Lord shall rest upon him (Christ), the Spirit of wisdom and understanding, the Spirit of counsel and might, the Spirit of knowledge and of the fear of the

Lord." Isaiah 11. 2. Who will deny that the Spirit, in this respect, is a competent witness to testify of the Lord Jesus to the church?

Is it another indispensable qualification that he who testifies to a fact should do so from a *personal knowledge* of the fact which he attests? The Holy Spirit, the Witness, is intimately acquainted with every fact which He relates, and with the nature and the truth of the work to which He testifies. His testimony is not grounded upon the knowledge or the evidence of others (what He has *heard*) but upon His own personal knowledge—upon what He *knows* of the great facts, to the truth of which He witnesses. He reveals to His people what no creature eye ever saw, nor ear heard, nor heart conceived, unless first enlightened and renewed by Him. "Eye hath not seen, nor ear heard, neither have entered into the heart of man, the things which God hath prepared for them that love him. But God hath revealed them unto us by his Spirit : for the Spirit searcheth all things, yea, the deep things (τα βαθη, *the depths*) of God." As a distinct person in the Godhead, it is impossible that it should be otherwise. He must know all that passes within the hidden recesses of the Divine mind. No "depths of God" but He fathoms them; all the designs of Jehovah's mind, the counsels of His will, the thoughts of His heart, the purposes of His grace, and the acts of His love, are known to the eternal Spirit. By Him, as far as the revelation involves the happiness and the holiness of the saints, they are disclosed to them. His knowledge, let it be remembered, arises from His essential union with the Divine Essence, without which He must have remained eternally ignorant. The "judgments of God are a great deep," which no creature line—not the most capacious finite intellect—could ever fathom. The reasonableness of accounting in this way for the secret knowledge of the Spirit is thus argued by the apostle. Referring to the same principle in man, he reasons : "For what man knoweth the things of a man, save the spirit of man which is in him? Even so the things of God knoweth no man, but the Spirit of God." It requires no further argument or illustration to show that a full and minute personal knowledge of the facts to which He witnesses is a qualification belonging to the Spirit.

One more qualification is essential. He who assumes the character of a witness should be known for the strictest probity. If the veracity of the witness cannot bear the closest investigation, " his witness is not true." Pre-eminently does this qualification attach itself to the blessed Spirit. Truth in relation to Him is an adjunct, but an essential characteristic. It is His very essence: to deprive Him of it, or, in the slightest degree, to question it, would be to undeify Him. He cannot exist without being true. As sustaining this character, He is emphatically spoken of in the Word. " Howbeit, when he, the Spirit of truth, is come, he will guide you into all truth." John 16. 13. " And I will pray the Father, and he shall give you another Comforter, that he may abide with you for ever, even the Spirit of truth." John 16. 16, 17. " And it is the Spirit that beareth witness, because the Spirit is truth." 1 John 5. 6. Thus does the Spirit possess all the essential qualifications of a competent witness. He is the Spirit of wisdom and understanding; He searches the depths of God; He is the Spirit of truth.

We proceed to specify some of those important facts to which especially the Spirit witnesses. And in the first place, *the Spirit is a witness to the truth of God's Word.* It is no small attainment to arrive at the full belief of the heart in the truth of the Divine record. We are not speaking now of the historical credence which an enlightened judgment may yield, but of a higher faith than this. Nor do we confine ourselves to that entire assent of the mind, and trembling belief of the heart, upon the grounds of which the soul may have ventured an humble reliance upon Christ, although this is no small attainment; but we allude to that firm, unmoved, and inmovable belief of the truth, which is often an after-work, a work of time and of deep experience, before the heart becomes thoroughly schooled into it. Let it not be supposed that we undervalue the smallest degree of faith. To believe that God's Word is true, and on the strength of that belief to be willing to renounce all other dependence, and to rest simply and implicitly upon its revealed plan of salvation, is a blessed attainment—an attainment only to be realised by the power of the Holy Ghost; but to know it from a deep experience of its sanctifying power, from the heartfelt preciousness and fulfilment of its promises, from its sustaining and soothing influence in sorrow, its all-sufficient light in darkness and perplexity, to be brought to trust the naked promise because God has spoken it, to believe, and to go forward, because He has said it, is a still higher step in faith's ladder, and a more illustrious display of the grace and power of the Spirit. It is an unspeakable mercy to be well grounded in the belief of the truth. Let those speak who have thus been blessedly taught. Let them testify that God's Word was, when they first believed, as a sealed book compared with what it is now; that, since they have advanced in the Divine life, led and instructed by the Spirit of truth, it has opened to their minds with all the light and freshness of a new revelation. Doctrines once mysterious, are now beautifully lucid; promises once unfelt, are now sweetly consolatory; precepts once insipid, are now powerfully persuasive. And to what is this maturity of the heart in the full belief of the truth to be ascribed? We unhesitatingly reply, to the witness of the Spirit, the Holy Ghost deepening His work in the heart, teaching the soul more experimentally, and guiding it more fully into all truth—in a word, bringing the truth more vividly to the mind with convincing power.

Nor can we refrain from remarking that this deeper experience of the truth of God is frequently the result of sore but sanctified trial. A believer knows but imperfectly what he is in himself, or what the truth of God is to him, until placed in circumstances favourable to the development of both. The Lord will have His people, and especially the ministers of His gospel, experimentally acquainted with His truth. They shall not testify of an unknown, unfelt and unexperienced Saviour. They shall be enabled to say, "That which we have heard, which we have seen with our eyes, which we have looked upon, and our hands have handled of the word of life, declare we unto you." And more valuable and precious is one grain of the truth of God experienced in the heart, than the whole system occupying a place only in the judgment. To deepen, then, their knowledge of the truth, to ground and settle them in it, to bring it out in all its practical power, a good, a covenant God often places His children in sore trial and temptation. It is in the storm and the hurricane, amid rocks and shoals, that the mariner becomes practically acquainted with his science. All that he knew before he launched his vessel on the ocean, or encountered the storm, was but the theory of the school; but a single tempest, one escape from shipwreck, has imparted more experimental knowledge than years of mere theoretical toil. So learns the believer. Oh, how theoretical and defective his views of Divine truth; how little his knowledge of his own heart, of his deep corruptions, perfect weakness and little faith; how imperfect his acquaintance with the fulness, preciousness, all-sufficiency and sympathy of Jesus until the hand of God falls upon him! And when, as with Job, messenger after messenger has brought the tidings of disaster upon disaster; then, brought down and laid low like him, he is brought to confess, " I have heard of thee by the hearing of the ear; but now mine eye seeth thee. Wherefore I abhor myself, and repent in dust and ashes." Job 42. 5, 6.

But before we pass to consider the testimony the Spirit bears for Christ, there is yet another step, so to speak, which must ever precede the manifestation of Jesus to the soul, and that is—the witness which the Spirit bears to the holiness, spirituality and justice of the Divine law. This is a preliminary step. *Conviction of sin by the law of God*, in the hands of the eternal Spirit, must ever precede faith in the Lord Jesus Christ. It is, with many, a favourite theory to deny that the Holy Spirit is the convincer of sin; but to deny this is to oppose the mind and conscience to the clear and express testimony of God's Word: " And when he (the Comforter) is come, he will reprove (marg. *convince*) the world of sin." John 16. 8. This is the great office of the Spirit—this is His first work, prior to His bringing the soul to rest on the great sacrifice for sin. Not a step will the soul take to Christ, until it has been brought in guilty and condemned by the law of

God. And this is the work of the Spirit. "No man," wrote the excellent John Newton, "ever did, or ever will feel himself to be a lost, miserable and hateful sinner, unless he be powerfully and supernaturally convinced by the Spirit of God." And what is the instrument by which the Spirit thus powerfully and supernaturally convinces of sin? We reply, THE LAW. "By the law is the knowledge of sin." Rom. 3. 20. " The law was our schoolmaster to bring us unto Christ." Gal. 3. 24. The law, brought into the conscience by the Holy Ghost, condemns the man, and leads him to condemn himself; it holds up to view the holiness of God, the purity and inflexibility of every precept, contrasts it with the unrighteousness, guilt and misery of the sinner, until the soul, prostrate in the dust, exclaims in all the lowliness of self-accusation, "'the law is holy, just and good'—I am guilty, guilty, guilty." What need have we of further testimony than that of the apostle: " What shall we say then? Is the law sin? God forbid. Nay, I had not known sin but by the law: for I had not known lust, except the law had said, Thou shalt not covet. But sin, taking occasion by the commandment, wrought in me all manner of concupiscence. For without the law sin was dead. For I was alive without the law once: but when the commandment came, sin revived, and I died." Rom. 7. 7-9. Through this instrument—the law of God—the Holy Spirit effectually convinces the soul of sin and lays it low before God.

We now come to show in what particular way the Spirit testifies of Christ to the believer. Our warrant for believing this comes from our dear Lord's own words: " But when the Comforter is come, whom I will send unto you from the Father, even the Spirit of truth, which proceedeth from the Father, *he shall testify of me*." John 15. 26. " He shall glorify me; for he shall receive of mine, and shall shew it unto you." John 16. 14.

First, *the Spirit in witnessing to the glory of the person of Christ testifies to His supreme, absolute Deity*. Strong is the testimony of the Holy Ghost in the Word to the essential Deity of our blessed Lord. And if *He* has laid such amazing stress upon it, surely it should be a solemn matter with us how we think of, and treat it. The great, the grand glory of Immanuel is His essential glory—the glory of His Godhead. It is only in this light that we can approach Him with the hope of pardon and acceptance. It is *then* we talk of Him as a Mediator, it is *then* we view Him as the great Sin-bearer of His people; it is *then* we contemplate Him as their Surety, their Righteousness, their covenant Head. In vain should we speak of His atoning blood, of His finished righteousness, of His mediatorial fulness, if we could not look up to Him in the glory He had with the Father before the world was." It is this that imparts such efficacy to His work, and throws such a surpassing lustre around it. And what is the witness of the Spirit to this doctrine? It is this; that all the names, the perfections, the works and the worship proper only to Deity belong to Christ, thus proclaiming Him with a loud voice to be what He really is—JEHOVAH JESUS. Consider the evidence. Jesus of Nazareth, the anointed Saviour of poor sinners, is emphatically styled the "GREAT GOD" (Tit. 2. 13), the "MIGHTY GOD" (Isa. 9. 6), the "ONLY WISE GOD" (Jude 25), the "TRUE GOD" (1 John 5. 20), and the "ONLY LORD GOD" (Jude 4). The name JEHOVAH peculiarly belongs to God: it is never in a solitary instance applied to a mere creature. "I am JEHOVAH, that is my name." And yet the very name is ascribed to Jesus by the Holy Ghost—"This is the name whereby he shall be called, JEHOVAH OUR RIGHTEOUSNESS." He is then JEHOVAH Jesus, "God over all, blessed for evermore." Could testimony be more clear and decisive? O precious truth on which to live; O glorious rock on which to die! Jesus is JEHOVAH—He is "Immanuel, God with us"— "God manifest in the flesh." Hold fast to this truth, reader. Let nothing weaken your grasp upon it. It is your *plank*, your *life-boat*, your *ark*, your all. This gone, all goes with it! You will need it when you come to die. In that solemn hour when all else fails you, when sin in battle array rises before you, and you think of the holiness of a holy God, *then* you will want a rock to stand upon. Then, as the Spirit leads you to Jesus the Rock, testifies to your soul of His blood, witnesses to His Godhead, unfolds Him in His essential glory, you will be enabled to shout "Victory! Victory!" as you pass safely and triumphantly over Jordan. The blood that speaks peace will be felt to be efficacious, the righteousness that justifies will be seen to be glorious, and the Rock that sustains will be felt to be firm and immovable, as the blessed Glorifier of Christ witnesses to the truth of His deity. O *then* to see the Law-giver in the character of the Law-fulfiller! To behold the God-Man obeying, suffering, dying, and therefore the law honoured, justice satisfied, and the Father well pleased! Truly may the believing soul adopt the triumphant language of the apostle, and take up his challenge: "who is he that condemneth? it is Christ that died." Set a high value on the doctrine of our Lord's Deity, guard it with a jealous eye, pray to be established in the full experimental belief of it; for the more you see of the dignity of His person, the more you will see of the glory of His work.

The Spirit witnesses to the personal glory of Christ as GOD-MAN. There are many believers who unhesitatingly admit the doctrine of our Lord's humanity, but do not delight to linger around those passages in the sacred Word which prove and unfold it, lest an essential inferiority in Jesus should be implied, and an impression should be left upon the mind unfavourable to His personal dignity. But this arises from the want of an enlarged, harmonious and scriptural view of the Divine method of salvation. Viewed in its proper aspect, the humanity of our Lord will be found to occupy a place in that scheme, as important and essential to its perfection as His Deity. The humanity was pure humanity, and the Deity absolute Deity, but the mysterious union of the two in the person of the Lord Jesus Christ constituted Him the proper and the "one Mediator between God and man." Glorious is this aspect of our Lord's complex person. And full and clear is the testimony of the Spirit to its truth. Thus we read, "The Word was made flesh, and dwelt among us (and we behold his glory, the glory as of the only begotten of the Father) full of grace and truth." John 1. 14. In the following passages Christ is evidently spoken of as subordinate to the Father, but only His mediatorial character is under consideration. There cannot be the slightest essential inferiority. It would be fatal to His entire work. The following passage would seem to imply an inferiority in Christ, but an inferiority only of *office*, not of *nature*: "Verily, verily, I say unto you, The Son can do nothing of himself, but what he seeth the Father do: for what things soever he doeth, these also doeth the Son likewise." John 5. 19. That these words of our Lord refer to His Divine nature we cannot believe, since in another place we find Him declaring, "All power is given unto me in heaven and in earth." Matt. 28. 18. So that where Christ speaks of Himself as inferior to the Father, as having "received glory from the Father," as "receiving life from the Father" and of "the Father being greater than he," He must invariably be regarded as alluding to Himself in His *mediatorial office* only, and not in His Divine character. He is equal with the Father in nature, subordinate to Him only in office. On this truth hinges all the glory and efficacy of redemption.

It was, then, essential to His fitness as the Surety and Mediator of His covenant people that He should be "bone of their bone and flesh of their flesh." Forasmuch as the children are partakers of flesh and blood, He also Himself likewise took part of the same; "it behoved Him to be made like unto His brethren." The nature of His office, and the success of His undertaking, required that every Divine and human perfection should meet and centre in Him. He was to be the middle person between God and man. He was to bring together these two extremes of being—the Infinite and the finite. He was to mediate for the offended Creator and the offending creature. How could He possibly accomplish this great and peculiar work without a union of the two natures—the Divine and the human? Jehovah could admit of mediation only by one of equal holiness and glory, and man could only negotiate in this great business of reconciliation with one "in all points (sin excepted) like unto himself." Behold this wondrous union in the person of Jesus. *As man*, He was made under the law—honouring it in its precepts by His obedience and in its penalty by His sufferings. *As God*, He imparted a

F

dignity to that obedience and a virtue to those sufferings
which rendered them eternally efficacious in the salvation of
men, glorious in the sight of angels and infinitely satisfactory
to law and to justice.

You must not stand aloof, reader, from the pure *humanity* of
your blessed Lord. It was *humanity* that obeyed, that bled and
died for you. Cling to the doctrine of His *deity*. It was *God*
in the man that rendered His obedience meritorious for your
justification, and His death effectual for your redemption. O
glorious person of the God-Man-Mediator! What a foundation is here laid for a poor condemned sinner to build upon!
What a "new and living way" to God is opened! What a
wide door he has to His very heart! He may come now and
feel that not a perfection of Jehovah is trampled upon in his
coming, that not an iota of His law is dishonoured in his salvation. Instead the law appears in its richest lustre and every
perfection shines in its resplendent glory in the full and free
redemption of a sinner through the blood and righteousness
of the Son of God. Is it any wonder that over the door of
mercy should be written in letters of brightness that might
dazzle an angel's eye, "*Whosoever believeth in him shall not
perish, but have everlasting life*"? The Holy Ghost witnesses
to the personal glory of Jesus, when He brings a soul to count
all other glory as loss, and to hang upon Christ as all his salvation. "What things were gain to me, those I counted loss
for Christ. Yea doubtless, and I count all things but loss for
the excellency of the knowledge of Christ Jesus my Lord." Phil.
3. 7, 8.

The Spirit witnesses to the atoning work of Jesus in His
priestly office. We have already seen that the foundation of
the work of Christ is the Godhead of His nature. It is important that the eye be kept immovably fixed upon this, as we
survey the atoning work of our Lord. Every step we take in
developing that work introduces us to new wonders as we
keep the glory of the person of Christ in view. The transcen-
dent efficacy of the sacrifice arose from the infinite dignity of
the Priest. The priests under the law could impart no personal
efficacy or glory to their sacrificial offerings. Their sacrifices

were only available for the atonement of transgression, as they were offered up in obedience to the command of God. But the sacrifice which Christ presented derived all its efficacy and glory from His person. It is this doctrine that attaches such importance to the death of Jesus and that throws such surpassing glory around His obedience. The blood of the Lord Jesus "cleanses us from all sin" because it is the blood of the God-Man; the righteousness of the Lord Jesus "justifies us from all things" because it is the "righteousness of God." From this arises the *costliness* of the sacrifice which Jesus presented to God.

It was also an *entire* sacrifice. It was *Himself* He offered. "Walk in love, as Christ also hath loved us, and hath given *Himself* for us an offering and a sacrifice to God for a sweet-smelling savour." Eph. 5. 2. It was Himself He offered up. More He could not give, less would not have sufficed. He gave Himself—all that He possessed in heaven, and all that belonged to Him on earth, He gave in behalf of His people. His life of obedience, His death of suffering, He gave as "an offering and a sacrifice to God." It was an entire surrender.

It was a *voluntary* offering. "He *gave* Himself." It was not by compulsion or by constraint that He surrendered Himself into the hands of Divine justice; he did not go as a reluctant victim to the altar; they did not drag Him to the cross. He went voluntarily. It is true that there existed a solemn necessity that Jesus should die in behalf of His people. It grew out of His covenant engagement with the Father. Into that engagement He voluntarily entered. His own ineffable love constrained Him. But after the compact had been made, the covenant of redemption ratified, and the bond given to justice, there was a *necessity* resting upon Jesus compelling Him to finish the work. His word, His honour, His truth, His glory, all were pledged to the entire fulfilment of His surety-ship. He had freely given Himself into the power of justice; He was therefore, on His taking upon Him the form of a servant, under obligations to satisfy all its claims; He was legally bound to obey all its commands.

And yet it was a *voluntary* surrender of Himself as a sacrifice for His people. It was a willing offering. If there was a necessity, and we have shown that there was, it grew out of His own voluntary love to His church. It was, so to speak, a voluntary necessity. See how this blessed view of the death of Jesus is sustained by the Divine Word. "He was oppressed, and he was afflicted, yet he opened not his mouth: he is brought as a lamb to the slaughter, and as a sheep before her shearers is dumb, so he openeth not his mouth." Isaiah 53. 7. His own declaration confirms the truth. "Therefore doth my Father love me, because I lay down my life, that I might take it again. No man taketh it from me, but I lay it down of myself. I have power to lay it down, and I have power to take it again." John 10. 17, 18.

Nor was it a voluntariness founded on ignorance. He well knew what the covenant of redemption involved and what stern justice demanded. The entire scene of His humiliation was before Him, in all its dark and sombre hues—the manger, the blood-thirsty king, the scorn and reproach of His country-men, the unbelief of His own kinsmen, the mental agony of Gethsemane, the bloody sweat, the bitter cup, the wayward-ness of His disciples, the betrayal of one, the denial of an-other, the forsaking of all; the mock trial, the purple robe, the crown of thorns, the infuriated cry, "Away with him, away with him, crucify him, crucify him"; the heavy cross, the painful crucifixion, the cruel taunts, the vinegar and the gall, the hidings of His Father's countenance, the concentrated horrors of the curse, the last cry of anguish, the bowing of the head, the giving up the ghost—all, all was before the om-niscient mind of the Son of God, with a vividness equal to its reality, when He exclaimed, "Save him from going down to the pit; I have found a ransom." And yet He willingly rushed to the rescue of ruined man. He voluntarily (though He knew the price of pardon was His blood) gave Himself up thus to the bitter, bitter agony. And did He regret that He had under-taken the work? Never! It is said that it repented God that He had *made* man, but in no instance is it recorded that it repented Jesus that He had *redeemed* man. Not an action, not a word, not a look betrayed an emotion like this. Every step He took from Bethlehem to Calvary did but unfold the willingness of Jesus to die. "I have a baptism to be baptized with, and how am I straitened till it be accomplished!"

Oh, how amazing was the love of Jesus! This, *this* was the secret why He loved not His own life unto the death. He loved sinners too well. He loved us better than Himself. With all our sinfulness, guilt, wretchedness and poverty, He yet loved us so much as to give Himself an offering and sacrifice unto God for us. Here was the springhead whence flowed these streams of mercy. This was the gushing fountain that was opened when He died. And when they taunted Him, and said, "If thou be the King of the Jews, save thyself," O what a reply did His silence give: "I came not to save myself, but my people. I hang here, not for My own sins, but for theirs. I *could* save myself, but I came to give My life a ransom for many." They *thought* the nails alone kept Him to the cross; He *knew* it was His own *love* that fastened Him there. Behold, reader, the strength of Immanuel's love. Come, fall prostrate, adore and worship Him. O what love was His! O the depth! Do not be content merely to stand upon the shore of this ocean : enter into it, drink deeply from it. It is for *you*, if you are truly feeling your nothingness, your poverty and your vileness; this ocean is for you. It is not for angels, it is for men. It is not for the righteous, but for sinners. Then drink to the full from the love of Jesus. Do not be satisfied with small supplies. Take a large vessel to the fountain. The larger the demand, the larger the supply. The more needy, the more welcome. The more vile, the more fit to come. Then plunge into this ocean, and count all things else but loss for Jesus, and sing, as you do so—

> *The cross! the cross! oh that's my gain,*
> *Because on that the Lamb was slain;*
> *'Twas there my Lord was crucified,*
> *'Twas there my Saviour for me died.*
>
> *What wondrous cause could move Thy heart*
> *To take on Thee my curse and smart?*

Well knowing that my soul would be
So cold, so negligent to Thee!

The cause was love, I sink with shame
Before my sacred Jesu's name;
That Thou shouldst bleed and slaughter'd be,
Because, because Thou lovedst me.

(Clare Taylor.)

We have yet to show in what way the Spirit witnesses to the atoning work of Jesus. He does so *by leading the guilty, condemned and broken-hearted sinner to rest on Jesus alone for salvation.* In this way He testifies of Christ. He first convinces the soul of sin, bringing the holy law of God with a condemning, slaying power into the conscience; then, having wounded and laid low, He leads the soul to Jesus as an all-sufficient Saviour. He opens the understanding to comprehend and the heart to welcome His own recorded testimonies of that all-sufficiency, and the readiness of the Lord Jesus Christ to save the vilest of the vile. He leads to the fountain of Immanuel's precious blood, plunges the guilty sinner beneath its cleansing stream, and then raises him to newness of life—" washed, sanctified, justified in the name of the Lord Jesus, and by the Spirit of our God." And this is the testimony: " As Moses lifted up the serpent in the wilderness, even so must the Son of man be lifted up: that whosoever believeth in him should not perish, but have eternal life. For God so loved the world, that he gave his only begotten Son, that whosoever believeth in him should not perish, but have everlasting life." John 3. 14-16. " All that the Father giveth me shall come to me; and him that cometh to me I will in no wise cast out." John 6. 37. " He that believeth . . . shall be saved." Mark 16. 16. " Wherefore he is able also to save them to the uttermost that come unto God by him." Heb. 7. 25. What a witness is this to the power and readiness of Christ to save! And this is the testimony of the Holy Ghost to the blessed Son of God. But He does more than this. He brings home the record with power to the soul. He writes the testimony on the heart. He converts the believing soul itself into a witness that " Christ Jesus came into the world to save sinners."

And what a gospel is this for a poor sinner! " There is not,' says an old divine, " an ill word in it against a poor sinner stripped of his self-righteousness." It speaks of pardon, of acceptance, of peace, of full redemption here, and unspeakable glory hereafter. It proclaims a *Saviour* to the *lost*; a *Redeemer* to the *captive*; a *Surety* to the *insolvent*; a *Physician* to the *sick*; a *Friend* to the *needy*; an *Advocate* to the *criminal* —all that a self-ruined, sin-accused, law-condemned, justice-threatened, broken-hearted sinner wants, this " glorious gospel of the blessed God " provides. It reveals to the *self-ruined* sinner, One in whom is his help, Hos. 13. 9. To the *sin-accused*, One who can take away all sin, 1 John 1. 7. To the *law-condemned*, One who saves from all condemnation, Rom. 8. 1. To the *justice-threatened*, One who is a hiding place from the wind, and a covert from the tempest, Isa. 32. 2. To the *broken-hearted*, One who bindeth up, and healeth, Isa. 61. 1. That One is—JESUS. O name ever dear, ever sweet, ever precious, ever fragrant, ever healing to the " poor in spirit "!

The blessed Spirit witnesses to the all-sufficiency of Christ, for all the wants of His people. He testifies that " it pleased the Father that in him should all fulness dwell." He takes of the things of Christ, and shows them to the believer. Perhaps this is His greatest witness to a child of God in reference to Jesus. And why? because the highest act by which a believing soul glorifies Christ is a life of daily faith upon Him. There is a vast difference between an acknowledgment of Christ in the judgment, a bowing of the knee to Him outwardly, and a real, experimental, daily living upon Him. The very essence of experimental religion is living upon Christ daily as a poor, empty sinner. We live in a day of easy and splendid profession, a day in which the many can speak well of Christ and " profess and call themselves Christians." But all is not gold; there is much tinsel, much that is only dross, much that is counterfeit. And while many a man has been applauded for his money, admired for his philanthropy, worshipped for his talent and followed for his eloquence, God has said, "I see no lowliness of spirit, no brokenness of heart, no humbling views of self; I hear no voice of prayer, no acknowledgment of My power; I behold no crowning of My Son, no honouring of Me with the glory." And while many a man has been as the scum and the offscouring of all things; despised for his feeble gifts, his poor talents, his humble sphere; looked down upon by the great and the wise and the haughty; the "high and lofty One who inhabiteth eternity, whose name is Holy," has said, "I see a broken heart, I see a lowly mind, I see the work of My Spirit, I see the image of My Son, I dwell with him that is of a humble and contrite spirit." O yes! a poor believer, going to Jesus in all his emptiness and weakness; going to Him, leaning on His blood and righteousness, going to Him in the face of all opposition, pleading His worth and worthiness; going with all his sins, with all his infirmities, with all his backslidings, with all his wants, has more real glory in it than all the glory of all worlds collected in one blazing focus. What a witness, then, is this which the eternal Spirit bears to Jesus! He assures the believer that all he can possibly want is treasured up in Christ, that he has no cross but Christ can bear it, no sorrow but Christ can alleviate it, no corruption but Christ can subdue it, no guilt but Christ can remove it, no sin but Christ can pardon it, no want but Christ can supply it. Lift up your heads, you who are poor, needy and disconsolate! Lift up your heads, and rejoice that Christ is ALL to you, all you need in this vale of tears, all you need in the deepest sorrow, all you need under the heaviest affliction, all you need in sickness, all you will need in the hour of death and in the day of judgment. Indeed, Christ is *in all* too. He is *in all* your salvation, He is *in all* your mercies, He is *in all* your trials. He is *in all* your consolations and *in all* your afflictions. What more can you want? What more do you desire? A Father who loves you as the apple of His eye! A full Saviour to whom to go, moment by moment! A blessed indwelling, sanctifying, comforting Spirit to reveal all to you, and to give you Himself as the "earnest of your inheritance until the redemption of

the purchased possession, unto the praise of his glory"!
"Happy is that people that is in such a case: yea, happy is
that people, whose God is the Lord."

Another and an important witness which the eternal Spirit
bears for Christ is *when He impresses upon the believer the
image of Christ.* It is the peculiar work of the Spirit to
glorify Christ; and this He does in various blessed ways, but
perhaps in none more strikingly than in drawing out the likeness of Christ upon the soul. *He glorifies Christ in the believer.* He witnesses to the power of the grace of Christ in
its influence upon the principles, the temper, the daily walk
and the whole life of a man of God. The image of Christ—
what is it? In one word, it is HOLINESS. Jesus was the holiness of the law embodied. He was a living comment on the
majesty and purity of the Divine law. The life He lived,
the doctrines He proclaimed, the precepts He enjoined, the
announcements He made, the revelations He disclosed, all,
all were the very inspiration of holiness. Holiness was the
vital air He breathed. Although in a world of impurity, all of
whose influences were hostile to a life of holiness, He yet
moved amid the mass of corruption, not only untouched and
untainted, but reflecting so vividly the lustre of His own
purity, as to compel the forms of evil that everywhere flitted
athwart His path either to acknowledge His holiness and
submit to His authority or to shrink away in their native
darkness. And *this* is the image the Holy Spirit seems to
draw, though it be but an outline of the lineaments, upon the
believing soul. What a testimony He bears for Christ, when
He causes the image of Jesus to be reflected from every faculty
of the soul, to beam in every glance of the eye, to speak in
every word of the tongue, and to invest with its beauty every
action of the life! O that every child of God might more
deeply and solemnly feel that he is to be a *witness for Jesus!*
—a witness for a cross-bearing Saviour, a witness to the spotless purity of His life, the lowliness of His mind, His deep
humility, self-denial, self-annihilation, consuming zeal for
God's glory, and yearning compassion for the salvation of
souls, a witness to the sanctifying tendency of His truth, the

holiness of His commands, the purifying influence of His precepts, the elevating power of His example. It may not be that *all* these Divine characteristics centre in one person, or that all these lovely features are reflected in a single character. All believers are not alike eminent for the same peculiar and exalted graces of the Spirit. It was not so in the early and palmy days of the Gospel, when Jesus Himself was known in the flesh, and the Holy Ghost descended in an extraordinary degree of sanctifying influence upon the church. It would therefore be unwise to expect it now. And yet we have a right to look for one or more of the moral features of our dear Lord's character in His people : some resemblance to His image; something that marks the man of God; some lowliness of mind, gentleness of temper, humility of deportment, charity, patience in the endurance of affliction, meekness in the suffering of persecution, forgiveness of injuries, returning good for evil, blessing for cursing—in a word, some portion of " the fruit of the Spirit " which is " love, joy, peace, long-suffering, gentleness, goodness, faith, meekness, temperance." If one or more of these are not " in us and abound, so that they make us that we shall neither be barren nor unfruitful in the knowledge of our Lord Jesus Christ," and in a resemblance to His likeness, we have great reason to doubt whether we have ever " known the grace of God in truth." That is indeed a melancholy profession in which can be traced nothing that identifies the man with Jesus; nothing in his principles, his motives, his tone of mind, his spirit, his very looks, that reminds one of Christ, that draws the heart to Him, that makes the name of Immanuel fragrant and that lifts the soul in ardent desires to be like Him too. This is the influence which a believer exerts who bears about with him a resemblance to his Lord and Master. A holy man is a blessing wherever he may go. He is a savour of Christ in every place. It is a mercy to be brought in contact with him. We extract a blessing from him. We get, it may be, a drop of oil from his vessel, or a single ray from his heart. And although it is more blessed to possess the solar beam, to ascend to the " fountain of light," yet a reflected warmth in this wintry world is too valuable and blessed to be lightly esteemed. Would that the saints of God who may have drawn largely upon the fulness of Christ, who have been made to possess some peculiar manifestations of His loving-kindness, some special revivings of His Spirit, were more ready to pass on the same blessing to others. A believer is not his own, nor is he to live to himself. And when the Lord imparts a gift or a grace to any one member, it is for the edification and comfort of the whole body. " Come and hear, all ye that fear God, and I will declare what he hath done for my soul " is an invitation that has often refreshed the spirit, revived the heart, kindled the love and " strengthened the things that remained that were ready to die," in the saints of God.[1] Thus is the Spirit a Witness for Christ in His people by conforming them to His image.

It would only be presenting a limited view of the Spirit's work as a witness if we confined His work in this character to the testimony He bears for Christ. He is not only a witness for Christ, but *He witnesses to the saints of God.* This is clear from His own sacred word, " He that believeth on the Son of God hath the witness in himself." 1 John 5. 10. " Hereby know we that we dwell in him, and he in us, because he hath given us of his Spirit." 1 John 4. 13. " Who hath also sealed us, and given the earnest of the Spirit in our hearts." 2 Cor. 1. 22. But the most direct allusion to this truth is this: " The

---

[1] The history of American revivals presents a striking and beautiful illustration of this fact. The author can testify, from personal observation and experience, that some of the most gracious and remarkable outpourings of the Spirit with which that honoured land has been favoured, have resulted from the simple testimony to a special reviving of the Lord's work in his own soul, borne by some individual member of the church, moving, it may be, in a humble and limited sphere of influence. God has honoured his testimony. His narrative has awakened interest, his zeal has rebuked indolence, his fervour has excited to prayer, his tears and pleadings have moved to exertion; and thus an impulse has been created which has gone on strengthening and expanding until it has embraced and blessed an entire community. It was but as a small pebble cast into the stagnant water; yet the circle included a family, it widened, until it embraced a church, and still it grew wider, until an entire village, or town, felt the power of the Spirit, and every house became vocal with " thanksgiving and the voice of melody."

Spirit itself beareth witness with our spirit, that we are the children of God." Rom. 8. 16. Let us present a brief outline of this subject; beyond this, we cannot venture.

The doctrine of an *assured* belief of the pardon of sin, of acceptance in Christ and of adoption into the family of God, has been, and still is, regarded by many as an attainment never to be expected in the present life; and when it is expressed, it is viewed with a suspicion unfavourable to the character of the work. But this is contrary to the Divine word, and to the actual experience of millions, who have lived and died in the full assurance of hope. The doctrine of assurance is a doctrine of undoubted revelation, implied and expressed. That it is enforced as a state of mind *essential to the salvation of the believer*, we cannot admit; but that it is insisted upon as essential to his comfortable and holy walk, and as greatly involving the glory of God, we must strenuously maintain. Otherwise why do we have these marked references to the doctrine? In Col. 2. 1, 2, Paul expresses " great conflict" for the saints, that their "hearts might be comforted, being knit together in love, and unto all riches of the *full assurance of understanding*." In the epistle to the Hebrews 6. 11, the writer says, "We desire that *every one* of you do show the same diligence to the *full assurance of hope unto the end*." And in chap. 10. 22, he exhorts them, "Let us draw near with a true heart, in *full assurance of faith*." And to crown all, the apostle Peter thus earnestly exhorts his readers, "Wherefore the rather, brethren, give *diligence* to make your calling and election SURE." 2 Peter 1. 10. No further proof from the sacred Word is required to authenticate the doctrine. It is written as with a sunbeam that "the Spirit itself beareth witness with our spirit, that we are the children of God." Let us present a brief explanation of these words.

Three important things are involved in them, first, the Witness; second that with which He witnesses; and lastly, the great truth to which He witnesses. First, "the Spirit itself beareth witness." The great business of making known to a poor sinner his acquittal in the high court of heaven and his adoption into the King's family is entrusted to no inferior agent. No angel is commissioned to bear the tidings, no mortal man may disclose the secret. None but God the Holy Ghost Himself! The *Spirit itself*!" He that rests short of this testimony, wrongs his own soul. See that you rely on no witness to your " calling and election " but this. Human testimony is feeble here. Your minister, your friend, schooled as they may be in the evidences of experimental godliness, cannot assure your spirit that you are " born of God." God the eternal Spirit alone can do this. He alone is competent, He alone can fathom the " deep things of God," He alone can rightly discern between His own work and its counterfeit, between grace and nature, He alone can make known the secret of the Lord to them that fear Him. All other testimony to your sonship is uncertain, and may fearfully and fatally deceive. " It is the Spirit that beareth witness, because the Spirit is truth." Again and yet again would we solemnly repeat it; take nothing for granted touching your personal interest in Christ; do not rest satisfied with the testimony of your own spirit, or with that of the holiest saint on earth; seek nothing short of " the Spirit itself." This alone will do for a dying hour.

The second thing to be observed in the declaration is, that *with which* He witnesses—" the Spirit itself beareth witness *with our spirit*." It is a personal testimony, not borne to others, but to *ourselves*, " with our spirit." The adoption of the believer into the family of God is so great a privilege, involving blessings so immense, for beings so sinful and in all respects unworthy, that, if their heavenly Father did not assure them by His own immediate testimony of its truth, no other witness would suffice to remove their doubts, quiet their fears and satisfy them as to their real sonship. The eternal Spirit of God descends and enters their hearts as a witness to their adoption. He first renews our spirit, applies the atoning blood to the conscience, works faith in the heart, enlightens the understanding, and thus prepares the believing soul for the revelation and assurance of this great and glorious truth—his adoption into the family of God. As it is " with our spirit" the Holy Ghost witnesses, it is necessary that, in order to perfect agreement and harmony, he who has the witness within himself should first be a repenting and believing sinner. He who says that he has this witness, but who still remains "dead in sins"—a stranger to faith in the Lord Jesus, to the renewings of the Holy Ghost, in a word, who is not *born of God*—is wrapping himself up in an awful deception. The witness we plead for, is the *holy* testimony, in concurrence with a *holy* gospel, by a *holy* Spirit, to a *holy* man, and concerning a *holy* truth. There can be no discrepancy, no want of harmony between the witness of the Spirit and the Word of God. He witnesses according to, and in agreement with, the truth. Vague and fanciful impressions, visions and voices, received and rested upon as evidences of salvation are fearful delusions. Nothing is to be viewed as an evidence of our Divine sonship which does not square and harmonise with the revealed Word of God. We must have a " thus saith the Lord" for every step we take in believing that we are the children of God. Let it be remembered, then, that the Spirit bears His testimony to *believers*. His first step is to work repentance and faith in the heart; then follows the sealing and witnessing operation: " In whom also *after that ye believed*, ye were sealed with that Holy Spirit of promise."

The last aspect is the great truth to which He testifies, namely " *that we are the children of God*." The Spirit is emphatically spoken of as a Spirit of adoption. "For ye have not received the spirit of bondage again to fear; but ye have received the Spirit of adoption, whereby we cry, Abba, Father." Rom. 8. 15. And again, " And because ye are sons, God hath sent forth the Spirit of his Son into your hearts, crying, Abba, Father." Gal. 4. 6. Now it is the peculiar office of the Spirit to witness to the adoption of the believer. Look at the blessed fact to which He testifies—not that we are the *enemies*, the *aliens*, the *strangers*, the *slaves*, but that we are " the CHILDREN of God." High and holy privilege! "The children of God"! Chosen from all eternity: " having predestinated us unto the adoption of children by Jesus Christ to himself, according to the good pleasure of his will," all their iniquities laid on Jesus their blessed Surety, justified by the "Lord our righteousness," called by the effectual operation of the eternal Spirit, inhabited, sanctified and sealed by God the Holy Ghost. O exalted state! O holy privilege! O happy people! Pressing on, it may be, through strong corruptions, deep trials, clinging infirmities, fiery temptations, sore discouragements, dark providences and often the hidings of a Father's countenance—and yet "the children of God" now, and soon to be glorified hereafter.

Reader, in closing, let me ask you, *have you the witness of the Spirit?* Has He convinced you of sin by the law? Has He made you acquainted with your guilt and pollution? Is it written upon your conscience as solemnly and as undoubtedly as it is written in the Bible, that you are guilty and condemned, lost and undone, and must finally and awfully perish, without Christ? Have you sought a secret place for humiliation and confession and supplication before God, the eternal and holy God, the Sovereign of all worlds, the Judge of the quick and dead, at whose tribunal you soon must stand? Ah, solemn, searching questions! You may evade them, you may frame some vain excuse, you may wait for "a more convenient season," you may even seek to stifle the seriousness and the thoughtfulness which these questions have occasioned, by another and a deeper plunge into the world; but they will follow you *there*, and will be heard amid the din of business and the loud laugh of pleasure. They will follow you to your dying bed, and they will be heard *there*, amid the gloom and the silence and the terror of that hour. They will follow you up to the judgment-seat, and will be heard *there* amid the gatherings and the tremendous disclosures of that scene. They will follow you down to the abode of the lost, and will be heard *there*, amid the "weeping, and the wailing, and the gnashing of teeth." Sinner! from an enlightened, but guilty and accusing conscience, you can never escape. It will be the "worm that never dies"! From the wrath of God you can then find no shelter. It will be the "fire that never shall be quenched." Again we earnestly inquire—have you the witness of the Spirit? Has He testified to you of Jesus, of His renewing grace, pardoning love, sin-cleansing blood, justifying righteousness and full redemption? Have you joy and peace in believing?

To the child of God we would say, *covet earnestly the witness of the Spirit.* Do not be cast down, nor cherish rash and hasty conclusions as to your adoption, if you do not possess it so fully and clearly as others. The holiest believer may walk for many days without the sun. Read the record of the experiences of David and of Job and of Jeremiah, and of the *last moments* of our dear and adorable Immanuel, and mark what shadows at times fell upon their souls, how a sense of comfort failed them, how joys fled, and they *mourned an absent God.* But were they the less dear to the heart of Jehovah? Were they the less His beloved children because they were thus tried? No! God forbid! Still, we plead for the full enjoyment of the witness of the Spirit. It is the high privilege of the children of God—let no one rob them of it—to look up to God, and humbly yet unceasingly cry, " Abba, Father!"

CHAPTER VIII

The Spirit the Author of Prayer

THE BELIEVER DRAWING NEAR TO GOD

> " *Likewise the Spirit also helpeth our infirmities: for we know not what we should pray for as we ought: but the Spirit itself maketh intercession for us with groanings which cannot be uttered.*"—Rom. 8. 26.

THAT God should have erected in this lower world a throne of grace, a mercy-seat, around which may gather, in clustering and welcome multitudes, the helpless, the burdened, the friendless, the vile, the guilty, the deeply necessitous—that no poor comer, be his poverty never so great, his burden never so heavy, or his case never so desperate, should meet with a refusal of a hearing or a welcome, does greatly develop and magnify the riches of His grace, His wisdom and His love to sinners. *What* a God our God must be, thus to have appointed a meeting-place, an audience chamber for those upon whom all other doors are closed!

More wonderful still is it that He should have appointed *Jesus* the door of approach to that throne, should have given His only begotten and well-beloved Son to be the " new and living way " of access, thus removing all obstruction in the way of the soul's coming, both on the part of Himself, and on the part of the sinner; that the door should be a crucified Saviour —the wounds of the Son of God—that through blood (and that blood the blood of the incarnate Deity) the guilty should approach. Wonder, O heavens, and be astonished, O earth!

Shall we say even more than this? For there is a yet lower depth in this love and condescension of God—His sending of His *Spirit* into the heart, the Author of prayer, putting the petition into words, breathing in the soul, implanting the desire, convincing of the existing necessity, unfolding the character of God, working faith in the heart and drawing it up to God through Jesus, all of which seems the very perfection of His wisdom, benevolence and grace.

It must be acknowledged by the spiritual mind that all true prayer is of the leading of the Spirit—that He is the Author of all real approach of the soul to God. And yet how perpetually we need to be reminded of this! Prayer is one of the most spiritual employments that can possibly engage the mind. It is that holy act of the soul which brings it immediately in contact with a holy God. It has more directly to do with the "high and lofty One" than any other exercise. It is that state of mind, too, that most deeply acknowledges its dependence on God. Prayer is the expression of *want*, the desire of *need*, the acknowledgment of *poverty*, the language of *dependence*, the breathing of a soul that has nothing in itself, but hangs on God for all it wants. It must therefore be a highly spiritual and holy exercise. But this will appear still more so if we consider that true prayer is *the breathing of the life of God in the soul of man*. It is the Spirit dwelling and breathing in him. It is the new nature pouring out its vital principle, and that into the ear of the God whence it came. It is the cry of the feeble child turning to the Father it loves, and in all its conscious weakness, dependence and need, pouring out the yearnings of its full heart into the bosom where dwells nothing but love. In a word, it is God and the creature meeting and blending in one act of blessed, holy and eternal fellowship.

Now, that on a subject so spiritual and involving so deeply the happiness and the holiness of a child of God, the believer should at times be greatly and seriously harassed and tempted, as much by the weaknesses of his nature as by the influence of Satan, is not to be wondered at. We desire therefore, before going into the consideration of the Spirit's operation in this holy exercise, to glance at some of those peculiar infirmities which so frequently and so painfully lessen the habit, and weaken the power, and keep back the answer of prayer. May the Spirit now teach us!

There is a state of mind often enfeebling to the exercise of prayer, *arising from the difficulty of forming proper views of the spiritual nature of the Divine Object of prayer.* Through the weakness of our nature, the spirituality of God has been felt by some to be a stumbling-block in the approach of the soul. "God is a Spirit" is the solemn announcement that meets them at the very threshold, and so completely overawes and abashes the mind as to congeal every current of thought and of feeling, and well-nigh to crush the soul with its inconceivability. Nor is this surprising. Prayer is the approach of finity to Infinity; and although it is the communing of spirit with Spirit, yet it is the finite communing with the Infinite, and that through the organs of sense. Is it any marvel, then, that at periods a believer should be baffled in his endeavour to form some just conception of the Divine existence, some faint idea of the nature of that God to whom his soul addresses itself; and, failing in the attempt, should turn away in sadness, sorrow and despair? The remedy for this state of mind we believe is at hand. It is simple and scriptural. To enlarge our thoughts with any adequate idea of the nature and the appearance of the Divine Spirit is an utter impossibility. He that attempts it, and thinks he has succeeded, lives in the region of fancy and opposes himself to the revelation of God Himself, which expressly declares, "No man hath seen God at any time." John 1. 18. "Who only hath immortality, dwelling in the light which no man can approach unto; whom no man hath seen, nor can see." 1 Tim. 6. 16. This being then admitted, as it must be by all reflective minds, the question arises, "How am I to view God? what idea am I to form of His existence in approaching Him in prayer?" In reply, two things are necessary in getting proper thoughts of God as the Object of prayer. First, that the mind should resign all its attempts to comprehend the *mode* of the Divine existence, and should concentrate all its powers upon the contemplation of the *character* of the Divine existence. In what *relation* God stands to the creature, not in what *way* he exists in Himself, is the point with which we have to do in approaching Him. Let the mind be wrapt in devout contemplations of His holiness, benevolence, love, truth, wisdom, justice, and there will be no room for vain and fruitless imaginations respecting the fathomless and inconceivable mode of His existence.

The second thing necessary is that *the mind should view God in Christ*. If it is baffled and perplexed, as it surely will be, in its attempts to unravel the spiritual nature of God, let it seek a resting-place in the " incarnate mystery." This was one part of the gracious design of God in assuming human nature. It was to bring, so to speak, the Infinite in a direct angle with the finite, so that the two lines should not merely run parallel, but that the two extremes of being should meet. It was to embody His essential and surpassing glories in such a way as to present an object which man could contemplate without fear, worship without distraction, and look upon and not die. The Lord Jesus Christ is " the image of the invisible God," " the brightness of his glory, the express image of his person." " He that hath seen Me " (His own declaration) "hath seen the Father." Wondrous stoop of the great God! In all approach to God, then, in prayer, as in every other kindred exercise, let the eye of faith be fixed upon Him who fills the middle seat upon the throne—the Day's-Man—the Mediator —the incarnate Son of God. How quieting to the mind of a praying soul is this view of God! What a mildness invests the throne of grace, and what an easy access to it presents itself, when the eye of faith can behold " the glory of God in the face of Jesus Christ"! And if the mind be embarrassed in its attempts to conceive an idea of His spiritual nature, it can soothe itself to repose in a believing view of the glorified humanity of Jesus, " God manifest in the flesh." To this resting-place he Himself invites the soul—" I am the way, the truth, and the life: no man cometh unto the Father, but by Me." And thus too He calmed the fears of His exiled servant who, when the splendour of His glorified humanity broke upon his view, fell prostrate to the earth: " And when I saw him," says John, " I fell at his feet as dead. And he laid his right hand upon me, saying unto me, Fear not; I am the first, and the last: I am he that liveth, and was dead; and, behold,

I am alive for evermore, Amen; and have the keys of hell and of death."

Another infirmity which often impedes the free course of prayer, *is the manifest want of wisdom that may mark the petition of a child of God.* For example, when Paul prayed for the removal of the thorn in the flesh, he asked that of God which betrayed a want of wisdom in his petition. Who would have suspected this in the apostle of the Gentiles? But the Lord knew best what was for the good of His dear servant, and saw that, on account of the special revelations that were given him in his visit to glory, the discipline of the covenant was needed to keep him low in the dust. When His child petitioned three times for the *removal* of the thorn in the flesh, he for a moment overlooked, because of the painful nature of the discipline, its needed influence to keep him " walking humbly with God." So that we see even an inspired apostle may ask those things of God which He may see fit to refuse. We may frequently expect some trial, something to keep us low before God, after a season of peculiar nearness to Him or some other manifestation of his loving-kindness to our souls. There is a proneness to rest in self-complacency after close communion with God, and the gentle hand of our Father is needed to shield us from ourselves. It was so with Paul; why may it not be with us? We may be assured of this, however, that in withholding the thing we ask of Him, He will grant us a perfect equivalent. The Lord saw fit to deny the request of the apostle, but He granted him an equivalent, indeed more than an equivalent to that which He denied him —*He gave him His all-supporting grace.* " My grace is sufficient for thee." Have you asked many times for the removal of some secret, heavy, painful cross? Perhaps you are still urging your request; and yet the Lord does not seem to answer you. And why? because the request may not be in itself wise. Were he now to remove that cross, He might, in taking away the cross, close up a channel of mercy which you would never cease to regret. O what secret and immense blessing may that painful cross be the means of conveying into your soul! Is it *health* you have often petitioned for?

And is the request denied you? It is *wisdom* that denies. It is *love* too, tender unchangeable love to your soul, that refuses a petition which a wise and gracious God knows, if granted, would not be for your real good and His glory. Do you not think that there is *love* and *tenderness* enough in the heart of Jesus to grant you what you desire, and ten thousand times more, if He saw that it would promote your true holiness and happiness? Could He *resist* that request, that desire, that sigh, that tear and that beseeching look, if infinite wisdom did not guide Him in all His dealings with your soul? O no! But He gives you an equivalent to the denied request. He gives you *Himself*. Can He give you more? His grace sustains you, His arm supports you, His love soothes you, His Spirit comforts you; and your chamber of solitude, though it may not be the scene of health and buoyancy and joyousness, may yet be the secret place where a covenant God and Father pours His grace into your soul, and where Jesus meets you with the choicest unfoldings of His love. Could He not, would He not, heal you in a moment, if it would be for your good? Then ask for a submissive spirit, a will swallowed up in God thy Father's. It may be that when the lesson of secret and filial submission has been learned, so that health is only desired as a means of glorifying God, He may put forth His healing power and grant you your request. But do not forget the Lord best knows what will most promote His own glory. *You* may have thought that health of body would better enable you to glorify Him. *He* may think that the chamber of solitude and the bed of languishing are most productive of glory to His name. The patience, resignation, meek submission and child-like acquiescence which His blessed Spirit through this means works in your soul, may more glorify Him than all the active graces that ever were brought into exercise.

A believer may urge a request that is in itself wrong. The mother of Zebedee's children did so, when she asked the Lord that her two sons might sit, the one on His right hand, and the other on the left, in His kingdom, Matt. 20. 20, 21. Who does not notice the *self* that appears in this petition? And although it was a mother's love that prompted it, and, as such, presents a beautiful and touching picture, yet it teaches us that a parent, betrayed by his love for his child, may ask that of God which is really wrong in itself. He may ask worldly distinction, honour, influence, wealth for his child (which a godly parent should never do), and this may be a wrong request, which God in His infinite wisdom and love withholds. Such was the petition of the mother, which our Lord saw fit to deny. Her views of the kingdom of Christ were those of earthly glory. To see her children sharing in that glory was her high ambition, which Jesus promptly but gently rebuked. Let a Christian mother ask for *spiritual* blessings for her children, and whatever else is needful the Lord will grant. Let converting, sanctifying and restraining grace be the constant petition presented at the footstool of mercy, and then she cannot ask too much, or press her suit too frequently or too fervently.

To allude to another illustration of our remark—It was wrong of Job to ask the Lord that he might *die*. "Oh that I might have my request!" (are his words) "and that God would grant me the thing that I long for! Even that it would please God to destroy me; that he would let loose his hand, and cut me off." Job 6. 8, 9. It was an unwise and sinful petition, which the Lord in great mercy and wisdom denied him. Truly "we know not what we should pray for as we ought." What a mercy that there is One who knows!

A child of God may ask for a wise and good thing in a wrong way. There may be no faith in asking. There may be a wrong attitude of mind: no sense of God's freeness in bestowing, no filial approach, no going as a child, as one pardoned and "accepted in the Beloved," as one dear to the heart of God. There may be no honouring of the Father in Himself, no honouring of Him in the Son, no honouring of the blessed Spirit. There may be no resting upon the cross, no pleading of the atoning blood, no washing in the fountain, no humble, grateful recognition of the "new and living way" of access. There may be a want of humility in the mind, of brokenness in the spirit, of sincerity in the heart, of reverence in the manner and of sobriety in the words. There may be no confession of sin, no acknowledgment of past mercies and no faith in the promised blessing. Oh, how much there may be in the prayer of a dear child of God that operates as a blight upon his request, that seems to close the ear and the heart of God! But oh, to go to Him with filial confidence, with sweet faith, with love flowing from a broken heart; to go to Him as the people of His choice, dear to Him as the apple of His eye, as those who are viewed each moment in His Son who would, for the love He bears us, *undeify Himself*, if that would be for our real good, and His own glory. Did He not once empty Himself of His glory, did He not become poor, did He not humble himself, did He not take upon Him human nature—all for the love He bore His people? That was approaching so near, in appearance, the cessation of Deity, that, as we gaze upon the spectacle, we wonder what another step might have produced! We might well think that He could not have gone further without ceasing to be God. Behold the broad basis, then, upon which a child of God may approach Him in prayer. His love, O how immense! it is past finding out!

Yet again, *a believer may present a right petition in a right way, and yet he may not wait for the Lord to answer in His own time*. The believer may appoint a time, and if the Lord does not answer within that period, he turns away, resigning all expectation of an answer. There is such a thing as waiting for the Lord. "It is good that a man should both *hope* and *quietly wait* for the salvation of the Lord." Lam. 3. 26. And the apostle alludes to, and enjoins the same holy patience, when he speaks to the Ephesians of " praying always with all prayer and supplication in the Spirit, and watching thereunto with all perseverance," ch. 6. 18. A believer may present his request, may have some degree of nearness in urging it, may press it with fervency, and yet, forgetting the *hoping*, *quiet*, *waiting* patience which ought invariably to mark a praying soul, he may lose the blessing he has sought. There is such a thing as "waiting upon the Lord." O how long have we made Him wait for us! For years, it may be, we kept Him knocking and standing and waiting at the door of our hearts, until His own Spirit took the work in His own hands and unlocked the heart and the Saviour entered. The Lord would now often have us *wait His time* in answering prayer. And, if the vision tarry, let us still *wait, hope* and *expect*. Let the delay stimulate hope, and increase desire, and exercise faith, and multiply petitions at the mercy-seat. The answer will come when the Lord sees best.

Lastly, a believer may lose the answer to his prayer *by dictating to the Lord the mode* as well as the time of answering. The Lord has His own mode of blessing His people. We may prescribe *the way* the Lord should answer, but He may send the blessing to us through an opposite channel, in a way we never thought of and should never have selected. Sovereignty sits ruling upon the throne, and in no aspect is its exercise more manifestly seen than in selecting the *way* and the *means* by which the prayers of the saints of God are answered. Do not dictate to the Lord. If you ask a blessing through a certain channel or in a prescribed way, let it be with the deepest humility of mind and with perfect submission of the will to God. Be satisfied to receive the blessing in any way which a good and covenant God may appoint. Be assured that it will be in the way that will most glorify God Himself, and secure to you the greatest amount of blessing.

Many and endearing are the characters or offices ascribed to the Spirit in the Word, but none are found more sweet or appropriate by a child of God than that which He fills as *the Intercessor for His saints*. We have already remarked that all true prayer is put into words by the Spirit. He is the Author of prayer in the soul. A brief reference to the Divine testimony will clearly substantiate this. "Likewise the Spirit also helpeth our infirmities: for we know not what we should pray for as we ought: but *the Spirit itself maketh intercession for us*, with groanings which cannot be uttered. And he that searcheth the hearts knoweth what is the mind of the Spirit, because *he maketh intercession for the saints* according to the will of God." Rom. 8. 26, 27. "For through him we both have access *by one Spirit* unto the Father." Eph. 2. 18. "Praying always with all prayer and supplication *in the Spirit*."

Eph. 6. 18. " But ye, beloved, building up yourselves on your most holy faith, *praying in the Holy Ghost.*" Jude 20. And our dear Lord encouraged His disciples in view of their approaching persecutions, with the same truth—" It is not ye that speak, but *the Spirit of your Father which speaketh in you.*" Matt. 10. 20. The consideration of two or three points will sufficiently unfold His work as the Author of prayer in the believer.

First, *it is the Spirit who leads the soul to an acquaintance with its wants.* Such is the fallen condition of the soul and such is its poverty, ignorance and infirmity that it does not know its real weakness and deep necessity until taught it by the Holy Ghost. This is even so after conversion. A dear child of God (and it is awfully true, without any qualification, of an unrenewed man) may fall into the state of the Laodicean church, to whom it was said, " Because thou sayest, I am rich, and increased with goods, and have need of nothing: and *knowest not* that thou are wretched, and miserable, and poor, and blind, and naked." Rev. 3. 17. A believer may not know his real condition, his absolute need. There may be a secret declension in his soul, the enfeebling and decay of some spiritual grace, the slow but effective inroad of some spiritual enemy, the cherishing (like Achan) of some forbidden thing, the feeding of some worm at the root of his holiness—and all the while he may remain ignorant of the solemn fact. And how is he to know it unless someone teaches him? And who is that teacher but the Spirit? As He first convicted of sin, so in each successive stage of the believer's experience He convicts of the daily want, the spiritual necessity, the growing infirmity, the increasing power of sin and the deepening poverty. Do not overlook this important part of His work. To go to the throne of grace, we must have something to go for, some errand to take us there, some sin to confess, some guilt to mourn over, some want to supply, some infirmity to make known and (we must not leave this out) some blessing to acknowledge. How is all this to be brought about but by the blessed Spirit? O what an unspeakable mercy to have One who knows us altogether, and who can make us acquainted

with ourselves!   It is a far advanced step in grace when we
know our real undisguised condition. A man may lose a grace,
and may travel far and not be aware of his loss. The world
has come in and filled up the space.   Some carnal joy or pursuit has occupied the mind, engrossed the affections and the
thoughts; and the soul has not been conscious of the loss it
has sustained. Thus have many lost the sense of adoption,
pardon and acceptance. The graces of faith, love and humility have become enfeebled until the description of Ephraim
may truly and painfully apply to them—" Ephraim, he hath
mixed himself among the people; Ephraim is a cake not
turned. Strangers have devoured his strength, and he knoweth
it not; yea, grey hairs are here and there upon him, yet he
knoweth it not." Hos. 7. 8, 9. But the blessed Spirit at length
reveals to the soul its loss, convinces it of its departure, makes
known its real condition, and in this way leads it to the throne
of grace. Cherish high views of the work of the Spirit. To
have one near at hand, indeed in you, as He is; to detect so
faithfully and lovingly as He does, the waning grace, the
feeble pulse, the spiritual decay; to awaken the conscience,
arouse godly sorrow, and draw out the heart in confession,
is to possess one of the most valuable blessings. Honour the
blessed Spirit, praise Him for his work, extol His faithfulness
and love, and treat Him as your tenderest, dearest Friend.

He stirs up the slumbering spirit of prayer. This is either
perpetually declining, or exposed to declension in the believer.
And it needs as perpetual a supply of grace from the Author
of prayer to keep it in vigour, as to restore it when it has de-
clined. " And I will pour upon the house of David, and upon
the inhabitants of Jerusalem, the Spirit of grace and of sup-
plications." Zech. 12. 10.

He teaches the believer to plead the atoning blood of Christ.
He puts this great and prevailing argument in his mouth; and
when sin seems a mountain, and unbelief would suppress the
aspiration, and a deep consciousness of unworthiness would
cause the soul to " stand afar off," He opens to his view this
precious encouraging truth—the prevalency of the blood of
Jesus with God on behalf of His people. In a moment the

mountain is levelled, unbelief is checked, and the soul, unfettered and unrestrained, draws *near* to God, yea, rushes into the bosom of its Father. What a view does this give us of the love of the Spirit as the Author of prayer! Who has not experienced it, who is not a stranger to the blessed exercise of communion with God? How often has guilt caused the head to hang down, and a sense of utter vileness and worthlessness covered the soul with shame! Even the sense of destitution has kept back the believer, just as the penury, the wretched covering and the loathsomeness of the poor beggar have kept him from the door! *Then* does the blessed Spirit, in the plenitude of His grace and tenderness, unfold Jesus to the soul as being all that it wants to give it full, free and near access to God. He removes the eye from self, and fixes and fastens it upon the blood that pleads louder for mercy than all his sins can plead for condemnation; He brings, too, the righteousness near, which so clothes and covers the soul as to fit it to appear in the presence of the King of kings, not merely with acceptance but with delight. Beholding him thus washed and clothed, God rests in His love and rejoices over him with singing.

Nor must we overlook *the understanding which exists between God the Father and the Spirit.* " And he that searcheth the hearts knoweth what is the mind of the Spirit, because he maketh intercession for the saints according to the will of God." There is a perfect agreement or understanding between the Father and the interceding Spirit. First, the Father, the Searcher of hearts, knows the mind of the Spirit. He understands the desire and the meaning of the Spirit in the souls of the saints. He understands the "groanings which cannot be uttered." He can interpret their sighs; He can read the meaning of their very desires. And when feeling has been too deep for utterance, and thought too intense for expression, and the soul could but groan out its wants and desires, *then* has God understood the mind of the Spirit. O the inconceivable preciousness of a throne of grace! To have a God to go to, who knows the mind of the Spirit, a God who can interpret the groan and read the language of desire; to have promise upon promise inviting the soul to draw near—how precious this is! When from the fulness of the heart the mouth has been dumb, and from the poverty of language thought could not be expressed, *then* God, who searches the hearts and knows what is the mind of the Spirit, has said, " Never before did you, My child, pray to Me as you did then; never before was your voice so sweet, so powerful, so persuasive; never before were you so eloquent as when My Spirit made intercession for you with groanings which you could not utter." It was, perhaps, your last resource. Refuge failed you, no man cared for your soul. Friends failed you, feelings failed you, all forsook you and fled, and in your extremity you went to God—and He did not fail you. You found the throne of grace accessible; you saw a God of grace upon it, and the sweet incense of the Redeemer's precious merits going up; and you drew near, sighing and groaning and breathing out your wants, and said, " It is good for me to draw near to God." Yes! " He knows the mind of the Spirit." The secret desire for Jesus, the longing for Divine conformity, the hidden mourning over the existence and power of indwelling sin, the feeblest rising of the heart to God, the first sign of the humble and contrite spirit—all are known to God. " He searcheth the heart, and he knoweth the mind of the Spirit." O let this encourage you, when you feel you cannot pray by reason of the weakness of the flesh, or the depth of your feeling; if the Spirit is interceding in you, your heavenly Father knows the mind of the Spirit, and not a sigh or a groan can escape His notice.

There is yet another vital principle connected with the perfect agreement of the Father and the Spirit in this important matter of prayer; it is that the Spirit " maketh intercession for the saints *according to the will of God*." Whatever the Spirit may say, the believer can be assured that it is according to God's will. The worldly desires which sometimes take possession of a child of God must not be included in this. He may sometimes be left to ask God for worldly distinction, influence and wealth, and for places of temporal honour and aggrandisement, as the mother of Zebedee's children did. But who will dare assert that, in presenting such petitions, he is asking for those things which are " according to the will of God "? No believer, if he is in a truly spiritual frame, thirsting for God, crucifying the world, and living as a stranger and a pilgrim here, can go to the throne of grace and plead for *these*. It would be a carnal petition for carnal things, and there must be a dearth of spirituality in the soul that can urge it.

But, in *spiritual things*, how vastly different is it! When we draw near to God, and ask for more love, more zeal, an increase of faith, a reviving of God's work within us, more resemblance to Christ, the subjection of some enemy, the mortification of some evil, the subduing of some iniquity, the pardon of some guilt, more of the spirit of adoption, the sprinkling of the atoning blood, the sweet sense of acceptance, we know and are assured that we ask for those things which are according to the will of God, and which it is in the heart of God fully and freely to bestow. There need be no backwardness here, there need be no restraint here, there may be no misgiving here. When the believer is pleading for such blessings and spreading out such wants before the Lord, he may with " boldness enter into the holiest by the blood of Jesus." He may draw near to God, not standing afar off, but, in the spirit of a child, drawing *near* to God. He may come with large requests, large desires, hopeful expectation. He may open his mouth wide, because he asks those things which it is glorifying to God to give, which glorify Him when given, and which we know from His own Word it is according to His blessed will to bestow. O the unspeakable encouragement of going to God with a request which we feel assured it is in His heart, and according to His will, freely to grant!

Do not forget that *it is the throne of grace* to which you come in prayer. It is a *throne*, because God is a *Sovereign*. He will ever have the suppliant recognise this perfection of His nature. He hears and answers as a Sovereign. He hears whom He will, and answers what and when He will. There must be no dictation to God, no refusing to bow to His sovereignty, no rebelling against His will. If the answer be delayed, or God should seem to withhold it altogether, remember that "He giveth no account of any of his matters," and that He has a right to answer or not to answer, as seems good in His sight. Glorious perfection of God, shining from the mercy-seat!

But it is also a throne of GRACE. And why? Because *a God of grace* sits upon it, and the *sceptre of grace* is held out from it, and all the favours bestowed there are the *blessings of grace*. God has many thrones. There is the throne of creation, and the throne of providence, and the throne of justice, and the throne of redemption; but this is the throne of *grace*. Just the throne we want! We are the poor, the needy, the helpless, the vile, the sinful, the unworthy. We have nothing to bring but our deep wretchedness and poverty; nothing but our complaints, our miseries, our crosses, our groanings, our sighs and tears. But it is the throne of *grace*. For just such is it erected. It is set up in a world of woe, in the midst of the wilderness, in the very land of the enemy, in the vale of tears. It is a God of grace who sits upon it, and all the blessings He dispenses from it are the gifts of grace. Pardon, justification, adoption, peace, comfort, light, direction—all, all is of *grace*. No worth or worthiness in the creature extracts these blessings; no price he may bring purchases them; no tears or complainings or misery move the heart of God to compassion —all is of *grace*. God is so full of compassion, and love, and mercy, He does not need to be moved to pour it forth. It gushes from His heart as from a full and overflowing fountain, and flows into the bosom of the poor, the lowly, the humble and the contrite, enriching, comforting and sanctifying their souls. Therefore whatever your case, *you* may come. If it is a throne of *grace* (as indeed it is) then why not come? Why stand a long way off? If the poor, the penniless, the disconsolate and the guilty are welcome here, if this throne is crowded by such—why make yourself an exception? Why not come too? What is your case, what is your sorrow, what is your burden? Ah! perhaps you can disclose it to no earthly ear. You can tell it to God only. Then take it to Him. Let me tell you for your encouragement that God has His *secret audience chamber*, where He will meet you alone, and where no eye shall see you and no ear shall hear you but

His, where you may open all your heart, and reveal your real case, and pour all your secrets into His ear. Precious encouragement! It comes from those lips into which grace was poured: " Thou, when thou prayest, enter into thy closet, and when thou hast shut thy door, pray to thy Father which is *in secret*; and thy Father which seeth *in secret*, shall reward thee openly." Then, armed with this promise, go to the throne of grace. Whether the want is temporal or spiritual, take it there. God loves your secrets. He delights in your confidence and will honour the soul that thus honours Him.

Remember, *the throne of grace is near at hand*. You have not to travel far to reach it; there is no lengthy and painful journey, no wearisome and mortifying pilgrimage. It is near at hand. Lying down or rising up, going out or coming in, in the streets or in the house, in public or in private, in the chamber or in the sanctuary, God is everywhere; and where He is, there is a prayer-hearing and a prayer-answering God. In a moment, in the greatest emergency, you may lift up your heart to the Lord, and in a moment your cry shall be heard and your request shall be granted. " And it shall come to pass, that before they call, I will answer: and while they are yet speaking, I will hear." Isa. 65. 24. " The eyes of the Lord are upon the righteous, and his ears are open unto their cry. The righteous cry, and the Lord heareth, and delivereth them out of all their troubles. The Lord is *nigh* unto them that are of a broken heart; and saveth such as be of a contrite spirit." Psa. 34. 15, 17, 18. Remember that the throne of grace is *everywhere*. On the land and on the sea, at home or abroad, in the publicity of business or in the privacy of retirement, " the eyes of the Lord are upon the righteous, and his ears are open unto their cry." Wherever a believer goes, he carries about with him the intercession of the Spirit below, and he has the consolation of knowing that he has the intercession of Jesus above.

Do not stay away from the throne of grace because of an unfavourable state of mind. If God is ready to receive you just as you are, if no questions are asked, and no examination is instituted, and no exceptions are made on account of the *badness* of the state, then count it a great blessing to be able to go to God even when you feel at your worst. To keep away from the throne of grace because of unfitness and un-preparedness to approach it, is to alter its character from a throne of *grace* to a throne of *merit*. If the Lord's ears are only open to the cry of the righteous when they seek Him in a certain good and acceptable state of mind, then He hears them because of their state of mind, and not because He is a God of *grace*. But He can never alter His character or change the foundation of His throne. It is the *mercy*-seat—the throne of *grace*; and not for any attitude either good or bad in the suppliant does He bow His ear, but for His own mercy's sake. Do not yield then to this device of your adversary to keep you from prayer. It is the privilege of a poor soul to go to Jesus at his *worst*, to go in darkness, to go in weak faith, to go when everything says " stay away," to go in the face of opposition, to hope against hope, to go in the consciousness of having walked at a distance, to press through the crowd to the throne of grace, to take the hard, the cold, the reluctant heart and lay it before the Lord. O what a triumph this is of the power and the grace of the blessed Spirit in a poor believer! What is your state? Are you weak in prayer? Are you tried in prayer? And yet is there anything at all of real want, of real desire in your heart? Is this so? Then draw near to God. Your state of mind will not be more favourable to-morrow than it is to-day. You will not be more acceptable or welcome at any future period than you are at this moment. Give yourself to prayer. Supposing your state is the worst that can be, your frame of mind the most unfavourable, your cross the heaviest, your corruption the strongest, your heart the hardest; still go to the throne of grace, and opening your case to the Lord with groanings that cannot be uttered, you shall adopt the song of David, who could say in the worst state, and in most pressing times, " But I give myself unto prayer "—" O magnify the Lord with me, and let us exalt his name together. I sought the Lord, and he heard me, and de-livered me from all my fears. They looked unto him, and were lightened; and their faces were not ashamed. This poor

G

man cried, and the Lord heard him, and saved him out of all his troubles." Psa. 34. 3-6.

The throne of grace is for the needy. It is always a time of need with a child of God. "Without me," says Jesus, "ye can do nothing." There is not a moment when, if he knows his real state, he is not in need of something. What a blessing then is the throne of grace! It is for the *needy*. It is for those who are in *want*, those to whom all other doors are closed, with whom all other resources have failed, who have nowhere else to look, nowhere else to fly. To such is the throne of grace always open. Is it a time of *trial* with you? then it is a time of *need*. Take your trial, whatever it be, simply to God. Do not brood over it. This will not make it sweeter or more easy to be borne, but taking it to Jesus will. The very act of taking it will lighten it, and casting it upon His tenderness and sympathy will make it sweet. Is it a time of spiritual *darkness* with you? Then it is a time of *need*. Take your darkness to the throne of grace, and "in His light" who sits upon it, you "shall see light." Is it a time of *adverse providences*? Then it is a time of *need*. And where can you go for guidance, for direction, for counsel and for light upon the intricacies of the way, but to the God of grace? Is it a time of *temporal distress* with you? Then it is a time of *need*. Take your temporal cares and necessities to the Lord, for He who is the God of grace is also the God of providence. "Let us therefore come boldly unto the throne of grace, that we may obtain mercy, and find grace to help *in time of need*."

Thank the Lord for every errand that takes you to the throne of grace. Whatever that be which sends you to prayer, count it one of your choice blessings. It may be a heavy cross, a painful trial, a pressing want; it may be a disappointment, a cold look, an unkind expression; yet, if it leads you to prayer, regard it as a mercy sent from God to your soul. Thank God for an *errand* to Him. It may be that you have not felt like praying for *yourself*. You have not been conscious of any special sense of being drawn to the throne for your own soul, but you have gone *on behalf of another*. The burden, the trial, the affliction or the immediate want of some member of God's family has pressed upon you, and you have taken his case to the Lord; you have borne him in your arms to the throne of grace, and, while interceding for your brother, the Lord has met you, and blessed your own soul. Perhaps you have gone and prayed for the *church*, for the peace of Jerusalem, for the prosperity of Zion, that the Lord would build up her waste places, and make her a joy and a praise in the whole earth. Perhaps it has been to pray for your *minister*, that the Lord would teach him more deeply and experimentally, and anoint him more fully with the rich anointing and unction of the Holy Ghost. Perhaps it has been to pray for *Christian missions* and for hard-working and self-denying *missionaries*, that the Lord would make them eminently successful in spreading the knowledge of a precious Saviour, and in calling in His people. And thus, while you have been besieging the throne of grace for *others*, and pouring out your heart before the Lord, the Lord Himself has drawn near to your own soul and you have been made to experience the blessing that ever goes with and rewards *intercessory prayer*. Then let every event, every circumstance, every providence be a voice urging you to prayer. If *you* have no wants, *others* have; take them to the Lord. If *you* are borne down by no cross, smitten by no affliction, or suffering from no want, *others* are; go and plead for them with your heavenly Father, and the petitions you send up to the mercy-seat on their behalf may return into your own soul laden with rich covenant blessings. Turn everything into an occasion for prayer. Whether it is a dark providence or a bright one, let it take you to God. Make the falls, the weaknesses and the declensions of others grounds for prayer. Thus, and thus only, can you expect to grow in grace, and grace to grow in you.

Above all, *cultivate the habit of secret prayer*. No other prayer can take its place. There are confessions that can be made, desires that can be expressed, sins that can be lamented, and wants that can be disclosed only in the secret place, shut in with God. He that confines himself to the altar of the sanctuary, the family, or the social circle, will find leanness come into his soul. It must necessarily be (the very nature of the case proves it) that there are states of mind which the believer can unfold to none but God, sins that can only be acknowledged in His presence, and wants that can only be poured into His ear. What a loser, then, is that professing Christian who lives in the daily and habitual neglect of secret prayer! It is the close and secret walk with God that marks the true and advancing believer. It is in that walk, and that only, that fresh grace, strength and love are poured into the soul. It is in *secret communion* with God that the believer becomes girded for the conflict, strengthened for the hour of trial, and prepared for the joys of heaven.

Let it be remembered that one essential and important part of the Spirit's work as the Author of prayer is *to unfold Jesus as the medium of prayer*. There is no access to God but through Jesus. If there is no honouring of Christ in His person, blood, righteousness and intercession in prayer, we can expect no answer to prayer. The great encouragement to draw near to God is Jesus at the right hand of God. Jesus is the door. Coming through Him, the poorest, the vilest and the most abject may approach the throne of grace, and ask what he will. The glorious Advocate is on the throne to present the petition and urge its acceptance, and plead for its answer on the basis of His own infinite and atoning merits. Come then, you who are poor; come, you who are disconsolate; come, you who are tried and afflicted; come, you who are wounded; come, you who are needy; come and be made welcome at the mercy-seat; for Jesus waits to present your petition and plead your cause. Ask nothing in your own name, but ask everything in the name of Jesus; " ask and you shall receive, that your joy may be full." The Father may reject *you*, but *His Son* He cannot reject. " Having therefore, brethren, boldness to enter into the holiest by the blood of Jesus, by a new and living way, which he hath consecrated for us, through the veil, that is to say, his flesh; and having an High-priest over the house of God, let us draw near." Heb. 10. 19-22.

Draw near, then, seeking soul, with boldness; not the boldness of a presumptuous, self-righteous man, but that of one chosen, called, pardoned and justified. Draw near with the lowly boldness of a child, with the humble confidence of a son. You are dear to your Father. Your voice is sweet to Him. You are precious to Him because you have been accepted in His Beloved. You cannot come too boldly, you cannot come too frequently, you cannot come with too large requests. You are coming to a King; that King is your Father; that Father sees you in His beloved Son. Do not hang back. Do not stand afar off. He *now* holds out the golden sceptre and says, "Come near, what is your request? Come with your temporal want. Come with your spiritual need. Ask what you will, it shall be granted you. I have an open hand and a large heart." Is this your desire—"Lord, I want more grace to glorify Thee. I want more simplicity of mind, singleness of eye. I want a more holy, upright, honest walk. I want more meekness, patience, lowliness, submission. I want to know more of Jesus, to see more of His glory, to feel more of His preciousness and to live more simply upon His fulness. I want more of the sanctifying, sealing, witnessing and anointing influences of the Spirit?" Blessed, holy desires! It is the Spirit making intercession in you according to the will of God; and as you enter into the holiest by the blood of Jesus, the Lord will fulfil the desires of your heart.

Watch diligently against the least declension in the spirit of prayer. If there be declension here, there will also be declension in every part and department of the work of the Spirit in your soul. It is *prayer* that keeps every grace of the Spirit in active, holy and healthy exercise. It is the stream, so to speak, that supplies refreshing vigour and nourishment to all the plants of grace. It is true that the fountain-head of all spiritual life and "grace to help in time of need," is Christ; "for it pleased the Father that in him should all fulness dwell." And Paul's encouragement to the Philippians was, "My God shall supply all your need, according to his riches in glory *by Christ Jesus*." But the channel through which all grace comes is *prayer*—ardent, wrestling, importunate, believing prayer. Allow this channel to be dry, permit any object to narrow or close it up, and the effect will be a withering and a decay of the life of God in the soul. Every plant will droop, every flower will fade and lose its fragrance, and the state of the soul will no longer resemble that of the church thus so beautifully described: " A garden enclosed is my sister, my spouse; a spring shut up, a fountain sealed. Thy plants are an orchard of pomegranates, with pleasant fruits; camphire with spikenard. Spikenard and saffron; calamus and cinnamon, with all trees of frankincense; myrrh and aloes, with all the chief spices: a fountain of gardens, a well of living waters, and streams from Lebanon. Awake, O north wind, and come, thou south; blow upon my garden, that the spices thereof may flow out. Let my beloved come into his garden, and eat his pleasant fruits." Sol. Song 4. 12-16. This is the true and glowing picture of a believing soul in which the spirit of prayer is flourishing and vigorous. Reverse this, and how melancholy would it appear! And yet that would be the exact state of every prayerless professing Christian. Guard, then, against the slightest decline of prayer in the soul. If prayer—family prayer, social prayer, most of all, secret prayer —is declining with you, no further evidence is needed of your being in a backsliding state of mind. There may not yet have been the outward departure, but *you are on the way to it*, and nothing but *a return to prayer* will save you. Oh, what alarm, what fearfulness and trembling, should this thought produce in a child of God, " I am on my way to an awful departure from God! Such is the state of my soul at this moment, such my present state of mind, such the loss of my spirituality, such the hold which the world has upon my affections, there is no length in sin to which I may not now go, there is no iniquity which I may not now commit. The breakers are full in view, and my poor weak vessel is heading for and rapidly nearing them!" What can shield you from the commission of that sin, what can keep you from wounding Jesus afresh, what can preserve you from foundering and making shipwreck of your faith, but an immediate and fervent return to prayer? *Prayer* is your only safety. Prayer for grace to help in your time of need. Prayer for reviving grace, for quickening, restraining, sanctifying grace. Prayer to be kept from falling, to be held up in the slippery paths. Prayer for the lowly mind, for the contrite spirit, for the broken heart, for the careful, close and humble walk with God.

Do you ask what are some of the *symptoms* of a decline of the spirit of prayer? We reply that the decay of any one grace of the Spirit in the soul—faith, love, zeal, patience, meekness, temperance, lowliness—marks the low and feeble pulse of prayer in a believer. There may not be a decay of *all* the graces at once, and because of this the believer may be greatly deceived. Outward *zeal* may continue long after other more hidden and spiritual graces have withered; and because this remains, the soul is deceived as to its real state before God. A secret and a fearful process of spiritual declension may be going forward in the soul, while for a time there may be nothing outward to mark it. There are many evidences, known only to the individual himself, by which the declining spirit of prayer may be detected. A distaste for the Word of God, for a spiritual and searching ministry, for intercourse with spiritual minds, for holy thought and meditation; all, and many more which cannot be unknown to the backsliding soul, indicate a neglected throne of grace.

Are you a *prayerless professing Christian?* Oh, what is all your profession worth if you are a prayerless soul? What is your zeal, your church membership, your talking well and loud, your gifts, your reputation as a 'live' Christian while you are dead to the true spirit and life of prayer, living in awful neglect of family prayer, social prayer and secret prayer? All your profession of godliness, your outward zeal, your splendid gifts, all is but a "fair show in the flesh," an empty name, while you live in neglect of prayer. Prayer is the breathing of the life of God in the soul. It is the pulse of the renewed man. It is the turning of the soul to God. Where this is missing, the great evidence of the actual existence of life is missing too.

This may catch the eye of someone *who has never yet truly prayed;* who all his life so far has neglected the throne of grace. What an awful condition! What a sad sight! Your

life, reader, has been a *prayerless life*. It has been a life devoted to self, to sin, to rebellion against God, to impenitence
and unbelief, to hardness of heart, and contempt of God's
Word, to a neglect of the great salvation, to a despising of
Christ, to a pursuit of happiness in a poor, dying, present evil
world. Not a breath of prayer has ever risen from your soul
to God. Not one pulse of love has ever beaten in your breast
for Jesus. You have lived as a lover of self, a lover of the
world, a lover of sin, a lover of wealth, pleasure and ambition,
rather than as a lover of God. And why are you at *this moment* out of hell? You have long been preparing for it. Your
character for years has been moulding for the society and the
sufferings of the lost. Why are you not there *now*, calling
for a drop of water to cool that parched tongue which never
once called in earnest supplication upon God? It is of the
Lord's mercies that you are not consumed. And because His
long-suffering patience has borne with you so long, you are
yet within the region of hope. " What meanest thou, O
sleeper? arise, and call upon God." The wrath of God here,
and its fearful outpouring hereafter, rests upon the soul that
does not come to the throne of grace. The hell of an *unpraying man* is a fearful hell. To go from the means of grace,
from the ordinances of religion, from a preached Gospel, from
a praying family, to the judgment-seat, an unpraying, unre-
penting, unbelieving soul, is to go to a special hell. The un-
taught, unenlightened and unwarned heathen, does not go to
the hell of that soul that dies surrounded by the means of saving grace, rejecting the Lord Jesus Christ, and a stranger to
prayer. "Of how much *sorer punishment*, suppose ye, shall
he be thought worthy," who has heard of the throne of grace
only to slight it; of Jesus only to despise him; of the Gospel
only to reject it; of God's love, long-suffering and grace only
to trample it under his feet? " It shall be more tolerable for
the land of Sodom in the day of judgment" than for that soul.
" Those mine enemies that would not that I should reign over
them, bring hither, and slay them before me." " Who shall
be punished with everlasting destruction from the presence of
the Lord, and from the glory of his power." " Depart from

me, ye cursed, into everlasting fire, prepared for the devil and his angels." "And I saw a great white throne, and him that sat on it, from whose face the earth and the heaven fled away; and there was found no place for them. And I saw the dead, small and great, stand before God; and the books were opened: and another book was opened, which is the book of life: and the dead were judged out of those things which were written in the books, according to their works. And whosoever was not found written in the book of life was cast into the lake of fire." Rev. 20. 11. This will be the doom and the portion of an *unpraying soul*! Remember, reader, that without prayer in your family, *your family is cursed*; that without prayer in your business, *your business is cursed*; that without prayer for your own soul, *the curse of God rests upon you*. If you have not *time* for prayer, then seek time, find time, make time. You *must pray*, or be lost! You *must pray*, or be eternally condemned! You *must pray*, or sink down overwhelmed with the wrath of God for ever and for ever! Seek time, find time, make time for prayer. Abstract it from business, take it from pleasure, even steal it from sleep. You *must pray*, or go to an awful, a special hell. A *sorer punishment* than all others will be yours, if you die a prayerless soul!

Are you conscious of the slightest movement of your heart towards God? Cherish it as your most valuable mercy. It is the first gentle breathing of the blessed Spirit in your soul. It is the first pulse of spiritual life. It may be feeble; it may be only a desire, a misgiving, a solemn thought, a feeling after God; a cry, "God be merciful to me a sinner!" Oh, it is the life-giving Spirit overshadowing you; let it lead you to the mercy-seat. O precious longing after God! O blessed and gentle drawing of the Spirit! Let it lead you at once to the throne of grace. Go there and spread your case before the Lord. Confess your sins, acknowledge your iniquity, humble yourself at His feet, and for Jesus' sake God will receive you graciously, pardon you freely and seal you as His child.

Lastly, *pray expectantly, diligently and perseveringly*. Expect an answer to your prayer, a promise to your request, a compliance with your suit. Be as much assured that God will answer, as that you have asked or that He has promised. Ask in faith; only believe; watch daily at the gates for the answer; look for it at any moment, and through any providence; do not expect it in your own way, but in the Lord's; do not be astonished if He should answer your prayer in the very opposite way that you had anticipated and (it may be) dictated. With this view, watch every providence, even the smallest. You do not know when the answer may come, at what time, or in what way. *Therefore watch.* The Lord may answer in a great and strong wind, in an earthquake, in a fire, or in a still small voice; therefore watch every providence to know which will be the voice of God to you. Do not pray as if you asked for or expected a *refusal.* God delights in your holy fervency, your humble boldness and your persevering importunity. "The effectual *fervent* prayer of a righteous man availeth much." Pray submissively, expect hopefully, watch vigilantly, and wait patiently.

Behold, then, the throne of grace! Was ever spot so verdant and so sunny? Was ever resting-place so sacred and so sweet? Could God Himself invest it with a richer or greater attraction? Behold it yet again. *It is the throne of grace.* There are dispensed all the blessings of sovereign grace—pardon, justification, adoption, sanctification, and all that connects the present state of the believer with eternal glory. There is dispensed grace itself—grace to guide, to support, to comfort and to help in time of need. *There sits the God of grace,* proclaiming Himself "the Lord God, merciful and gracious, long-suffering, and abundant in goodness and truth; keeping mercy for thousands, forgiving iniquity, transgression and sin." *There is extended the sceptre of grace,* welcoming the sons and daughters of want, the weary and the heavy laden, the guilty, the broken in heart, the poor, the friendless, the bereaved. *There stands Jesus the High-priest and Mediator,* full of grace and truth, waving to and fro his golden censer, from which pours forth the fragrant incense of His atoning merits, wreathing in one offering as it ascends the name, the wants and the prayer of the lowly worshipper. *And there, too, is the Spirit of grace,* breathing in the soul, making known the want, putting the petition into words, and making inter-cession for the saints according to the will of God. Behold, then, the throne of grace, and draw near! You are welcome. Come with your cross, come with your infirmity, come with your guilt, come with your want, come with your wounded spirit, come with your broken heart, come and welcome to the throne of grace! Come without price, come without worthiness, come without preparation, come without fitness, come in a bad state of mind, come with a hard heart, come and welcome to the throne of grace! God, your Father, makes you welcome. Jesus, your Advocate, makes you welcome. The Spirit, the Author of prayer, makes you welcome. All the happy and the blessed who cluster around it make you welcome. The spirits of just men made perfect in glory make you welcome. The ministering spirits sent forth to minister for them who shall be heirs of salvation make you welcome. All the holy below, and all the holy above, all, all make you, poor trembling soul, welcome, thrice welcome, to the throne of grace!

CHAPTER IX

The Spirit a Comforter

THE BROKEN HEART BOUND UP

"*The Comforter, which is the Holy Ghost.*"—John 14. 26.

IN several parts of this work, we have had occasion to touch upon the sanctifying tendency of the discipline of the covenant. We have been led to trace the goodness, and to justify the wisdom of God, and to mark some of the blessed results in His appointing the *suffering state* to be the special allotment of His children. But there is one important view of the subject yet reserved. It is this: That in no one aspect does the happy tendency and indispensable necessity of that discipline more manifestly appear, than in the fact that through this channel the believer is brought into communion with, and into the enjoyment of, the *tenderness* and *sympathy* of the Spirit. The wisdom, the faithfulness and the power of the Spirit, the soul has been brought to acknowledge and experience in conversion; but to know the Spirit as a *Comforter*, to experience His tenderness and sympathy, His kindness and gentleness, we must be placed in those special circumstances that call it into exercise. In a word, we must know what sorrow is, to know what comfort is; to know what true comfort is, we must receive it from the blessed and eternal Spirit, the Comforter of the church.

The God and Father of His people foreknew all their circumstances. He knew that He had chosen them in the furnace of affliction, that this was the particular path along which they should all walk. As He foreknew, so He also fore-arranged for all those circumstances. In the eternal purposes of His wisdom, grace and love, He went before His church, planning its history, allotting its path and providing for every possible position in which it could be placed; so that we cannot imagine an exigency, a trial, a difficulty or a conflict which is not amply provided for in the covenant of grace. Such is the wisdom and the goodness of God towards His covenant family!

The great provision for the suffering state of the believer is the Holy Spirit, the special, personal and abiding Comforter of the church. It was to this truth our dear Lord directed the sorrowing hearts of His disciples, when on the eve of His return to glory. He was about to withdraw from them His bodily presence. His mission on earth was fulfilled, His work was done, and He was about to return to His Father and to their Father, to His God and to their God. The prospect of separation absorbed them in grief. Thus did Jesus speak of it, and thus, too, he consoled them: "But now I go my way to him that sent me; and none of you asketh me, Whither goeth thou? But because I have said these things unto you, sorrow hath filled your heart. Nevertheless I tell you the truth; it is expedient for you that I go away: for if I go not away, the Comforter will not come unto you; but if I depart I will send him unto you." John 16. 5-7. Note the *circumstances* of the disciples; *it was a season of deep sorrow*. Then observe *how* Jesus mitigated that sorrow, and chased away the dark cloud of their grief—*by the promise of the Spirit as a Comforter*—assuring them that the presence and abiding of the Spirit as a Comforter would more than recompense the loss of His bodily presence. What the Spirit then was to the sorrowing disciples, He has been in every successive age, is at the present moment, and will continue to be to the end of time—the personal and abiding Comforter of the afflicted family of God. May He now sanctify and comfort our hearts, by leading us into the consideration of this great and most precious doctrine.

In the sacred Word great stress is laid upon the subject of comfort. It is clearly God's revealed will that His people should be comforted. The fulness of Christ, the exceeding great and precious promises of the Word, the covenant of grace and all the dealings of God are closely related to the comfort and consolation of the saints. A brief reference to the Divine Word will convince us of this. This is the very character God Himself bears, and this is the blessed work He accomplishes. Thus, "Blessed be God, even the Father of our Lord Jesus Christ, the Father of mercies, and the *God of all comfort*; who comforteth us in all our tribulation, that we may be able to comfort them which are in any trouble by the comfort wherewith we ourselves are *comforted of God.*" 2 Cor. 1. 3, 4. Similarly we have those striking words in Isaiah 40. 1, "Comfort ye, comfort ye my people, saith your God." This was God's command to the prophet. It was His declared will that His people should be comforted, even though they dwelt in Jerusalem, the city which had shed the blood of the prophets, and more than that, which was later to witness the crucifixion of the Lord of life and glory. What an unfolding does this give us of Him who is the God of all comfort, who comforts us in all our tribulation, and that, too, in every place!

The comforting of the saints is one important purpose of the Scriptures. "Whatsoever things were written aforetime were written for our learning, that we through patience and *comfort* of the Scriptures might have hope." Rom. 15. 4. And thus the exhortation runs—"*Comfort* the feeble minded." "Wherefore *comfort* yourselves together, and edify one another, even as also ye do." "Then we which are alive and remain shall be caught up together with them in the clouds, to meet the Lord in the air; and so shall we ever be with the Lord. Wherefore *comfort* one another with these words." Thus has the Holy Ghost testified to this subject. Thus it is clear that it is the will of God and in His heart that His people should be comforted.

The *necessity* of comfort springs from the existence of sorrow in some one or more of its varied and multiplied forms. For each and every kind of sorrow the blessed Spirit is the Comforter; but as He comforts in various ways according to the nature of the sorrow, we would select a few of the prominent sources of grief, common alike to all the Lord's people, and show how He binds up, heals and comforts.

With regard to the *spiritual sorrows* of a child of God, those peculiar to a believer in Jesus, we believe that a *revelation of Jesus* is the great source of comfort to which the Spirit leads the soul. He comforts all the spiritual grief of a believer, dries up all his spiritual tears, by testifying of Christ, and that according to the peculiar feature of the case. Our Lord told His sorrowing disciples this: "But when the Comforter is come, whom I will send unto you from the Father, even the Spirit of truth, which proceedeth from the Father, he shall testify of me." John 15. 26. Notice that He was to comfort their hearts *by testifying of Jesus*. Here is the true source of comfort. What higher comfort do we need? What more can we have? This is enough to heal every wound, to dry up every tear, to assuage every grief, to lighten every cross, to fringe with brightness every dark cloud, and to make the roughest place smooth—that a believing soul has Jesus. Having Jesus, what has a believer?

He has the entire blotting out of all his sins. Is not *this* a comfort? Tell us what can give comfort to a child of God apart from this. If this fail, where can he look? Will you tell him of the world, of its many schemes of enjoyment, of its plans for the accumulation of wealth, of its domestic happiness? Wretched sources of comfort to an awakened soul! Poor empty channels to a man made acquainted with the inward plague of sin! That which *he* wants to know is, the sure payment of the ten thousand talents, the entire cancelling of the bond held against him by stern justice, the complete blotting out, as a thick cloud, of all his iniquity. Until this great fact is made sure and certain to his conscience, all other comfort is but as a dream of boyhood, a shadow that vanishes, a vapour that melts away. But the Holy Ghost comforts the believer by leading him to this blessed truth—the full pardon of sin. This is the great controversy which Satan has with the believer. To bring him to doubt the pardon of sin, to unhinge the mind from this great fact, is the constant effort of this arch-enemy. And when unbelief is powerful, and inbred sin is powerful, and outward trials are many and sore, and, in the midst of it all, the single eye is removed from

Christ, then is the hour of Satan to charge home upon the conscience of the believer all the iniquity he ever committed. And how does the blessed Spirit comfort at that moment? By unfolding the greatness, perfection and efficacy of the one offering by which Jesus has for ever blotted out the sins of His people, and perfected them that are sanctified. O what comfort does this truth speak to a fearful, troubled, anxious believer, when (the Spirit working faith in his heart) he can look up and see all *his* sins laid upon Jesus in the solemn hour of atonement, and no condemnation remaining! However poor and worthless you may feel yourself to be, this truth is still for *you*. O rise to it, welcome it, embrace it, do not think that it is too costly for one so unworthy. It comes from the heart of Jesus, and cannot be more free. " Blessed is he whose transgression is forgiven, whose sin is covered." Having Jesus, what has the believer more?

He possesses a righteousness in which God views him complete and accepted, from the beginning of the year to the end of the year. Is it not a comfort to stand " complete in Him," in the midst of many and conscious imperfections, infirmities, flaws and proneness to wander? What a comfort for the sorrowing and trembling heart to turn and take up its rest in this truth, that " he that believeth is justified from all things," and stands accepted in the Beloved, to the praise of the glory of Divine grace. God beholds him in Jesus without a spot, because He beholds His Son in whom He is well pleased, and viewing the believing soul in Him, can say, " Thou art all fair, my love; there is no spot in thee!" The blessed Comforter unfolds this truth to the troubled soul, bringing it to take up its rest in it. And as the believer realises his full acceptance in the righteousness of Christ, and rejoices in the truth, he weeps as he never wept and mourns as he never mourned, over the perpetual bias of his heart to wander from a God that has so loved him. The very comfort poured into his soul from this truth lays him in the dust, and draws out the heart in ardent longings for holiness.

And what a Comforter is the Spirit *in seasons of temptation*! Few of the children of God are ignorant of Satan's devices. Few are exempt from the "fiery darts" of the adversary. Our Lord Himself was not. Many, peculiar and great are Satan's temptations. They are often those which touch the very vitals of the gospel, which attempt to undermine the believer's faith in the fundamentals of Christianity, and which affect his own personal interest in the covenant of grace. Satan is the sworn enemy of the believer. He is his constant, unwearied foe. There is a subtlety, a malignity, which is not present with other enemies of the soul. The Holy Ghost, in Rev. 2. 24, speaks of the "depths of Satan." There are "depths" in his malice, in his subtlety, in his sagacity, which many of the beloved of the Lord are made in some degree to plumb. The Lord may allow them to go down into those "depths," just to convince them that there are depths in His wisdom, love, power and grace which can outfathom the "depths of Satan."

But what are some of the devices of the wicked one? What are some of his fiery darts? Sometimes he fills the mind of the believer with the most blasphemous and atheistical thoughts, threatening the utter destruction of his peace and confidence. Sometimes he takes advantage of periods of weakness and trial and perplexity to stir up the corruptions of his nature, bringing the soul back as into captivity to the law of sin and death. Sometimes he suggests unbelieving doubts respecting his adoption, beguiling him into the belief that his professed conversion is all a delusion, that his religion is all hypocrisy, and that what he had thought was the work of grace is only the work of nature. But by far the greatest and most general controversy which Satan has with the saint of God, is to lead him to doubt the ability and the willingness of Christ to save a poor sinner. If the anchor of his soul is removed from this truth, he is driven out upon a rough sea of doubt and anguish, and is at the mercy of every wind of doctrine and of every billow of unbelief that may assail his storm-tossed bark. But in the midst of it all, whence flow the comfort and the victory of the tempted believer? From the promise which assures him that "when the enemy shall come in like a flood, the Spirit of the Lord shall lift up a standard against him." Isaiah 59. 19. And what is the standard which the Spirit, the Comforter, lifts up to stem this flood? A dying, risen, ascended, exalted and ever-living Saviour. This is the standard that strikes terror into the foe; this is the gate that shuts out the flood. So the disciples proved. This is their testimony: "And the seventy returned again with joy, saying, Lord, even the devils are subject unto us *through thy name*." Luke 10. 17. Immanuel is that name which puts to flight every spiritual foe. And the Comforter, which is the Holy Ghost, leads the tempted soul to this name, to shelter itself beneath it, to plead it with God, and to battle with it against the enemy. Are you a mark against which the fiery darts of the devil are levelled? Are you strongly tempted? Do not be astonished as though some strange thing had happened unto you. The holiest of God's saints have suffered as you are now suffering; indeed even your blessed Lord—your Master, your Pattern, your Example, and He in whose name you shall be more than conqueror—was once assailed as you are, and by the same enemy. And let the reflection console you, that temptations only leave the traces of guilt upon the conscience, and are only regarded as sins by God, as they are yielded to. The mere suggestion of the adversary, the mere presentation of a temptation, is no sin, so long as (in the strength that is in Christ Jesus) the believer firmly and resolutely resists it. "Resist the devil, and he will flee from you." "Above all, take the shield of faith, wherewith ye shall be able to quench all the fiery darts of the devil." Jesus has already fought and conquered for you. He well knew what the conflict with Satan was. And He remembers too what it is. Lift up your head, tempted soul! You shall obtain the victory. The Seed of the woman has bruised the serpent's head, has crushed him so that he can never obtain supremacy over you again. He may harass, annoy and distress you, but pluck you from the hollow of the hand that was pierced for you he never can.

But in seasons of deep trial and affliction, the Spirit specially shows Himself the Comforter of His people. It was under circumstances of peculiar and keen trial that Jesus promised the Spirit as a Comforter. Nor is He confined to any peculiar trial. Whatever is a cause of depression to the believer, whatever grieves his heart, wounds his spirit or casts him down, is a trial. If it is only a cold look from eyes that once shone with love, it is still a trial. If it is only an unkind word from the tongue that once flowed with affection, it is still a trial; and in proportion to the heart's tenderness the keenness of the trial is felt.

Many of the saints of God tend to forget the appointed path of believers through the world. They forget that that path is to be one of tribulation; that far from being a smooth, a flowery and an easy path, it is rough, thorny and difficult. The believer often expects all his heaven on earth. He forgets that—whatever spiritual enjoyment there may be here, related in its nature to the joys of the glorified, and of this he cannot expect too much—the present is only the wilderness state of the church. The life that now is is only that of a pilgrimage and a journey. Kind was our Lord's admonition : " In the world ye shall have tribulation "; and equally so that of the apostle, " we must through much tribulation enter into the kingdom." Affliction, in some of its many and varied forms is the lot of all the Lord's people. If we do not have it, we lack an evidence of our true sonship, for the Father " scourgeth every son whom He receiveth." But whatever the trial or affliction is, the Spirit is the Comforter.

Now, how does He comfort the afflicted soul? *He unfolds the love of his God and Father in the trial.* He shows the believer that his sorrow, so far from being the result of *anger*, is the fruit of *love*; that it comes from the *heart* of God, sent to draw the soul nearer to Himself, and to unfold the depths of His own grace and tenderness; that " whom He loveth He rebuketh." And oh, how immense the comfort that flows into a wounded spirit when love—deep, unchangeable, covenant love—is seen in the hand that has stricken; when the affliction is traced to the covenant, and through the covenant to the heart of a covenant God!

He comforts by revealing the purpose for which the affliction is sent. He convinces the believer that the discipline, though painful, was yet needed; that the world was, perhaps, making inroads upon the soul, or earthly love was shutting out Jesus; some indulged sin was perhaps crucifying Him afresh, or some known spiritual duty was neglected. The Comforter opens the believer's ears to hear the voice of the rod, and Him who has appointed it. He begins to see why the Lord has smitten, why He has caused His rough wind and His east wind to blow, why He has blasted, why He has wounded. And now the Achan is discovered, cast out, and stoned. The heart, disciplined, returns from its wanderings and, wounded, bleeding, suffering, seeks more fondly than ever a wounded, bleeding, suffering Saviour. Who can fully estimate the comfort which flows from the sanctified discipline of the covenant when the purpose for which the trial was sent is accomplished? Accomplished, it may be, in the discovery of some departure, or in the removal of an obstruction to the growth of grace, of some object that obscured the glory of Jesus, and that suspended His visits of love to the soul. " Blessed discipline," he may exclaim, " that has produced so much good; gentle chastisement that has corrected so much evil; sweet medicine that has produced so much health!"

But it is *in unfolding the tenderness and sympathy of Jesus* that the Spirit most effectually restores comfort to the tried, tempted and afflicted soul. He testifies of Christ especially in the sympathy of His manhood. There can be no question that, in His assumption of our nature, Jesus had in view, as one important end, a closer affinity with the suffering state of His people with a view to their more immediate comfort and support. The great object of His incarnation, we are well assured, was obedience to the law in its precept, and the suffering of its penalty. But connected with, and resulting from this, is the channel that is thus open for the outflowings of that tenderness and sympathy of which the saints of God so constantly stand in need, and as constantly receive. Jesus is the " brother born for adversity "—" it behoved him to be made like unto his brethren, that he might be a merciful and faithful High-priest "—" in that he himself hath suffered, being tempted, he is able to succour them that are tempted "—

" we have not an High-priest which cannot be touched with the feeling of our infirmities, but was in all points tempted like as we are, yet without sin."

Here is the true and blessed source of comfort in the hour and the circumstance of sorrow. The Lord's people are a tried people; Jesus was a tried Saviour. The Lord's people are an afflicted people; Jesus drank deeply of affliction's bitter cup. The Lord's people are a sorrowing family; Jesus was a " man of sorrows, and acquainted with grief." He brought Himself down on to a level with the circumstances of His people. He completely identified Himself with them. However, we are not to suppose that in every peculiarity of trial there is an identity with our dear Lord. There are trials growing out of peculiar circumstances and relations in life to which he was a stranger. But Jesus took upon Himself pure humanity in its suffering form and was deeply acquainted with sorrow as sorrow; and from these two circumstances He became fitted in all points to succour, to sustain and to sympathise with His afflicted, sorrowing people, whatever the cause of that affliction or sorrow was. It is enough for us that He was " bone of our bone, and flesh of our flesh." It is enough for us that His heart was composed of all the tenderness and sympathy and gentleness of our nature, and that, too, freed from everything growing out of the infirmity of sin that could weaken, impair and blunt the sensibilities. It is enough for us that sorrow was no stranger to His heart, that affliction had deeply furrowed His soul, and that grief had left its traces upon every line of His countenance. What more do we require? What more can we ask? Our *nature*? He took it. Our *sicknesses*? He bore them. Our *sorrows*? He felt them. Our *crosses*? He carried them. Our *sins*? He pardoned them. He went before His suffering people, trod out the path and left his footprint; and now invites them to walk in no way, to sustain no sorrow, to bear no burden and to drink no cup in which He has not Himself *gone before*. It is enough for Him that you are a child of *grief*, that *sorrow* is the bitter cup that you are drinking. He asks no more. A chord is in a moment touched in His heart, which vibrates to that touched in yours, whether its note be a pleasing or a mournful one. For let it be ever remembered that Jesus has as much sympathy for the *joys* as He has for the *sorrows* of His people. He rejoices with those that rejoice and He weeps with those that weep. But how does Jesus sympathise? Not in the sense in which some may suppose, that when we weep He actually weeps, and that when we suffer He actually suffers. This may once have been so, but we no more know Christ in the flesh, as He was once known. Ah! there was a period when " Jesus wept"! There was a period when His heart wrung with anguish, and when His body agonised in pain. That period is no more. However there still is a sense (and an important one) in which Jesus feels sympathy. When the believer suffers, the tenderness of Jesus is drawn forth. His sustaining strength, sanctifying grace and comforting love are all unfolded in the experience of His child while passing through the furnace. The Son of God is with him in the flames. Jesus of Nazareth is walking with him on the billows. He has the HEART of Christ. And *this* is sympathy—*this* is fellowship—*this* is to be ONE with Christ Jesus.

What is your sorrow? Has the hand of *death* smitten? Is the beloved one removed? Has the desire of your eyes been taken away with a stroke? But who has done it? Jesus has done it. Death was only His messenger. *Your Jesus has done it*. The Lord has taken away. And what has He removed? Your wife? Ah, Jesus has all the tenderness that your wife ever had. Hers was only a drop from the ocean that is in His heart. Is it your husband? Jesus is better to you than ten husbands. Is it your parent, your child, your friend, your all of earthly bliss? Is the cistern broken? Is the earthen vessel dashed to pieces? Are all your streams dry? Jesus is still enough. He has not taken *Himself* from you, and never, never will. Take your bereaved, stricken and bleeding heart to Him, and rest it upon His, once bereaved, stricken and bleeding, too; for He knows how to bind up the broken heart, to heal the wounded spirit and to comfort those that mourn.

What is your sorrow? Has health failed you? Has property forsaken you? Have friends turned against you? Are you tried in your circumstances? Perplexed in your path? Are providences thickening and darkening around you? Are you anticipating seasons of approaching trial? Are you walking in darkness, having no light? *Simply go to Jesus.* He is an ever open door. A tender, loving faithful friend, ever near. He is a brother born for *your* adversity. His grace and sympathy are sufficient for *you.* The life you are called to live is that of *faith;* that of *sense,* you have done with. You are now to walk by faith and not by sight. This, then, is the great secret of a life of faith—to hang upon Jesus daily, to go to Him in every trial, to cast upon Him every burden, to take the infirmity, the corruption, the cross as it rises, simply and immediately to Jesus. You are to set Christ before you as your Example to imitate; as your Fountain to wash in; as your Foundation to build upon; as your Fulness to draw from; as your tender, loving and confiding Brother and Friend, to go to at all times and under all circumstances. To do this daily, constitutes the life of faith. O to be enabled with Paul to say, " I am crucified with Christ: nevertheless I live; yet not I, but Christ liveth in me: and the life which I now live in the flesh, *I live by the faith of the Son of God,* who loved me, and gave himself for me." O holy, happy life! O unearthly, heavenly life! The life Jesus Himself lived when below, the life all the patriarchs and prophets and apostles and martyrs and the spirits of just men made perfect once lived, and the life every true-born child of God is called and privileged to live, while yet a stranger and pilgrim on the earth!

There are three important aspects in which a believer should never fail to view his present lot. The first is to remember *that the present is, by the appointment of God, the afflicted state of the believer.* It is God's ordained, revealed will that His covenant children should be here in an afflicted condition. When called by grace, they should never take into their account any other state. They become the disciples of the religion of the *cross;* they become the followers of a *crucified* Lord; they put on a *yoke,* and assume a *burden.* They must, then, expect the cross inward and the cross outward. To escape it, is impossible. To pass to glory without it, is to go by another way than God's ordering, and, in the end, to fail of arriving there. The gate is strait, and the way is narrow, which leads to life, and a man must become nothing if he would enter and be saved, Matt. 7. 14. He must deny himself. He must become a fool that he may be wise, 1 Cor. 3. 18. He must receive the sentence of death in himself, that he should not trust in himself, 2 Cor. 1. 9. The wise man must cease to glory in his wisdom, the mighty man must cease to glory in his might, the rich man must cease to glory in his riches. Their only ground of glory in themselves must be their insufficiency, infirmity, poverty and weakness; and their only ground of glory out of themselves must be that " God so loved the world, that he gave his only begotten Son, that whosoever believeth in him should not perish, but have everlasting life." The believer in Jesus, then, must not forget that if the path he treads is rough and thorny, if the sky is wintry and the storm is severe, and if the cross he bears is heavy, that *this is the road to heaven*. He is only in the wilderness; why should he expect more than belongs to the wilderness state? He is on a journey; why should he look for more than a traveller's fare? He is far from home; why should he murmur and complain that he has not all the rest, the comfort and the luxuries of his Father's house? If your covenant God and Father has allotted to you *poverty*, be satisfied that it should be your state; indeed, rejoice in it. If bitter *adversity*, if deep *affliction*, if the daily and the heavy *cross*, still do not breathe one murmur, do not shed one tear, do not heave one sigh, but rather rejoice that you are led into the path that Jesus Himself walked in, that you " go forth by the footsteps of the flock," and that you are counted worthy thus to be one in circumstance with Christ and His people.

The second aspect in which the suffering believer should view his present lot is that *a state of humiliation or casting down invariably follows a state of exaltation or lifting up*. The Lord empties before He fills. He makes room for Himself, for His love and for His grace. He dethrones the rival, casts down the idol and claims to occupy the temple, filled and radiant with His own ineffable glory. Thus does He bring the soul into great straits, lays it low, but only to school and discipline it for richer mercies, higher service and greater glory. Be sure of this, that when the Lord is about to favour you with some great and peculiar blessing, he may prepare you for it by some great and peculiar trial. If He is about to advance you to some honour, He may first lay you low that He may exalt you. If He is about to place you in a sphere of great and distinguished usefulness, he may first place you in His school, that you may know how to teach others. If He is about to bring forth your righteousness as the noon-day, He may cause it to pass under a cloud, that, emerging from its momentary obscuration, it may shine with richer and more enduring lustre. Thus does He deal with all His people. Thus He dealt with Joseph. Intending to elevate him to great distinction and influence, He first cast him into a dungeon, and that, too, in the very land in which he was so soon to be the gaze and the astonishment of all men. Thus, too, he dealt with David and Job; and thus did God deal with his own Son, whom He advanced to His own right hand from the lowest state of humiliation and suffering. "It is the way of God to work by contraries, to turn the greatest evil into the greatest good. To grant great good after great evil, is one thing, and to turn great evils into the greatest good, that is another; and yet that is God's way. The greatest good that God intends for His people, many times He works it out of the greatest evil; the greatest light is brought out of the greatest darkness."

The third aspect is *to regard the present suffering as only preparatory to future glory*. This will greatly mitigate the sorrow, reconcile the heart to the trial and tend materially to secure the important purpose for which it was sent. The life of a believer is only a disciplining for heaven. All the covenant dealings of his God and Father, are only to make him a partaker of His holiness here, and thus to prepare him to be a partaker of His glory hereafter. Here he is only being trained for a high position in heaven. He is only preparing for a more holy and (for all we know) a more active and essential service in the upper world. So every infirmity overcome, every sin subdued, every weight laid aside and every step advanced in holiness only strengthens and matures the life of grace below, until it is fitted for, and terminates in, the life of glory above. Let the suffering believer then see that he emerges from every trial of the furnace with some dross consumed, some iniquity purged and with a deeper impress of the blessed Spirit's seal of love, holiness and adoption on his heart. Let him see that he has made some advance towards the state of the glorified; that he is more perfected in love and sanctification—the two great elements of heaven; and that therefore he is becoming fit for the inheritance of the saints in light. " Every branch that beareth fruit, he purgeth it, that it may bring forth more fruit." Blessed and holy tendency of all the afflictive dispensations of a covenant God and Father towards a dear and covenant child!

But there is a sorrow, even keener and deeper than this, in which the Spirit the Comforter is seen directly and manifestly to work. *It is the sorrow of a heart broken on account of sin.* A wounded conscience, a humble and contrite spirit, a broken heart—who can adequately describe? Though he may have experienced it, yet no mortal can fully unfold it, as no mortal can alone heal and comfort it. It is the deep and wonderful work of God the Holy Ghost; and he who approaches a spirit wounded by sin, either to describe the state, or to attempt its healing, has need of much wisdom, tenderness and sympathy. This part of our work addresses itself especially to the poor in spirit, to the humble and the contrite, to the wounded conscience, to the broken heart; let it then be read, as it is written, in the spirit of prayer, that the Comforter (which is the Holy Ghost) may take the work into His own hands, and heal where He has wounded and bind up where He has broken.

Shall we attempt a faint description of your feelings? Suffer one who has walked to some degree the path you are now treading, and who is prepared to sympathise with every tear and sigh that comes from a convinced and wounded conscience, with all tenderness and humility to draw aside the veil which conceals the deep and conflicting emotions that now agitate your heart, with a view to leading you to Jesus, whose voice alone can hush the tempest, and say to the waves of conviction and guilt, "peace, be still."

You feel yourself to be the very chief of sinners. You seem to stand out from the great mass a lone and solitary being, more vile, polluted, guilty and lost than all the rest. Your sentiments in reference to yourself, to the world, to sin, to God and to Christ, have undergone a rapid, total and surprising change. *Yourself*, you see to be guilty and condemned; the *world*, you feel to be a worthless portion, a cheat and a lie; *sin*, you see to be the blackest and most hateful of all things; *God*, you regard in a light of holiness, justice and truth, as you never did before; and *Christ*, as possessing an interest entirely new and overpowering. Your views in relation to the *law of God* are reversed. You now see it to be immaculately holy, strictly just and infinitely wise. Your best attempts to obey its precepts you now see are not only utterly powerless, but in themselves are so polluted by sin, that you cannot look at them without the deepest self-loathing. The *justice of God* shines with a glory unseen and unknown before. You feel that, in now bringing the condemnatory sentence of the law into your conscience, He is strictly holy, and were He now to send you to eternal woe, He would be strictly just. But ah! what seems to form the greatest burden? What is that which is more bitter to you than wormwood or gall? Oh, it is the thought that you should ever have lifted your arm of rebellion against so good, so holy, so just a God as He is. That you should ever have cherished one treasonable thought, or harboured one unkind feeling. That your whole life, thus far, should have been spent in bitter hostility to Him, His law, His Son, His people, and that yet, in the midst of it, yea, all day long, He has stretched out His hand to you, and you did not regard it! O the guilt that rests upon your conscience! O the burden that presses your soul! O the sorrow that wrings your heart! O the pang that wounds your spirit! Is there a posture of humility more lowly than all others? You would assume it. Is there a place in the dust more humiliating than all others? You would lie in it. Now you are looking wistfully around for a refuge, a resting place, a balm, a quietness for the conflict in your soul. Is this your real state? Are these your true feelings? Then the Lord is blessing you! "Blessing, do you say?" Yes! Those tears are a blessing! Those convictions are a blessing! Those humbling, lowly views are a blessing! That broken heart, that contrite spirit, that awakened, convicted and wounded conscience, despite all its guilt, is a blessing! Why? because the Spirit that convicts men of sin, of righteousness and of judgment has entered your soul and worked this change in you. He has opened your eyes to see yourself lost and wretched. He has broken the spell which the world has woven around you. He has dissolved the enchantment, unveiled the delusion and made you feel the powers of the world to come. Then you have received a blessing.

But "is there no balm in Gilead? is there no physician there?" *There is!* The Physician is Jesus, the balm is His own most precious blood. He binds up the broken heart, He heals the wounded spirit. See how the Holy Ghost testifies to this, and how He comforts by the testimony: "The Spirit of the Lord God is upon me; because the Lord hath anointed me to preach good tidings unto the meek: he hath sent me to *bind up the broken-hearted*, to proclaim liberty to the captive, and the opening of the prison to them that are bound; to proclaim the acceptable year of the Lord, and the day of vengeance of our God; *to comfort all that mourn*; to appoint unto them that mourn in Zion, to give unto them beauty for ashes, the oil of joy for mourning, the garment of praise for the spirit of heaviness." Isa. 61. 1-3. And if the reader will compare this precious announcement with Luke 4 from the 16th verse, he will find our Lord quoting it, and declaring that it was then fulfilled in Himself. "This day," says He, "is this scripture fulfilled in your ears."

Jesus is the binder-up of a broken heart. All the skill, all the efficacy, all the tenderness and acute sympathy needed for the office, meet and centre in Him in their highest degree. Here then you can bring your wounded heart. Bring it simply to Jesus. One touch of His hand will heal the wound. One whisper of His voice will hush the tempest. One drop of His blood will remove the guilt. Nothing but applying to Him in faith will do for your soul *now*. Your case is beyond the skill of all other physicians. Your wound is too deep for all other remedies. It is a question of life and death, heaven or hell. It is an emergency, a crisis, a turning point with you. Oh, how solemn, how eventful is this moment! Eternity seems suspended upon it. All the intelligences of the universe, good spirits and bad, seem to be gazing upon it with intense interest. Decide the question by closing *immediately* with Jesus. Submit to God. All things are ready. The blood is shed, the righteousness is finished, the feast is prepared, God stands ready to pardon, indeed He advances to meet you, His returning child, to fall upon your neck and embrace you with the assurance of His full and free forgiveness.

Do not let the *simplicity* of the remedy keep you back. Many stumble at this. It is only a *look* of faith: " *Look* unto me, and be ye saved." It is only a *touch*, even though with a paralysed hand: "And as many as *touched* Him were made whole." It is only believing the broad declaration that " Christ Jesus came into the world to save *sinners*." You are not called to believe that He came to save *you*; but that He saves *sinners*. Then if you inquire, "But will He save *me*? How do I know that if *I* come I shall meet a welcome?" Our reply is, *only test Him*. Do not settle down with the conviction that you are too far gone, too vile, too guilty, too unworthy, until you have gone and tried Him. You do not know how you wound Him, how you dishonour Him, and grieve the Spirit, by yielding to a doubt, even a shadow of a doubt, as to the *willingness* and the *ability* of Jesus to save you, until you have gone to Him believingly and put His readiness and His skill to the test.

Do not let the *freeness* of the remedy keep you away. This, too, is a stumbling-block to many. Its very freeness holds them back. But it is " without money, and without price." The simple meaning of this is that no worthiness on the part of the applicant, no merit of the creature, no tears, no convictions, no faith, is the ground on which the healing is bestowed. O no! It is all of grace—all of God's free gift, irrespective of any worth or worthiness in man. Your *warrant* to come to Christ is your very sinfulness. The *reason* wherefore you go to Him is that your heart is broken, and that only He can bind it up; your spirit is wounded, and only He can heal it; your conscience is burdened, and only He can lighten it; your soul is lost, and only He can save it. And that is all you need to recommend you. It is enough for Christ that you are covered with guilt; that you have no plea that springs from yourself; that you have no money to bring in your hand, but have spent your all upon physicians and are no better; that you have wasted your substance in riotous living and are now insolvent; and that you really feel a drawing towards Him, a longing for Him. You ask, you seek, you crave, you earnestly implore His compassion—*that is enough for Him*. His heart yearns, His love is moved, His hand is stretched out. Come and welcome to Jesus, come.

Let this thought keep you from despair : your present convictions, being the work of the blessed Spirit, must end in your *full conversion* to God. The Lord never leaves His work unfinished. He never wounds except to heal. He never convicts of sin except to lead the soul into the pardon and peace of the Gospel. Do not think that He has brought you thus far, to leave you and abandon you; that He has excited emotions only to smother them, and has awakened hopes only to disappoint. Oh no! The first tear of godly sorrow you shed was a link in the golden chain of eternal glory. The first sigh you heaved from your broken heart was a pulse of that life that shall never end. May you be encouraged to go on (like the author of Psalm 138) by the thought that the Lord will perfect that which concerns you; He will conduct you out of the dark storm into the serene sunlight of His precious love. Only we would remind you that He chooses His own way and time. Do not be impatient. Press hard after Him— seek Him in His word, seek Him at the throne of grace, seek Him diligently—but seek Him with a patient, submissive and childlike spirit. It is as certain that you WILL find Him as it is that He is now exalted upon His throne, "a Prince and a Saviour, to give repentance to Israel, and forgiveness of sins."

A word in conclusion. The Spirit comforts the believer by revealing *the nearness of the coming glory*. Heaven is near at hand. It is only a *step* out of a poor, sinful, sorrow-stricken world into the rest that remaineth to the people of God. It is only a *moment*, the twinkling of an eye—and we are absent from the body and present with the Lord. *Then* will the days of our mourning be ended, *then* sin will grieve no more, affliction will wound no more, sorrow will depress no more, and God will hide Himself no more. *There* will be the absence of all evil, and the presence of all good; and they who have come out of great tribulation, and have washed their robes, and made them white in the blood of the Lamb, shall take their stand before the throne of God, and shall " serve him day and night in his temple : and he that sitteth on the throne shall dwell among them. They shall hunger no more; neither thirst any more; neither shall the sun light on them, nor any heat. For the Lamb which is in the midst of the throne shall feed them, and shall lead them unto living fountains of waters: and God shall wipe away all tears from their eyes." Wherefore, beloved in the Lord, let us comfort one another with these words and with this prospect.

Geneva Series of Commentaries

"In order to be able to expound the Scriptures, and as an aid to your pulpit studies, you will need to be familiar with the commentators: a glorious army, let me tell you, whose acquaintance will be your delight and profit. . . ."—C. H. Spurgeon, from *Commenting and Commentaries*.

OLD TESTAMENT:

NEW TESTAMENT:

* *American editions of these titles are available, and therefore this British edition is not for sale in the U.S.A. or Canada.*